Your positive and negative traits can be interpreted through

NUMBERS AND YOU

The Number 1
Positive: ambitious, daring, generous, fearless, dynamic
Negative: arrogant, selfish, cold, bullying, manipulating

The Number 2
Positive: mild-mannered, considerate, peace-maker, persuasive, charming
Negative: petty, deceptive, hoarding, cruel, insincere

The Number 3
Positive: creative, popular, confident, articulate, musical
Negative: vain, dictatorial, self-indulgent, jealous

(more)

The Number 4

Positive: honest, disciplined, practical, loyal, steady

Negative: dull, crude, hateful, insensitive, melancholy

The Number 5

Positive: versatile, literary, curious, spontaneous, freedom-loving

Negative: self-indulgence related to sex, irritable, abusive

The Number 6

Positive: loving, magnetic, sociable, artistic, understanding

Negative: domestic tyrant, cynic, self-righteous, jealous

The Number 7
Positive: intuitive, refined, secretive, philosophical, probing
Negative: sarcastic, recluse, no depth, cunning, too critical

The Number 8
Positive: authoritative, conservative, executive ability, religious
Negative: greedy, power-hungry, intense, scheming

The Number 9
Positive: humanitarian, courageous, competitive, resourceful, spiritual
Negative: impulsive, argumentative, heartless, narrow-minded.

NUMBERS AND YOU™

A Numerology Guide for Everyday Living

Lloyd Strayhorn

BALLANTINE BOOKS • NEW YORK

Library of Congress Catalog Card Number: 80-18386

ISBN 0-345-34593-2

Manufactured in the United States of America

First Ballantine Books Edition: October 1987
Seventh Printing: December 1990

To my wife, Kathy,
and my wonderful children, Rahsaan, Keirra,
Amaar, Llanice, and . . .

Special Thanks:

To the CREATOR who led me down this path and made it all possible.

To the countless authors on the subject of Numerology who I consider my teachers.

To my editor, Cheryl Woodruff, who gave deeper insight and dimension to this present work.

To Juanita Grant-Townes, editor of the Yama Publishing edition of NUMBERS AND YOU.

To my countless students, readers of my newspaper columns, listeners to my daily radio shows, and to my personal clients.

To my copyeditor Barbara Shor, for her clarity and craft.

To Terrence Warner, many thanks—may your 22 destiny be fulfilled.

Saving the best for last—to my family and friends.

Introduction

It gives me great pleasure to present *Numbers and You*
in this new, revised, and expanded edition. A little over
seven years has gone by since the original publication of
this work, and I have been gratified to see how consistent
and accurate the information has been. I have added
more than thirty brand new chapters to the original work,
and most of the original chapters have been revised, clari-
fied, and expanded.

I am presenting many new and original concepts, such
as "Parenting," the "Personal Week," "U.S. Presidents,"
"Money," "Products," and "Gift Giving" to name a few,
based upon my eighteen years of study, research, and observation of this fascinating subject. I have also added
new material on familiar topics, such as family, health,
career, and historical events.

The purpose of this book is still to help you help yourself to understand what makes you so special, and to answer the basic questions you have about yourself and your
loved ones with clarity and insight.

Table of Contents

Introduction   viii
How to Use This Book   xiii
Introduction: The Philosophical Origins and   1
    History of Numerology

PART I. NUMEROLOGY SYSTEMS

How to Add in Numerology   7
Numerology Systems: A Brief Introduction   12
The Pythagorean Approach: The Whole You   16
The Chaldean Approach   23
What's in a Name?   26
Name Attraction   34
Numbers and Their Rulership   39
The Planes of Power   56
Numerology and the Elements   60

PART II. CORRESPONDENCE SYSTEMS

Numerology and the Occult Sciences   65
Numerology and Astrology   72
Astrological and Numerological   75
    Correspondences
Biorhythms in Action   78
Lucky Colors, Gems, and Metals   90

PART III. YOUR PERSONAL NUMBERS

Birth Numbers and Their Meanings 95
The Life Cycles 100
A Rosicrucian Approach to the Life Cycles 110
Your Personal Destiny Number 113
The Master Numbers 117
Your Personal Year Forecast 120
Your Personal Month Forecast 141
Your Personal Week Forecast: A New Concept 149
Personal Changes in Your Life 153
What Day of the Week Were You Born? 157
Careers and Occupations 160
Your Home and Office 164
The Best Place to Live 167
Vacation Spots 171

PART IV. YOUR FAMILY

Tracing Your Roots 177
Attraction and Compatibility 182
Numerology and Marriage 188
Numerology and Sex 192
Parenting 197
Numerology and Childbirth 202
Your Child 206

PART V. YOUR HEALTH

Health and Illnesses 215
Herbs and Fruits: A Natural Way to Eat 218
Health: The Rosicrucian Way 221

PART VI. THE SUBJECT OF MONEY

Numerology and Money 227
How to Use Your Lucky Numbers 235
Analysis of a Lottery 237
What Does It Take to Be a Winner 253
Gambling and Horse Racing 255
Numerology and Horse Racing 259

PART VII. NUMEROLOGY IN HISTORY AND EVENTS

In the Beginning . . .   265
Friday the 13th   268
Numerology and the United States   272
Numerology and the Dollar Bill   274
Lincoln-Kennedy: A Common Thread   276
A Presidential Chart: Ronald Reagan   279
Failure of a Shuttle Mission   283
Dr. Martin Luther King, Jr.:   287
    A Numerical Biography
Numbers in Human Achievements   289
Numerology and Plane Crashes   291
Numerology and Fires   294
Numerology Tidbits from Real Life   296
Trends and Predictions   303

PART VIII. THINGS OF INTEREST

Music, Music, Music   313
Numerology and Hobbies   317
Numerology and Sports   320
Numerology and Cars   323
Numerology and Gift Giving   326
Numerology and Consumer Products   331
Questions Asked of Me   333

PART IX. NUMEROLOGY AND BEYOND

The Sacred Number 7   339
The Secrets of Thought Reading   342
Finding Lost Objects   347
Your Passions and Weaknesses   351
Failure and Success   357
Numerology and Success   360
Numerology and Meditation   362

A Closing Word   366
Appendix: Perpetual Calendar   367

How to Use This Book

Numbers and You: A Numerology Guide for Everyday Living is divided into nine parts for easy reference. Parts III through VI of the book deal with you, the individual —your name, birth, family, health, and career. Unlike most Numerology books, the section dealing with *YOUR NAME* uses both the Pythagorean and Chaldean systems of numbers.

The section on *YOUR PERSONAL NUMBERS* helps you learn how to time the events in your life by understanding your birth and destiny numbers, as well as the cycles, ages, and years that will surely affect your life. This book should be used over and over again as a reference, but more importantly, as a better way of understanding you.

Lloyd Strayhorn
New York City

Introduction: The Philosophical Origins and History of Numerology

Imagine getting up and starting your day in a world without numbers. Like many things, we take numbers for granted. From time to time I challenge my "Numbers and You" radio listeners to go through their day without using numbers. No, you can't lie in bed all day. The trick is to carry on a normal day and not use numbers. Don't look at your clock or wristwatch upon rising. Don't turn on your radio or TV set. Don't call anyone. When you leave home, don't buy gum, a newspaper, a candy bar, cigarettes. Don't get on a bus or subway, or drive to work. Don't ride an elevator, or keep that important appointment. Get the point?

From birth to death, you're a number—and in most cases, a series of numbers. The examples I've just given represent the physical side of numbers, where they're used in some concrete way. Take a case in point—without numbers telephone companies would fold in a very short time. After all, aren't they in the business of numbers?

However, there's another side to numbers — an invisible side. In the world of the occult this is known as Numerology, an ancient and accurate science. It seems numbers and Numerology have always existed together. In my large collection of books on this subject, authors have given credit to various sources, such as Pythagoras, the Greek philosopher, the ancient Chaldeans, the mystic and mysterious Brahmins of India, and the sages of ancient China.

It's hard to pinpoint exactly where, when, why, and how numbers and Numerology truly began. The common consensus is that they began, and I quote, "in antiquity." The references to the seven days of creation in the Scriptures may have been the very first use of Numerology. Others in this field suggest that Numerology began when "man walked with God"—that's a nice way of saying, before we got stuck in our 9 to 5, Blue Cross/Blue Shield, high-tech lifestyle.

Although the exact origin of Numerology hasn't been truly determined, there are strong clues. The Pythagorean and Chaldean schools of numbers are the most commonly used. Chaldean Numerology is older, but the Pythagorean system of numbers is far more popular.

Pythagoras was considered a master mathematician. Born in Greece in the 6th century B.C., he demonstrated a natural gift with numbers. Many people are familiar with his theorems in geometry. However, he is also considered to be the Father of Modern Numerology. It has been recorded that he spent many years of study in Egypt and other parts of the world learning the ancient science of numbers. He later brought this knowledge back to Greece, where he taught for nearly forty years, and established a college and philosophy of numbers that would bear his name to this very day.

It was said that Pythagoras taught in secret. That each student, selected with care, had to go through a five-year period of perfect silence for the purpose of contemplation to develop a deep sense of faith. Furthermore, his students had to commit his teachings to memory, for it was forbidden to put any of it in writing. It was only after his death, around the year 500 B.C., that his faithful followers broke with this tradition.

The Chaldean system of numbers—better known as Mystic Numerology—gives us an even stronger clue to the age of this science. Astrology, Numerology, and other occult studies were considered a religion, but not in the way we would know it today. Many Chaldean priests were also famous astrologers. They held the belief that all things were part of Divine Providence, and that the planets were simply heavenly interpreters. In the time of Alexander the Great, around 356 B.C., the Chaldeans believed that their knowledge of Numerology and Astrology went back at least 473,000 years. Perhaps it was no accident that, in time, Chaldea and the occult became synonymous. The Chaldean system of numbers is still in use today.

There are other schools of Numerology as well, all reflecting their individual places of origin as well as how they're applied. For instance, there were the ancient Brahmins of India. Cheiro (1866–1936), a leading palmist, numerologist, and psychic of his day, credited these mystic men of the East for much of what he knew. In ancient Japan, there's a system known as Ki, based upon certain numerical patterns found in the birth date. This system is slowly coming back into public notice. Then there is the sacred system of Hebrew Numerology, better known as the Kabalah, which is based upon the meanings of letters and sounds. And there's still another system coming from Africa that uses numbers for divination purposes. No matter what part of the world we look at, there's a system of Numerology that had its beginnings in the dawn of time.

Numerology has been attacked as a "pseudo science." Nothing could be further from the truth. *Webster*'s dictionary defines science as: "systematized knowledge of any one department of mind or matter; acknowledged truths and laws, *especially as demonstrated by induction, experiment, or observation* [italics mine]; any branch of knowledge considered as a distinct field for the investigation of facts concerning it." What could be a better description for Numerology? After perhaps tens of thousands of years, there has been more than enough time to observe, investigate, and report that Numerology is definitely a science.

Numerology has also been attacked for going against the laws and teachings of God. In fact, just the reverse is true. The Bible, the Talmud, the Koran, even the Egyptian Book of the Dead, have alluded to numbers in ways that required interpretation by people of wisdom.

After eighteen years as a student of this subject, I have discovered entirely new numerological concepts dealing with such subjects as childbirth, the family tree, and the personal week, which I described in later chapters. This book offers you the opportunity to find out what makes you special among the tens of millions of people in this world. There is without a doubt an exceptional relationship between *Numbers and You*.

I.

Numerology Systems

How to Add in Numerology

Of all the branches of mathematics, Numerology—the occult study of numbers—is perhaps the easiest to learn and apply. Where other branches of mathematics deal with addition, subtraction, multiplication, and the like, Numerology in the majority of cases uses only simple addition to arrive at its answer.

Even so, Numerology only follows the standard method of addition up to a point. For example, let's add the number 78. In standard addition you simply say $7+8=15$ for the correct answer. In Numerology this is not enough, it uses a further method of addition known as the "Fadic" system, or "natural addition." This simply means you keep adding two or more numbers together until you arrive at one single digit.

Taking our example of 78, $7+8$ adds up to 15, but the additional step is to $1+5$, and the final number is 6. That's how you add in Numerology. The beauty of this system is in knowing what each number from 1 to 9 represents. Just start by remembering at least seven key words or symbols out of the many for each number, and you're on your way.

There's an even deeper and more esoteric side of Numerology known as "compound" or "double" numbers. Let's take our example of 78 again. To find the compound or double number of 78, you simply add $7+8=15$. The compound or double number is 15, while the 6

$(1+5=6)$ expresses the essence or soul of the number 78.

Try the following brief exercise (the answers are at the end of this chapter):

Fadic Exercise in Natural Addition

A. Find the single digit for:

1. 059	2. 1	3. 23	4. 99763
5. 2984	6. 284	7. 28475	8. 28857
9. 003	10. 473	11. 6628	12. 37914

B. Find the compound numbers for:

1. 92	2. 815	3. 3266
4. 1289	5. 973	6. 408
7. 75873	8. 0258	9. 52825

Just as important single and double-digit numbers are found in your address, age, telephone number, and birth date, so your name has equal importance, for there are numbers assigned to the letters of the alphabet. In order to find the number of your name, you have to convert the letters into numbers then add up the total.

There are many systems used to translate letters into numbers, but perhaps the easiest and most popular method is the Pythagorean system of numbers, often referred to as "Modern Numerology." This system deals with the numbers 1 to 9 and the symbology they represent. This is how the Pythagorean system is laid out:

Pythagorean Number Values

1	2	3	4	5	6	7	8	9
A	B	C	D	E	F	G	H	I
J	K	L	M	N	O	P	Q	R
S	T	U	V	W	X	Y	Z	

If you study the Pythagorean system closely it's easy to understand why it has become so popular in the West. The complete alphabet has twenty-six letters. This numerology system goes in sequence with alphabet: The letter L is the 12th letter, or the number 3 $(1+2=3)$. The letter Z is the 26th letter, or 8 $(2+6=8)$.

The Pythagorean system is also popular because it's easy to remember by making associations. If you look closely at row 6, it spells "FOX." Take row 4, or DMV. The association to remember here might be the "Department of Motor Vehicles." Another reason for the popularity of this system is that should you forget the associations and the numbers, simply take a pen and paper and write each number from 1 to 9 across the top of the page leaving space between each number. Next, place the letter A under the 1, the B under the 2, and so on until you get to the letter I under the 9. Then continue on with the next row of letters.

Taking the name William, for example:

$$W \quad I \quad L \quad L \quad I \quad A \quad M$$
$$5 + 9 + 3 + 3 + 9 + 1 + 4 = 34$$
$$3 + 4 = 7$$

So the total of the name William is the number 7, while the compound or double number is 34.

Sometimes analyzing your name can be tricky! However, the general rule in Pythagorean numerology is to use the name "given at birth." During the course of one's life, one's name may change—through marriage, religious belief, legal name change, nicknames, etc. These new names are referred to as "angles of development."

Now starting with your first name, and then your last, look at the above chart and transpose your letters into numbers. The following are some helpful hints to avoid errors:

- Spread your name (as it appears on your birth certificate) out evenly, leaving a little space between each letter.

- Carefully place each corresponding number under each letter. Important: double check!
- Next, find the double or compound, if any, then the single number. The single number is the essence of who you are in character and other traits.

For an exercise, do the names of your family members and friends. We'll go more deeply into the subject of names in later chapters.

As another exercise, find the compound number, then the single number for the following:

1. Home address	2. Birth date	3. Age
4. Work address	5. Bank account	6. Weight
7. Social Security	8. Telephone	9. Salary

Sometimes analyzing your name can be tricky. Thus the system you use will determine the results you get. The Pythagorean system insists you use your ORIGINAL NAME AT BIRTH for analysis. However in my experience this edict isn't infallible, since by adulthood, most of us have decided upon the name we want to project before the public. The Chaldean system analyzes the name that's COMMONLY USED, rather than the name given at birth.

During the course of one's life, one's name may change—through marriage, religious belief, legal name change, nicknames, etc. These new names are referred to as "angles of development." But if possible, the original name given at birth should be analyzed first; however, do not summarily dismiss name changes. For example, I have a friend who will not reveal his FIRST NAME, but uses his middle and last name instead. What do you do in a case like this? I choose to analyze the name that client projects before the public.

In the case of a married woman her original maiden name should be analyzed first, followed by the changed name.

In regard to a legally changed name, such as Marvin

Hagler changing his name to Marvelous Marvin Hagler, this is valid basis for analysis, as long as he insists that everyone call him by that name.

Answers to:

A. Fadic system, or natural addition:

1. 5	2. 1	3. 5	4. 7
5. 5	6. 5	7. 8	8. 3
9. 3	10. 5	11. 4	12. 6

B. Answers to the compound numbers:

1. 11	2. 14	3. 17	4. 20
5. 19	6. 12	7. 30	8. 15
9. 22			

Numerology Systems: A Brief Introduction

There are many different systems of Numerology. There's an African, an Arabic, and a Hebrew system of numbers. There's the Abracadabra system, which uses the pyramid technique. There's even a system of Japanese Numerology.

The Numerology systems commonly used here in the West are the Pythagorean and Chaldean methods. Of the two, the Pythagorean system is the more popular and easier to use. This explains why one numerologist may tell you your name or birth number is a 7, while another will say that you're a 3. The question to bear in mind is what system was used to arrive at your key number or numbers, and what do they mean?

Both the Pythagorean and Chaldean systems are similar in some respects, yet they have fundamental differences. On the similar side, both systems take your name and month, day, and year in which you were born into consideration. Both agree that people's names affect their character, and the birth date affects their destiny. Both systems are equally good in their own way at giving advice. Finally, numbers in both systems carry the same meaning, quality, character, and nature—this seems to be universal under all the systems.

For example, let's take an individual named VANCE LOUIS WHEELER, born August 3, 1944.

DUAL SYSTEM NAME CHART

Pythagorean System

V A N C E
4 + 1 + 5 + 3 + 5 = 18
1 + 8 = 9

L O U I S
3 + 6 + 3 + 9 + 1 = 22
2 + 2 = 4

W H E E L E R
5 + 8 + 5 + 5 + 3 + 5 + 9 = 40
4 + 0 = 4

Total: 9 + 4 + 4 = 17
1 + 7 = **8**

Chaldean System

L O U I S
3 + 7 + 6 + 1 + 3 = 20
2 + 0 = 2

W H E E L E R
6 + 5 + 5 + 5 + 3 + 5 + 2 = 31
3 + 1 = 4

Total: 2 + 4 = **6**

Destiny Number Chart

8 (Birth Month)
3 (Birth Date)
<u>1944</u> (Birth Year)
1955 = 20; 2 + 0 = **2** Destiny Number

Now let's compare the difference under the two systems:

The Pythagorean System

Pythagorean, or "Modern Numerology," as it's often called, is used in the majority of cases. This system is very popular because it's easier to learn how to translate letters into numbers, and to master their meanings. The name, when analyzed under this system, gives a psychological bent to what motivates you, what you best express naturally, as well as the impression you're likely to make on others. Thus, this method defines the natural talents, abilities, and tools that you were given at birth. This is why using the *full name at birth* is very important under this system. Our sample name, Vance Louis Wheeler, is fully written out, translated into numbers, and then these numbers are added across. They total the single number of 8.

Next, the birth day is considered. The birth day number represents what must be learned or mastered in this life in order to be successful. This is often called the destiny or birth path number. In this case, Louis' destiny number is a 2.

The Chaldean System

Chaldean or "Mystic Numerology" is the older of the two systems. While it's considered more accurate, it's less popular. This is because the Chaldean system is not as easy to master, and the alphabet values are not in as systematic an order as the other. The name, when analyzed under this system, gives a more occult or metaphysical flavor to the destiny that's interwoven into the person's character. This method indicates the hidden forces or invisible strings at play behind the scenes.

The Chaldean method also differs in that it goes by the name you're most known by. Our sample person is known as Louis Wheeler to most people, and this is preferred under Chaldean analysis. As you see, his name under this system adds up to a 6.

After the name, the birth number—the day of the month on which you were born—is considered to be the next most important factor. In our case, Louis was born on the 3rd of the month. The birth day number affects the personality, health, and other factors that will be detailed in future chapters.

The Pythagorean Approach: The Whole You

Your name holds your fortune. Your name, in fact, is your most important form of recognition and identification. This is what makes each of us so special. When properly understood, your name holds the key that you need to answer many of the questions you have about yourself. For instance, what are your natural talents and abilities? What motivates your likes and dislikes? What type of impression do you make on others? These questions and many more can be answered from your name through the science of Numerology.

In Numerology, each letter in your name has a number value. When the letters of your name are transposed into numbers and added up, you can get an accurate picture of yourself. Below are the alphabet letters and their number value for each letter under the Pythagorean system of modern Numerology.

Pythagorean Number Values

1	2	3	4	5	6	7	8	9
A	B	C	D	E	F	G	H	I
J	K	L	M	N	O	P	Q	R
S	T	U	V	W	X	Y	Z	

In this system, there are three major parts to your name. They are called the EXPRESSION, MOTIVATION, and PERSONALITY numbers. Of the three, the most important is the EXPRESSION number. Your EXPRESSION number indicates your natural talents, skills, and abilities, regardless of education or training. The EXPRESSION number is found from the sum total of your name. For instance:

$$D \quad A \quad V \quad I \quad D$$
$$4 + 1 + 4 + 9 + 4 = 22$$
$$2 + 2 = 4$$

$$P \quad A \quad T \quad E \quad R \quad S \quad O \quad N$$
$$7 + 1 + 2 + 5 + 9 + 1 + 6 + 5 = 36$$
$$3 + 6 = 9$$

Total: $4 + 9 = 13$
$1 + 3 = 4$

As you can see, his first name totals 22 ($2 + 2 = 4$), and his last name totals 36 ($3 + 6 = 9$). Therefore, the single number of his first name (4) added to the single number of his last name (9) equals his EXPRESSION number. In this case the EXPRESSION number 4 ($9 + 4 = 13$; $1 + 3 = 4$).

The second major part to your name is the MOTIVATION number. The MOTIVATION number is found from the sum total of the vowels in your name. The vowels are A, E, I, O, U and sometimes Y (when used as a diphthong—the sound ay, ey, or oy in the syllables of a name, i.e., Ken ne dy). The MOTIVATION number represents your likes and dislikes, as well as deep inner desires, needs, and wants.

The final major part of your name is the PERSONALITY number. This is found from the sum total of the consonants in your name. It usually represents the first impression that you're likely to make on people upon first meeting. Taking Louis Wheeler's name again and dividing it into vowels and consonants:

```
        6 3 9           5 5   5
     L O U I S     W H E E L E R
     3         1     5 8     3   9
```

The sum (total of the vowels adds up to a 6 MOTIVA-TION number (total 33; 3 + 3 = 6). The sum total of the PERSONALITY number adds up to 29, which gives us a 2 PERSONALITY number (2 + 9 = 11; 1 + 1 = 2). Finally, add the MOTIVATION and PERSONALITY numbers together to get your EXPRESSION total. In Louis' case, the sum total EXPRESSION is an 8 (6 + 2 = 8). Now an-alyze your name in this manner, and then the names of your loved ones, family, and friends. Below you'll find a brief explanation of the meaning of the numbers—both positive and negative—from 1 to 9. Read each part of your name—EXPRESSION, MOTIVATION, and PER-SONALITY—separately.

Positive and Negative
Meaning of Numbers

NUMBER 1:

Positive: original, creative, leadership, forceful, in-ventive, ambitious, daring, active, visionary, dynamic, and independent.

Negative: bossy, headstrong, fearful, selfish, bullying, egotistical, dominating, tyrannical, impatient.

NUMBER 2:

Positive: gentle, understanding, artistic, romantic, loving, considerate, tactful, sensitive, persuasive, charming, and a good listener.

Negative: moody, critical, shy, deceptive, changeable, sloppy, petty, and insincere.

NUMBER 3:

Positive: proud, active, optimistic, joyful, creative, ambitious, conscientious, popular, expressive, sociable, and youthful.

Negative: boastful, wasteful, superficial, gossipy, dictatorial, careful, extravagant, scheming.

NUMBER 4:

Positive: practical, methodical, solid, studious, punctual, organized, structured, visionary, different, useful, and orderly.

Negative: narrow, slow, stubborn, moody, spiteful, negative attitude, and indifference.

NUMBER 5:

Positive: traveler, clever, adaptable, freedom loving, intellectual, quick to learn, crisis oriented, flexible, and literary.

Negative: vulgar, wanderer, irritable, wasteful, and a tendency to addictions.

NUMBER 6:

Positive: compassionate, magnetic, dependable, affectionate, concerned, loving, artistic, responsible and caring.

Negative: obstinate, dogmatic, stubborn, doubtful, irresponsible, and uncaring.

NUMBER 7:

Positive: analytical, silent, intuitive, spiritual, independent, truth seeking, love of nature, knowledgeable, an authority.

Negative: skeptical, sarcastic, cynical, deceptive, withdrawn, fault finding, nervous, self-doubting.

NUMBER 8:

Positive: determined, powerful, faithful, consistent, practical, capable with money and finance, authoritative, strong willed, and loyal.

Negative: misunderstood, cruel, greedy, morbid, destructive, revengeful, and hateful.

NUMBER 9:

Positive: organizer, energetic, dynamic, inspirational, good opinion of self, leadership oriented, daring, universal in outlook, and humane.

Negative: quick tempered, impulsive, day dreamer, narrow minded, combative, emotional, lack of direction.

Your First Name

If you concentrate for a moment on the numbers in your first name, much more information about yourself can be answered. Before going further, use the alphabet chart on page 16 to determine three important pieces of information from your first name alone. The most important is called the KEY. It is the sum total of your first name. For instance:

$$P \quad A \quad U \quad L$$
$$7 + 1 + 3 + 3 = 14$$
$$1 + 4 = 5$$

As you can see, Paul's first name totals 14 ($1+4=5$). The sum total of Paul's first name or KEY is 5. The KEY is what unlocks your individuality apart from the rest of your family members. The KEY also unlocks clues to your occupations and career.

The next important bit of information from your first name is your CORNERSTONE. The CORNERSTONE is the first letter of your first name. It represents the foundation that the rest of your name is built upon. The CORNERSTONE number also denotes your point of view, your approach to a situation and to life in general. Let's take the name:

$$L \quad U \quad C \quad I \quad L \quad L \quad E$$
$$3$$

The first letter in this name is L. In the Pythagorean alphabet, L = 3, which is her CORNERSTONE number.

The final bit of important information is your IN-

STINCTIVE DESIRE. This is found in the first vowel (A, E, I, O, U, or Y) in your first name. For instance:

5
K E I R R A

As you can see, the first vowel in this sample name is E, which has a number value of 5. Your first vowel tells how you act instinctively, under pressure and emergencies, it expresses your initial reaction to a situation.

Now, take your first name in this manner and discover the amazing insights your KEY, CORNERSTONE, and INSTINCTIVE DESIRE numbers will reveal to you. Below are the brief meanings and occupational clues from 1 to 9.

First Name Clues

NUMBER 1:

Individualist, daring, straightforward, desire to be "first," a take-charge attitude. You could be a lawyer, writer, manager, leader, supervisor, or director.

NUMBER 2:

Peaceful, loving, friendly, considerate, desire for partnership, warm, and gentle. You might be a cook, chemist, electrician, poet, painter, editor.

NUMBER 3:

Outgoing and expressive, cheerful attitude, desire to rise to the top, optimistic, youthful. Are you a photographer, artist, religious official, jeweler, judge, writer, or illustrator?

NUMBER 4:

Steadfast, dependable, unique way of doing things, deliberate, hard worker, serious minded. Could be an electrician, mathematician, aviator, reformer, radio or TV personality, mechanic or engineer.

NUMBER 5:

Changeable, carefree, strong desire for freedom and expression, quick thinking, ever alert. You might be a scientist, business person, importer-exporter, salesperson, public speaker, or investigator.

NUMBER 6:

Sense of duty and responsibility, helpful, appreciative, affectionate, comforting. Try being a realtor, banker, singer, musician, teacher, doctor, counselor, or lawyer.

NUMBER 7:

Need for privacy, analytical, unique way of thinking, intuitive, reflective, absorbing. Are you a researcher, occultist, accountant, analyst, spiritualist, traveler, scientist, or an authority on some subject?

NUMBER 8:

Philosophical and mature, determined and intense with a desire to endure, religious, desire for truth. You could be a banker, public figure, government official, farmer, policeman, or lawyer.

NUMBER 9:

Desire to inspire and lead, to control other's affairs, universal and giving, courageous and bold, action oriented, energetic, and strong willed. You might be an organizer, politician, firefighter, steelworker, plumber, well-known personality, or in the police force or the military.

The Chaldean Approach

The Chaldean approach is very ancient and accurate. This system was developed by the Chaldeans of long ago, who once occupied the southern part of Babylonia. Because of their long and diligent study of the occult, the people of Chaldea became well known for their contributions to astronomy, mathematics, and other sciences, particularly Astrology and Numerology. So adept were these Chaldean people in the metaphysical arts, that their name became synonymous with such studies.

The Chaldean system takes both your name and birthdate into consideration. The analysis of your name under this system uses only the name you are most known by, instead of your original name given at birth (a requirement of the Pythagorean system).

In the Chaldean system the numbers only go from 1 to 8, and not 1 to 9—this means the transposition of the numbers assigned to the alphabet is different than in the Pythagorean counterpart. Below is the Chaldean chart:

Chaldean Number Values

1	2	3	4	5	6	7	8
A	B	C	D	E	U	O	F
I	K	G	M	H	V	Z	P
J	R	L	T	N	W		
Q		S		X			
Y							

As you may already have noticed, no alphabet letter was assigned to the number 9. The reason why the number 9 was omitted under this system was because the Chaldeans felt the 9 was holy, sacred, and thus to be held apart from the rest. However, should your name or that of someone you know total 9, then the 9 remains. Let's analyze a sample name under this system:

$$L \quad E \quad S \quad L \quad I \quad E$$
$$3 + 5 + 3 + 3 + 1 + 5 = 20$$
$$2 + 0 = 2$$

$$E \quad R \quad I \quad C$$
$$5 + 2 + 1 + 3 = 11$$
$$1 + 1 = 2$$

$$S \quad C \quad O \quad T \quad T$$
$$3 + 3 + 7 + 4 + 4 = 21$$
$$2 + 1 = 3$$

Total: $2 + 2 + 3 = 7$

Under the Chaldean system, this name adds up to the single number 7. All numbers, whether found under this system or the Pythagorean one, have basically the same meanings, symbols, nature, and character. This seems to be the universal rule of all number systems.

However, under the Chaldean system, it isn't enough to know what the single numbers mean. One must also know what the "compound," or "double," numbers mean as well. The single number simply represents the physical, outward appearance of a person's name, whereas the compound number represents the deeper, metaphysical, hidden influences or forces behind the name. In our above example, although the name adds up to the single number 7, the name also has three compound numbers—20 in the first name, 11 in the middle name, and 21 in the last name.

Once the physical (single number) and metaphysical (compound number) aspects of your name have been determined, the next important step is your date of birth. Your date of birth means the day of the month you were born under, for it too has its own occult symbology and significance. So, Leslie Eric Scott, born on the 8th day of December, would also be considered a number 8 person under this system. Your date of birth is extremely important because it is unchangeable and therefore a constant, like the needle pointing north on a compass. A person may undergo a series of name changes over the years because of marriage, adoption, and the like, but the birth date remains the same.

What's in a Name?

What's in a name? You'd be surprised at the vast amount of information that can be obtained from a person's name. This is where Numerology is a most helpful guide. In Numerology, a name can reveal a person's natural talents, skills, and abilities, regardless of his or her educational background and training.

In the West, a person is usually given three names at birth. There is the first name, the middle, and the last (family) name. However, for whatever reason, as adults we generally use a first and last name only. The way to interpret a name in Numerology is to transpose the letters of the name into numbers. The following is a layout of the letters and their numbers.

Pythagorean Number Values

1	2	3	4	5	6	7	8	9
A	B	C	D	E	F	G	H	I
J	K	L	M	N	O	P	Q	R
S	T	U	V	W	X	Y	Z	

Using this chart, you can now transpose any name you wish to know about into numbers.

The First Name

In Numerology the first name of a person is called the "Key." It is the key that unlocks an individual's talents and traits and sets the person apart from the rest of the family members. The Key is determined from the sum of the letters of the first name. For instance, let's use the name "Mark."

$$M \quad A \quad R \quad K$$
$$4 + 1 + 9 + 2 = 16$$
$$1 + 6 = 7$$

As you can see, "Mark" adds up to 16, and further to 7 $(1+6=7)$.

Another curious bit of information can be found from the first name, and that is called the "Cornerstone." The Cornerstone is simply the first letter of the first name. In our example, the first letter of Mark's name is an M, which has the numerical value of 4. The Cornerstone represents the foundation or basic way in which you approach people or a situation.

One more interesting clue to your character determined from the first name is called the "Instinctive Reaction." This is derived from the first vowel in the name. It indicates the way you're likely to act under stress or crisis conditions. The first vowel in Mark's name is the letter A, and thus represents the number 1 .

The Last Name

Have you ever wondered about your last name? The science of Numerology can tell you quite a bit about your family's traits, occupational preferences, even inherited illnesses. The way to determine this is to take the sum total of the family name. Let's take the sample name of RILEY. Next, transpose the letters of the family name into numbers.

$$R \quad I \quad L \quad E \quad Y$$
$$9 + 9 + 3 + 5 + 7 = 33$$
$$3 + 3 = 6$$

The family name RILEY adds up to the number 6. This number denotes certain traits, tendencies, occupational clues, and even possible health problems that are likely to be part of the RILEY family makeup.

One important point to remember is that when you're adding up the numbers in any name, take note of which numbers are repeated the most. For instance in the RILEY family name, although it adds up to the number 6, the 6 is not repeated in the name. But the number 9 is repeated twice. As a result, the 9—as well as the 6, which is the sum total of the family name—should also be given importance.

The following is a brief description of family traits, job and health tendencies. Remember, study the numbers in your first name as well as the single digit.

Family Traits of the Number 1:

TRAITS:

Tendency in the family toward leaders, those who are aggressive and determined, and who don't like to lose or be last. A lot of "firsts" run in the family—first doctor, first lawyer, etc.

OCCUPATIONS:

Administrators, lawyers, writers, inventors, or leaders in any field. Many firsts achieved in the career.

HEALTH:

Heart problems or high blood pressure, also problems with the eyes, such as astigmatism; and problems with the lungs.

Family Traits of the Number 2:

TRAITS:

This is a meticulous type of family that gets into details and is usually particular about matters of dress, manners, living habits, and diet. Women in a 2 family are generally respected, held in high regard, and often have great influence in family matters.

OCCUPATIONS:

Artists, poets, musicians, those who work with computers or electronics, or are in the food industry in some way. Hobbies often turn into professions under this influence.

HEALTH:

Stomach and digestive problems, especially if a lot of 2's are repeated. Diabetes, tumors, ulcers, hemorrhoids. The women born into a 2 family may have tendencies toward disorders of the reproductive system.

Family Traits of the Number 3

TRAITS:

Generally, pride, optimism, and ambition run through the family. They have a strong desire to succeed and move toward positions of trust or authority over others. Three is the talkative number and may produce the same trait in this particular family.

OCCUPATIONS:

Government, religion, the arts or creative careers, occupations connected with the public are also dominant.

HEALTH:

Problems connected with the skin, feet, overindulgence, and low blood pressure. Cases of burnout tend to run in this family because of overwork as well as emotional upsets.

Family Traits of the Number 4:

TRAITS:

Tendencies toward the odd and unusual run in the 4 family. They enjoy doing everything—or at least most things—completely different from others.

OCCUPATIONS:

Mechanical and mathematical types of occupations; radio, television, electronics, computers, and gadgets of all kinds.

HEALTH:

Tendency toward odd and mysterious illnesses that are hard to pinpoint. Moody in the extreme. This can lead to deep depression or possible suicide, especially if three or four 4s are found in the family name.

Family Traits of the Number 5:

TRAITS:

Here we find family members who are usually varied in temperament as well as occupations. A changeable nature runs through the family. As 5 is the number of attractiveness, this family may be quite good-looking.

OCCUPATIONS:

Occupations associated with the public, and with travel and movement, as well as the sciences, business, commerce, and communications in all forms.

HEALTH:

Nervous tension, mental exhaustion, paralysis, dizziness, and twitching in some part of the face, particularly around the eyes and mouth. Drug or alcohol addiction may be pronounced if many 5s are repeated.

Family Traits of the Number 6:

TRAITS:

Like the 5 family, good-looking people tend to run in this family too. The 6 family line has a strong sense of duty and of family obligation. They want the best out of life.

OCCUPATIONS:

Service occupations, including teachers, nurses, doctors, social workers, cashiers, artists, singers, lawyers, and the like.

HEALTH:

Tendency toward asthma and bronchial discomfort; hay fever and other allergies as well as problems with the nose, throat, and upper part of the chest. Women born into a 6 family may also experience sensitivity in the breasts.

Family Traits of the Number 7:

TRAITS:

This family tends to be secretive or low key. There is a strong need to analyze others. Loners are often produced in this family line.

OCCUPATIONS:

Technicians, researchers, accountants, as well as those who specialize in computers, electronics, the sciences, as well as religious and philosophical fields.

HEALTH:

Night sweats, worry and annoyances, stomach and digestive problems brought about by imagining that things are worse than they really are.

Family Traits of the Number 8:

TRAITS:

Here, you're likely to have family members who look older than they really are. By temperament, they're conservative, traditional, solid, and not afraid to work hard for the things they want out of life.

OCCUPATIONS:

Areas connected with religion, real estate, banking, the government, or any form of public life. Businesspeople, persons of authority, and administrators are found here as well.

HEALTH:

Headaches, constipation, rheumatism, blood poisoning, depression; problems connected with the knees, teeth, and bones. This family name may also fall victim to wrong medical diagnoses, treatment, or drug prescriptions.

Family Traits of the Number 9:

TRAITS:

Here you're likely to find family members who are aggressive, active, and well traveled. This family has a strong sense of self-determination and is basically not afraid to fight for what it believes.

OCCUPATIONS:

Occupations of a risky nature have dominion over this family name—they become firefighters, police, electricians, machinists, steel and construction workers, and enter the military.

HEALTH:

Accidents are more the general rule here than contagious or malignant illnesses. The danger may come from weapons, explosives, knives and other sharp instruments, and machinery of all kinds, they are prone to fevers. This particular family may also develop tendencies toward alcoholism.

Name Attraction

The name of a person in Chaldean Nu-Numerology seems to have the power to draw to it persons who are born under certain days of the month and Zodiac signs. Take, for instance, the name Bill, which adds up to the value of 9 in this system. As a 9, Bill may find that he has a tendency to draw or attract persons whose birth number adds up to a 9 or those born on the 9th, 18th, or 27th of the month. Bill will find that those born in the months of April (Aries), November (Scorpio), and August (Leo) will be very much attracted to him as well.

In Numerology, your name is taken into account because each letter has a numerical value. Next, your birth date is also considered. Your name, as you already know, denotes your natural talents, gifts, skills, and abilities. Your name is the "teacher," it tells you what you're here to teach, how you're to show others the way. Your birth date, on the other hand, sees you as the "pupil," and indicates what you're here to study, learn and master.

With this in mind, you can understand how the birth number of a person (pupil), can be easily attracted to another person's name (teacher). Therefore, you'll find that persons with certain birth numbers tend to learn something from those who symbolically carry this number in their name.

First, find your date of birth number (i.e., a person born on the 15th of the month is a number 6; $1+5=6$). Next, check below for lists of names and their numerical value under the Chaldean system. Because there are literally thousands of names, only the more common ones have been listed. If there's a particular one you're drawn to—romantic, business, or otherwise—that's not on this list, use the Chaldean chart to add up the person's name and see what number you get.

Numbers for Common Names

NUMBER 1 PERSON

Born on the 1st, 10th, 19th, or 28th of the month, or under the sign of Aries or Leo, you'll often find yourself drawn to people with such names as: Albert, Alicia, Anthony, Audrey, Barbra, Basil, Billy, Brenda, Calvin, Carla, Carlos, Cheryl, Chuck, Clara, Claudia, Claudine, Craig, Curtis, Dan, Daniel, Debbie, Doreen, Eddie, Eleanor, Estelle, Fred, Gina, Gordon, Gwen, Juanita, Kevin, Lenny, Lydia, Mack, Marvin, Maureen, Mimi, Morris, Paula, Patricia, Ralph, Reggie, Roy, Stephanie, Steven, Sidney, Willie, William, and Zenobia.

NUMBER 2 PERSON

If you were born on the 2nd, 11th, 20th, or 29th of the month, or under the sign of Cancer, you'll sense a natural attraction to people with names such as: Aileen, Annette, Arthur, Barbara, Bob, Brian, Butch, Camille, Carmen, Cecile, Charlie, Charlene, Delores, Denny, Earl, Eleana, Elaine, Emanuel, Eric, Erika, Eugene, Fanny, Fern, Harry, Jasmine, Jimmy, Jerry, Johnnie, Jonathan, Joseph, Julius, LaMar, Leon, Les, Leslie, Louis, Melissa, Michelle, Noreen, Phillip, Ricardo, Ronna, Ruby, Sally, Shirley, Tina, Tracy, Vincent, Vivian, Yvonne, and Zelda.

NUMBER 3 PERSON

Those born on the 3rd, 12th, 21st, or 30th of the month, as well as those born under Pisces or Sagittarius, will find a feeling of creative expression with those whose names are: Anita, Anna, Ben, Carole, Debi, Dorothy, Duane, Ella, Ellen, Erica, Gus, Hazel, Isaiah, Jean, Julia, Laurence, Liza, Llonice, Majorie, Maxine, Mike, Monica, Muriel, Nathaniel, Patricia, Rebecca, Sarah, Scott, Shari, Tanya, Theodore, Walter, and Wendy.

NUMBER 4 PERSON

Those born on the 4th, 13th, 22nd, or 31st of the month, or under the sign of Aquarius, will be unexpectedly drawn to people with such names as: Abdul, Al, Allen, Beulah, Carolyn, Catherine, Charles, Conrad, Donna, Edward, Erick, Ethel, Felicia, Georgia, Gerri, Greg, Hank, Harold, Jackie, Jeff, Jennie, Joe, Kathy, Keirra, Kelvin, Kenneth, Laura, Lee, Lorne, Lucy, Luis, Lula, Marlon, Michael, Miriam, Pamela, Pat, Pete, Renee, Robert, Roland, Ronald, Rosa, Russel, Sammy, Samuel, Ted, Trudie, Vicky, Wallace, Winston, and Yolanda.

NUMBER 5 PERSON

If you were born on the 5th, 14th, or 23rd of the month, or under the signs of Gemini or Virgo, you'll be stimulated by those whose names are: Adrian, Alex, Ali, Andrew, Beatrice, Bernice, Bobby, Carrie, Cathy, Chris, Cliff, Dennis, Dora, Elliot, Emily, Emma, Etta, Fatisha, Floyd, Francis, Grace, Hannibal, Helen, Herb, Henrietta, Horace, James, Jennifer, Joan, Kendall, Lena, Linda, Maury, Mildred, Ned, Omar, Rickie, Ron, Russ, Sadie, Selvin, Sharon, Sheilah, Skip, Steve, Sue, Tammy, Terry, Valerie, and Victor.

NUMBER 6 PERSON

Born on the 6th, 15th, or 24th, or under the sign of Taurus or Libra, you'll probably find a romantic link with such names as: Adrianne, Alberto, Benjamin, Beverly, Billy, Cecil, Claire, Donald, Eileen, Elizabeth, Ernest, Esther, Faye, Frankie, Gladys, Howie, Hubert, Jim, Joanne, Johnny, Karen, Linwood, Lionel, Major, Mamie, Maybelle, Melba, Melvin, Mia, Nancy, Otis, Peter, Phyllis, Tom, Tyrone, Sydelle, Sylvia, Thomas, Vanessa, Vivien, Wardell, and Yosef.

NUMBER 7 PERSON

If you were born on the 7th, 16th, or 25th of the month, or under the sign of Cancer or Pisces, you may be mysteriously drawn to people with such names as: Aaron, Aida, Alfonso, Anne, Beth, Betty, Carlton, Carol, Charlotte, Cicely, Clyde, Danny, David, Diane, Don, Dottie, Eve, Fannie, Gary, George, Herbert, Howard, Iris, Jack, Jan, Janet, Janice, José, Kim, Louise, Luther, Malcolm, Marsha, Mickie, Mickey, Miles, Nailah, Priscilla, Rasheed, Russell, Sandra, Sallie, and Yvette.

NUMBER 8 PERSON

If your birth date is the 8th, 17th, or 28th of the month, or you were born under the sign of Capricorn, you may find yourself seriously attracted to those whose names are: Albert, Angel, Allen, Ave, Barry, Connie, Crystal, Deborah, Dianna, Doris, Elsie, Ernestine, Gail, Hector, Irma, Jason, Jesse, Jessica, Jill, Julian, Karl, Laurance, Lillian, Lisa, Loretta, Lorraine, Mary, Martha, Michele, Phil, Regina, Rick, Rita, Rowena, Sam, Sharrieff, Stephen, Toni, Tony, Trudy, Vaughn, Vernel, and Wanda.

NUMBER 9 PERSON

Those born on the 9th, 18th, or 27th, or under Aries
or Scorpio, you will feel activated by those whose names
are: Adele, Amaar, Bill, Carl, Clarence, Clive, Derek,
Douglas, Ed, Eli, Ernie, Flo, Frank, Frances, Gene,
Gerald, Henry, Inez, Isaac, Jesse, John, Larry, Leroy,
Lewil, Lloyd, Lorna, Maria, Mark, Patti, Paul, Rahsaan,
Richard, Ricky, Sheila, Susan, Teddy, Tim, and Vicki.

Numbers and Their Rulership

The Number 1

The number 1 is masculine in nature. It is ruled by the Sun and represents the sign of Leo in the 5th House.

THE POSITIVE:

On the positive side, the number 1 is ambitious, daring, commanding, original, inventive, forceful, independent, courageous, a leader, generous, action oriented, fearless, aggressive, dynamic, capable of mental foresight, bold, strong, and dynamic.

THE NEGATIVE:

The negative 1 can be arrogant, bossy, selfish, egotistical, cold, bullying, manipulating, stubborn, domineering, dependent, antagonizing, narrow, demanding, and insulting. The number 1 is usually a sore loser, as it loves to win or come in first.

OCCUPATIONS:

Lawyer, writer, leader, pioneer, administrator, director, supervisor, doctor, executive, officer, producer, manager, instructor, captain, entrepreneur, expert, scientist, president, the first in life.

HEALTH:

Astigmatism of the eyes, high blood pressure, irregular blood circulation, heart palpitations, or other heart disorders; lung problems. Care or caution should be taken in health matters during January, May, and October.

MATES/PARTNERS:

Those born on the 1st, 10th, 19th, or 28th of any month. Astrologically, Aquarius, Aries, and Leo are very attracted to you. Secondary attraction with those born on the 4th, 13th, 22nd, or 31st of the month, or in the months of February, April, or August.

TIMES OF THE YEAR:

The best day is Sunday, followed by Tuesday. February, April, and August are the important months. The time span covered by the number 1 is about six months.

CITIES/COUNTRIES:

Atlanta, Boston, New York, Addis Ababa, Reno, Dar es Salaam, Havana, Houston, Knoxville, St. Kitts, Nassau, and Birmingham.

TIDBITS:

The number 1 has rulership over large and imposing buildings, official residences and headquarters, royal palaces, hills, forests, and convention halls.

The colors associated with 1 are in the yellow, orange, and brown family.

The number 1 is at its best during daylight hours.

The Number 2

The number 2 is feminine in nature. The 2 is ruled by the moon and represents the sign of Cancer in the 4th House.

THE POSITIVE:

Easygoing, mild mannered, agreeable, patient, considerate, cooperative, gracious, kind, a peacemaker, caring, persuasive, charming, receptive, diplomatic, understanding, and modest.

THE NEGATIVE:

Petty, small-minded, deceptive, apathetic, shy, weak, hoarding, supersensitive, cruel, impatient, uncooperative, sly, insincere, and inconsiderate.

OCCUPATIONS:

The number 2 tends to find success as a poet, musician, psychic, editor, draftsperson, computer programmer, botanist, chemist, statistician, actuary, librarian, secretary, engineer, naval officer, mediator, accountant, healer, clerk, designer, caterer, cook or restaurant owner, actor, artist, cashier, hostess or host.

HEALTH:

Stomach and digestive problems of all kinds, female problems, ptomaine poisoning, diabetes, cancer, ulcers, tumors, hemorrhoids, and water retention. Care and caution related to health should be taken during January, April, and November.

MATES/PARTNERS:

In romance or partnerships of any kind the number 2 does well with those born in late February through March, late April through May, late June through July, late September through October—as well as those born on the 1st, 2nd, 7th, 10th, 11th, 16th, 19th, 20th, 25th, 28th, and 29th of the month, or in the months March, May, July, and October.

TIMES OF THE YEAR:

The best day for the 2 is Monday, followed by Friday as a second choice. March, May, July, August, and October are usually months of importance. In reference to time it means news of any nature could be expected in about an hour.

CITIES/COUNTRIES:

Austin, Baltimore, Barcelona, Bridgeport, Brooklyn, Cincinnati, Harlem, Los Angeles, Leningrad, Miami, Panama, Raleigh, St. Thomas, St. Vincent, Timbuktu, countries in North and West Africa.

OTHER TIDBITS:

The number 2 has rulership over lakes, ponds, streams, water towers, public places, beaches, docks, harbors, canals, oceans, milk products, and the fishing industry.

The colors associated with 2 are in the cream, green, and white family.

The number 2 is at its best during the night.

The Number 3

The number 3 is masculine in nature. The 3 is ruled by Jupiter and represents the signs of Pisces in the 12th House, and Sagittarius in the 9th House.

THE POSITIVE:

Expressive, creative, artistic, ambitious, positive, popular, confident, sociable, conscientious, hardworking, articulate, optimistic, musical, self-expressive, cheerful.

THE NEGATIVE:

Vain, dictatorial, wasteful, shallow and superficial, boastful, pessimistic, self-indulgent, jealous, unreliable, extravagant, show-off.

OCCUPATIONS:

Artist, actor, jeweler, poet, photographer, writer, illustrator, gardner, club owner, dancer, cartoonist, entertainer, circus performer, lawyer, government official.

HEALTH:

The number 3 in relation to health is usually associated with overstrained nerves brought on by overwork and emotional upsets; low blood pressure, skin problems, and foot discomfort. Guard the health during the months of February, June, and September.

MATES/PARTNERS:

In close relationships the number 3 person tends to have a strong affinity with those born from late February through March, late April through May, late September through October, late November through December, as well as those born on the 3rd, 6th, 12th, 15th, 21st, 24th, or 30th of the month, or in the months of March, May, October, and December.

TIMES OF THE YEAR:

The best day for the number 3 is Thursday, followed by Friday as a second choice. March, December, May, and October are usually the months of importance. In reference to time it means news received in about one month.

CITIES/COUNTRIES:

Antigua, Cuba, Guadeloupe, Manhattan, Aruba, Gambia, Haiti, Jamaica, Kingston, Martinique, Montego

Bay, Moscow, San Antonio, Staten Island, Red Bank, NJ, Montclair, Memphis, Toledo.

OTHER TIDBITS:

The number 3 has rulership over churches, temples, and other houses of worship, theaters, government buildings, circuses, and large institutions, children's centers and shelters, fairs, and exhibit halls.

The colors associated with 3 are in the lilac, purple, and mauve family.

The number 3 is at its best anytime.

The Number 4

The number 4 is feminine in nature. The 4 is ruled by the planet Uranus and represents the sign of Aquarius in the 11th House.

THE POSITIVE:

Hard working, diligent, punctual, honest, down to earth, exacting, methodical, mechanical, and mathematical talents, disciplined, practical, determined, organized, economical, loyal, steady, enduring, love of detailed work.

THE NEGATIVE:

Dull, slow to make decisions, crude, moody, violent, destructive, harsh, overly stern, rigid and unbending, hateful, insensitive, melancholy, cruel, brutal.

OCCUPATIONS:

TV or radio personality, aviator, engineer, computer expert, hypnotist, farmer, bricklayer, electrician, occultist, accountant, architect, sculptor, mechanic, printer, mathematician, mason, janitor, factory worker, electrician, plumber.

HEALTH:

The number 4 is generally a question mark when it comes to medical diagnoses. There's a tendency toward odd and unusual illnesses or diseases generally difficult to pinpoint in the early stages. There can be mood swings, despondency, suicidal tendencies or erratic behavior. The health should be especially watched during January, March, May, October, and December.

MATES/PARTNERS:

In matters of relationship, number 4 people have a strong affinity with persons older than themselves. This is especially true with those born in late January through February, late May through June and late July through August. Those born on the 1st, 4th, 10th, 13th, 19th, 22nd, 28th, or 31st of the month are also compatible, as well as those born in the months of February, June and August.

TIMES OF THE YEAR:

The best day for the number 4 is Sunday, followed by Wednesday. The months of February, June, July, and August usually prove to be significant in some way. In reference to time, the number 4 means news received in about six months or less.

CITIES/COUNTRIES:

Atlantic City, Trinidad, Mobile, Washington, D.C., Barbados, London, Jackson, Albany, Saratoga, Buenos Aires, Surinam, Richmond, Salt Lake City, Princeton, Dayton.

OTHER TIDBITS:

The number 4 has rulership over odd and unusual buildings, nuclear plants, generators, power stations, mental institutions, radio and TV stations, railway stations, assembly-line plants.

Electric shades and halftones are associated with 4.

The number 4 is generally at its best during the odd hours of the day.

The Number 5

The number 5 is masculine in nature. The 5 is ruled by the planet Mercury, which represents Gemini in the 3rd House, and Virgo in the 6th House.

THE POSITIVE:

Clever, adaptable, versatile, energetic, literary, expressive, curious, daring, spontaneous, freedom loving, quick reflexes, crisis oriented, enthusiastic, loves excitement and travel.

THE NEGATIVE:

Excessive, irritable, careless, vulgar, callous, self-indulgent in relation to sex, drugs, and drink, lack of discipline, inconsistent, nervous, abusive, lacks direction.

OCCUPATIONS:

Salesperson, reporter, communications expert, detective, public relations, pilot, writer, magician, gambler, instructor, personnel interviewer, stockbroker, import-export, scientist, racing driver, good on emergency or crisis teams.

HEALTH:

Mental exhaustion, nervous tension, insomnia, amnesia, paralysis, lung problems, stammering in speech, dizziness, twitching in some part of the face. Prone to injuries to the arms, shoulders, and hands. Health changes likely to occur more in January, March, and December than any other time.

MATES/PARTNERS:

In matters of romance, this number is considered the most adaptable of them all. Relationships are best with those born in late April through May, late May through June, late August through September and late September through October. This also includes those born on the 5th, 6th, 14th, 15th, 23rd, and 24th of the month, as well as those born in the months of May, June, September, and October.

TIMES OF THE YEAR:

The best day for the 5 is Wednesday, followed by Friday. Generally, the months of February, May, June, September, and October are important. In reference to time, the 5 means news will come in about two months.

CITIES/COUNTRIES:

Chicago, Oakland, Attica, Greensboro, Freeport, St. Croix, Acapulco, Nicaragua, Curaçao, Rio de Janeiro, Bimini, Cairo, Nashville, Trenton, Palm Beach.

OTHER TIDBITS:

The 5 has rulership over high places, public schools, highways, playgrounds, post offices, shopping malls, trade and science buildings, labs and plants, communications centers, places of commerce, race tracks of all kinds, centers of any general public activity.

Light, mixed colors are usually associated with the 5.

The number 5 is at its best both day and night.

The Number 6

The 6 is feminine in nature. It is ruled by the planet Venus and represents the signs of Taurus in the 2nd House, and Libra in the 7th House.

THE POSITIVE:

Dependable, loving, loyal, responsible, magnetic, comforting, balanced, thoughtful, stable, sociable, service oriented, family oriented, artistic, outgoing, kind, consistent, understanding.

THE NEGATIVE:

Stubborn, gossiper, judgmental, domestic tyrant, interfering, Doubting Thomas, meddlesome, worshiping persons and things, cynical, suspicious, dogmatic, jealous, complacent, self-righteous.

OCCUPATIONS:

Teacher, lawyer, artist, singer, doctor, nurse, advisor, tutor, voice teacher, public servant, dentist, host/hostess, athlete, social worker, counselor, realtor, union or labor leader, professor, surgeon, beautician, makeup artist, public speaker.

HEALTH:

General concerns with the nose, throat, and upper part of the lungs; asthma, bronchitis, hay fever, irregular blood circulation, heart palpitations; and sensitivity in breasts for women. Watch out for possible changes during February, April, and August.

MATES/PARTNERS:

As the nature of the 6 has a strong leaning toward affection, home, and family, the proper selection of a mate is most important. Those born in late February through March, late April through May, late September through October, and late November through December tend to become the best mates. This also includes those born on the 3rd, 6th, 12th, 15th, 21st, 24th, or 30th of the month, as well as in the months of March, May, July, October, and December.

TIMES OF THE YEAR:

The best day for the number 6 is Friday, followed by Thursday. Most often the months of March, May, October, and December hold important milestones and events in the life. In reference to time, the number 6 means news received in about two weeks.

CITIES/COUNTRIES:

Amherst, Bogota, Santo Domingo, Kansas City, Augusta, Bermuda, Hawaii, New Orleans, Dallas, Paris, Paradise Island, Baton Rouge, Dover, Milwaukee, Honolulu, San Francisco, Munich.

OTHER TIDBITS:

The number 6 has rulership over institutional buildings, hospitals, museums, beautiful homes, bedrooms, fields, pastures, day-care centers, neighborhood shelters, civil defense shelters, art galleries, health centers.

The colors strongly associated with the 6 lie the blue family—from the lightest to the darkest.

The number 6 is at its best during the day.

The Number 7

The number 7 is masculine in nature. It was under the rulership of the Moon in the past, but it has now been assigned to the planet Neptune. It represents the signs of Cancer in the 5th House, and Pisces in the 12th House.

THE POSITIVE:

Knowledgeable, intuitive, love of distant travel, refined, perfectionist, psychic, independent, discriminating, thorough, profound, religious, inspired, analytical, probing, secretive, researching, seeker of truth, philosophical, contented, an authority.

THE NEGATIVE:

Sarcastic, drifter, recluse, hermit, fault finding, too demanding, no depth, skeptical, crafty, cunning, deceitful, withdrawn, schemer, faithless, too critical.

OCCUPATIONS:

Researcher, analyst, astrologer, astronomer, scientist, religious leader, navigator, accountant, healer, writer, technician, magician, numerologist, surgeon, computer expert or operator, librarian, engineer, editor, marine biologist, teacher, cultural expert.

HEALTH

As a general rule, it's been found that worry and annoyance tends to get the best of 7s. They are also inclined to be overimaginative, thinking things are worse than they really are. Skin problems predominate, followed by night sweats and minor stomach problems. Watch the health during January, April, and August.

MATES/PARTNERS:

In matters of romance or partnership they are generally faithful, preferring monogamous relationships. Perhaps the 7's love of being alone accounts for this—in addition to a discriminating nature. Their best mates are usually born in late January through February and March, late June through July and August. This also holds true for those born on the 2nd, 4th, 7th, 11th, 13th, 16th, 20th, 22nd, 25th, and 31st of the month, and in the months of March and July.

TIMES OF THE YEAR:

The best day for the number 7 is Monday, followed by Sunday. Generally, the months of February, March, July, and August play an important role in the life. In reference to time, it means news received in about one hour or sooner.

CITIES/COUNTRIES:

Norfolk, Queens, Hollywood, Little Rock, Paramus, NJ, Barcelona, Brazil, Japan, Zaire, Senegal, Lusaka, Madrid, Santiago, Teaneck, NJ, Tallahassee, Canton.

OTHER TIDBITS:

The number 7 has rulership over the motion picture industry, the fishing and shipping industries, the pharmaceutical industry, undersea exploration, space exploration, gardens, cultural events, woods and forests, lakes and streams, all houses of worship, oil fields, science and research projects or conventions, psychic or occult fairs.

The colors of the number 7 fall into the green, cream, and white family; there is also a strong attraction to pastels.

The number 7 is at its best during the night.

The Number 8

The number 8 is feminine in nature. It's ruled by the planet Saturn and represents the sign of Capricorn in the 10th House.

THE POSITIVE:

Achieving, powerful, authoritative, businesslike, successful, determined, strong powers of concentration and sense of justice, conservative, builder, self-reliant, dependable, executive ability, religious, philosophical, salt of the earth.

THE NEGATIVE:

Greedy, fatalistic, intense, oppressive, domineering, material or financial obsession, power hungry, scheming, lack of value judgment, material selfishness, material or emotional jealousy, tendency to become victims of tragedy.

OCCUPATIONS:

Executive, realtor, banker, commodity broker, laborer, grave digger, ditch digger, archaeologist, antique dealer, prison warden, miner, sanitation worker, religious leader or official, politician, police officer, lawyer, manager, boxer, actor, dramatist.

HEALTH:

The number 8 is sometimes a puzzle to the medical profession. They usually experience headaches, despondency, constipation, toxic buildup in the blood system, rheumatism, trouble with the kidneys, bile, and excretory system. There's also a tendency for 8s to be given the wrong drug prescription or medical treatment. Health changes usually come during February, June, August, September, January, May and October.

MATES/PARTNERS:

Because of the maturity of mind, the 8 is often drawn to persons much older than themselves. As a result those born late December through January, late April through May and late September through October are generally their best mates. This also includes those born on the 6th, 15th, 17th, 24th, or 26th of the month.

TIMES OF THE YEAR:

The best day for the number 8 is Saturday, followed by Friday. As a general rule, the months of January, May, July, and October are significant in the life. In reference to time, the number 8 means news received in one year.

CITIES/COUNTRIES:

Buffalo, Cleveland, Jersey City, Rye, Tulsa, the Bahamas, Bombay, Cuba, Haiti, Lagos, India, Delta, Sacramento, Guyana, Montego Bay, Gambia, Akron, Bloomfield, China, Fairfax.

OTHER TIDBITS:

The number 8 has rulership over cemeteries and other burial sites, coal mines and mineral fields, old or haunted houses, prisons, caves, antique shops, archeological sites and explorations, business, real estate, and banking institutions, night life, falling objects, nursing homes, grandparents, matters dealing with old age.

The colors of the number 8 tend to be dark, such as black, navy, or dark blue, and dark browns.

The number 8 is at its best during the night.

The Number 9

The number 9 is masculine in nature. It is ruled by the planet Mars. It represents the signs of Aries in the 1st House, and Scorpio in the 8th House.

THE POSITIVE:

Humanitarian, generous, broad-minded, energetic, bold, courageous, competitive, inspirational, independent, good organizer, self-determining, strong, charitable, artistic, resourceful, global-minded, spiritual, strong willed.

THE NEGATIVE:

Impulsive, hasty, ill-tempered, argumentative, over-emotional, daydreaming, narrow-minded, aimless, heartless, cynical, resentful, selfish, all talk and no show.

OCCUPATIONS:

Police or military officer, firefighter, construction worker, politician, musician, artist, spiritual leader, publisher, journalist, cutler, steelworker, ballistics expert, surgeon, judge, occultist, professional athlete, union leader, TV or radio personality, entrepreneur, travel expert or guide.

HEALTH:

The number 9 has more of a tendency toward accidents and injuries than illnesses. The number 9 has dominion over danger from cuts, burns, knives, guns, explosions, fires, accidents from machinery, fevers, and other sorts of high temperatures. The months to be careful of such things are January, May, and October, but most especially July.

MATES/PARTNERS:

In matters of love and romance, the 9 prefers a mate with a dynamic, energetic nature. The 9 would also prefer to select a mate with a lot of self confidence. Therefore, those born late February through March, late March through April, late October through November and late November through December tend to make the best mates. This includes those born on the 3rd, 9th, 12th, 18th, 21st, 27th, or 30th of the month.

TIMES OF THE YEAR:

The best day for the number 9 is Tuesday, followed by Thursday. The months of March, April, November, and December, followed by May and October, are months of importance. In reference to time, the number 9 means news received in one day.

CITIES/COUNTRIES:

Denver, Detroit, Ft. Worth, Boise, Beijing, Philadelphia, Tampa, St. Louis, Phoenix, San Salvador, Algiers, Antigua, Puerto Rico, Rome, Silver Springs, Savannah, Dominica.

OTHER TIDBITS:

The number 9 has rulership over slaughterhouses, battlefields, fire and police stations, munitions plants, armories, the auto industry, steel mills, international movements, publishing houses, and the travel industry.

Colors for the number 9 usually fall in the red, rose, or crimson family—from the lightest to the darkest.

The number 9 is at its best during the night.

The Planes of Power

By nature, all of us are different, and as a result, we function on different planes or levels of thought. Some people may go about their activities in a practical, methodical way; while others do their work in a more mental, intellectual fashion. Some may be emotional in their outlook, while others find success along spiritual and intuitive lines. The plane where you function best in life can be determined in Numerology through the PLANES OF EXPRESSION. The Planes of Expression denote that level of life where your name finds its natural place of power and can best express itself.

There are basically four planes of thought or levels of living that we're involved in. These levels are called the PHYSICAL, MENTAL, EMOTIONAL, and INTUITIVE planes. It's on one of these levels, or in some cases more, that we all must function.

Below is the alphabet and its Pythagorean numerical value to use in transposing your name into the numbers that represent each PLANE OF EXPRESSION.

Pythagorean Numerical Values

1	2	3	4	5	6	7	8	9
A	B	C	D	E	F	G	H	I
J	K	L	M	N	O	P	Q	R
S	T	U	V	W	X	Y	Z	

The numbers 4 and 5 represent the PHYSICAL plane.
The numbers 1 and 8 represent the MENTAL plane.
The numbers 2, 3, and 6 represent the EMOTIONAL plane.
The numbers 7 and 9 represent the INTUITIVE plane.

Let's take the name Kathryn Anice Hill, for example.

K	A	T	H	R	Y	N		A	N	I	C	E		H	I	L	L
2	1	2	8	9	7	5		1	5	9	3	5		8	9	3	3

For Kathryn, the Planes of Expression are:
PHYSICAL: 3 (no 4s and three 5s = a total of 3 numbers on the physical plane)
MENTAL: 4 (two 1s and two 8s = 4)
EMOTIONAL: 5 (two 2s and three 3s = 5)
INTUITIVE: 4 (one 7 and three 9s = 4)

As you can see, Kathryn has 3 numbers on the PHYSICAL plane, 4 numbers on the MENTAL plane, 5 numbers on the EMOTIONAL plane and 4 numbers on the INTUITIVE plane. Therefore, her name is highest on the EMOTIONAL plane and lowest on the PHYSICAL plane, while her MENTAL and INTUITIVE plane are both the same. Lay your name out in this manner to discover what plane or level of life your name best expresses, as well as its natural place of power.

The Physical Plane:

This plane represents form, the body, and basic animal instincts. It deals only with those things that can be seen or touched. A name found high on this plane has a hard time relating to fancies, emotions, feelings, and imagination; generally, everything has to be proven before it is believed. Only those things that are real and tangible have appeal. This may explain the need for a conservative, cautious approach to life. When your name is higher on this plane than any other, it gives you stamina and the ability to endure hard conditions, as well as a strong, cautious, and practical nature.

The Mental Plane:

This level of function represents the mind, the plane of life that deals with logic, analysis, and reason. Will and determination are found on this level, as well as the ability to gather facts and weigh one against the other. Only that which can be proved or analyzed by the mind are important on this level. When your name is highest on this plane, it gives you fine reasoning powers, mental concentration, strong will, determination, and the ability to push things through to a final conclusion. Here, reason rules emotions.

The Emotional Plane:

This level of function responds to the heart and to feelings. This is the plane of life that deals primarily with imagination, inspiration, affection, and creative thoughts. Here, emotions prevail over reason, and come ahead of facts and practical ideas. When your name is highest on this plane, it suggests strong emotions, warmth, and sympathy. It also denotes a happy, sunny disposition, with a strong love of life, beauty, and art, and the finer things. A warm loving nature, as well as potential for artistic expression is generally found on this level.

The Intuitive Plane:

This represents the plane of spirit, metaphysics, and inner knowing. This is the plane of life that deals mainly with revelation, abstract impressions, or things from On High. This Plane of Expression is higher than logic and reason, even higher than feelings and imagination. Things on this level come through intuition, divine wisdom, and deep meditative thought. When your name is highest on the INTUITIVE plane, it gives great inner awareness and the ability to comprehend and penetrate the unseen. Great accomplishments are possible on this level, but not in the usual or traditional way.

Numerology and the Elements

Each of the individual numbers from 1 to 9 is governed by one of the 4 natural elements. Air, Water, Fire, and Earth. These four basic elements are essential to our survival.

Everyone needs the element of **Air** to breathe. No living thing can exist longer than five minutes without it. How long can you hold your breath?

Water, like air, is also a necessity. Most of our body weight is composed of Water, and we can live only a short time without it.

Earth is necessary, since all the natural and wonderful vegetation—trees, plants, herbs, fruits, and flowers— comes from the Earth. Even in death, we must return to the Earth from which we originated.

The last important element is **Fire.** Fire warms you, cooks for you, and provides comfort in the form of heat and energy. Fire can also protect and bring light into darkness.

However, when these elements of nature are abused, misused, and taken for granted, no power on this planet can cause greater harm to us than nature itself—hurricanes, storms, tempests, earthquakes, tremors, tidal waves, flash floods, heavy rains, fires, electrical storms, and volcanic eruptions.

On the more occult or mystic side of these elements,

each represents a certain human quality when properly understood. The element of Air, for example, represents mental qualities; the ability to respond to reason, logic, and order; to weigh one fact against the other in a logical, intelligent way.

Water represents our inner feelings, sensitivities, and responses to other people and the environment. Being fluid and changeable, Water also indicates the emotional side of our nature.

Earth in man represents the physical side of human nature, when we take a practical, down-to-earth approach to a situation. With an earthy element, there's a preference for dealing with life in tangible and concrete ways.

Fire, the last element, represents the energetic, active side of things. When you hear people described as "all fired up," that means they're inspired, they're ready to go. Fire also governs the intuitive and spiritual side of nature.

With this understanding, how can you determine the basic element of nature that is dominant in you? The answer to finding your element is determined by your day of birth. Let's say you were born on the 2nd of the month. A 2 person is ruled by the element of Water and is basically emotional, sensitive, artistic, and imaginative in disposition and behavior. Remember, we all have a mixture of the elements in us. However, the element most dominant in theme is found in the birth number. Look below to see which element represents you.

Dominant Elements

THE NUMBER 1

Born on the 1st, 10th, 19th, or 28th of the month— Fire is your natural element, representing energy and force.

THE NUMBER 2

Born on the 2nd, 11th, 20th, or 29th of the month—
Water is your natural element, representing feelings and
emotions.

THE NUMBER 3

Born on the 3rd, 12th, 21st, or 30th of the month—
Fire is your element ruling force and energy.

THE NUMBER 4

Born on the 4th, 13th, 22nd, or 31st of the month—
Air is your element, representing mental and intellectual
qualities.

THE NUMBER 5

Born on the 5th, 14th, or 23rd of the month—Air is
your natural element, ruling thinking and mental activities.

THE NUMBER 6

Born on the 6th, 15th, or 24th of the month—Earth is
your element governing practical and down-to-earth
ways of dealing with things.

THE NUMBER 7

Born on the 7th, 16th, or 25th of the month—Water is
your element, representing deep thoughts and inner feelings.

THE NUMBER 8

Born on the 8th, 17th, or 26th of the month—Earth is
your element ruling over methodical and practical ways.

THE NUMBER 9

Born on the 9th, 18th, or 27th of the month—Fire is
your element, denoting intuition, spirit, and energy.

II.

Correspondence Systems

Numerology and the Occult Sciences

I am often asked if there's a relationship between numbers and the other branches of the occult. I can say Yes from firsthand experience. My original interest in the occult, prior to Numerology, was in Astrology. When I was introduced to Numerology in 1969, I could easily see a relationship. First, both the Zodiac signs and numbers are ruled by given planets. So if you understand the nature of the planets alone, you can talk to both an astrologer and numerologist at the same time. And this is true in other cases. Let's explore just a few of the areas of the occult to see how they relate to Numerology.

Astrology

Planets	Ruling Numbers
Sun	1
Moon	2
Jupiter	3
Uranus	4
Mercury	5
Earth	6
Venus	6
Neptune	7
Saturn	8
Mars	9

This chart shows you the common correspondences between the planets and their ruling numbers. Once you know this the rest is easy. (For more on the subject of Astrology, see chapter on "Numerology and Astrology").

Palmistry

Perhaps my third love, after Numerology and Astrology, is Palmistry. In Palmistry, certain positions on the hand are ruled by the planets. As a Numerologist, I can verify this. For instance, using a person's birth date, I can look for certain indicators in their palm.

Numerology/Palmistry Chart

NUMBER 1 PERSON

If you were born on the 1st, 10th, 19th, or 28th, or if you're a Leo or Aries, the 1 dominates the mount of Apollo (under the base of the third finger). I would expect this mount to be well developed in some way, or your Apollo (third) finger to be long, denoting a love of the public as well as leadership and energy, especially if your lifeline is strong.

NUMBER 2 PERSON

In those born on the 2nd, 11th, 20th, or 29th, or under Cancer, the 2 dominates the mount of the Moon (fleshy area of palm opposite the thumb). Being born on a 2 date would probably emphasize this part of your hand in some way, indicating a warm, sensitive, emotional, and artistic type of person. A long head line (in between lifeline and heart line and ruling your thinking) curving toward this area of the hand adds imagination.

NUMBER 3 PERSON

In those born on the 3rd, 12th, 21st, or 30th, or coming under the sign of Pisces or Sagittarius, the 3 dominates the mount of Jupiter (under the first or "index" finger). If you were born on this date, your first finger may be longer than the others, denoting leadership ability. If the mount under the finger is large, it indicates an ambitious nature.

NUMBER 4 PERSON

If you were born on the 4th, 13th, 22nd, or 31st, or if you're an Aquarius, the 4 also dominates the mount of Apollo (under the third finger), as in the 1, but in a more cautious and deliberate way. Your birth number suggests that even if the mount under this finger is large, or the finger itself is long, you'd still prefer to use a slow, more methodical approach to success and problem solving.

NUMBER 5 PERSON

In those born on the 5th, 14th, or 23rd, or under Gemini or Virgo, the 5 dominates the mount of Mercury (under the fourth or "pinkie" finger). Your hand, according to your birth, would suggest that you have an enlarged mount there, as compared with the rest; or that the finger itself may be long, denoting a love of gambling, taking chances, and risks. It also denotes a love of travel, variety, commerce, and unattachment.

NUMBER 6 PERSON

If you were born on the 6th, 15th, or 24th, or you happen to be a Taurus or Libra, the 6 dominates the mount of Venus (the fleshy part under the thumb). If this area of your hand is enlarged, it denotes a warm, loving and expressive nature. Your birth number also rules the heart line (moving across the top of the palm), denoting matters of love and romance. It also suggests an artistic and creative temperament.

NUMBER 7 PERSON

If you were born on the 7th, 16th, or 25th, or if you're a Pisces or Cancer, the 7 dominates the mount of Moon, and basically fits the same description as the number 2.

However the 7 as your birth number would make you more analytical and independent.

NUMBER 8 PERSON

In those born on the 8th, 17th, or 26th, or under the sign of Capricorn, the 8 dominates the mount of Saturn (under the second finger). If your mount, according to your birth number, is larger, or the finger under this mount is longer, and you also have a well-developed fate line (runs up center of hand from wrist), you have all the markings of a very serious-minded and determined person. When any of the elements are strong on this mount, or fate line, it suggests you're ruled by the forces of fate, or destiny.

NUMBER 9 PERSON

Born on the 9th, 18th, or 27th, or your sign is Aries or Scorpio, the 9 dominates the mounts of Mars, found under both the mounts of Mercury and Jupiter. If you have a long, straight head line in your hand, it suggests you have a fighting spirit and a desire not to be controlled by anyone or anything. It also suggests an energetic personality.

The Tarot

In my personal opinion, perhaps the most difficult area of occult study is the Tarot. One must have a basic knowledge of Numerology to master the symbols of 1 to 9, one must have a basic knowledge of the many symbols on the Tarot cards; and one must understand the "compound" or "double" numbers that move beyond the 9. For example, the 10 in the more esoteric side of numbers is known as the "Wheel of Fortune," which is the image on the 10th card of the Tarot deck. Let's take another, the compound number 16, which is often dreaded by numerologists. The 16th card in the Tarot deck is known as "The Shattered Citadel," or "The Tower Struck by

Lightning." Although there is a positive, spiritual side to this number, it is usually an ominous symbol. For instance, the first President to be assassinated in office was Abraham Lincoln—the 16th President. Another compound number in Numerology that comes directly from the picture symbols of the Tarot is the "Death" card, or number 13.

The study of the Tarot can be a rewarding addition to your life. It's admired as an art form, a very popular method of fortune-telling, a system of serious divination and meditation, and it can even be played as a game. The Tarot deck consists of 78 cards, filled with symbols, suits, various mystical designs, and colors, each having a meaning of its own. Perhaps this is the reason why this branch of the occult requires years and years of study. The cards are generally separated into three divisions: The Major Arcana, with twenty-two cards, numbered 0 to 21; the Minor Arcana, with its four suits (Wands, Cups, Pentacles, and Swords, from ace to 10); the balance being the Court Cards of each suit (Page, Knight, Queen, King). The Major Arcana represents the psychological, philosophical, and metaphysical side of individuals and their environment. The Minor Arcana deals with a person's character and daily life; and the Court Cards, which show the interplay of all the cards in a person's life. This area of the occult requires time, attention to details, and learning spreads (techniques of laying out the cards) among a host of other things. There are numerous books on this subject now at many bookstores for those of you who want to know more.

The I Ching

Perhaps one of the most profound systems of the occult is the I Ching, or the *Book of Changes*. Considered to be over 4000 years old, having its origin in China, it's still a popular method of divination. The interpretation of this ancient system is based upon Oriental philosophy, and differs from the approach here in the West. One has to throw three coins six times, then, according to the arrangement of heads and tails in each throw, you obtain a specific hexagram for interpretation. These 64 hexagrams are formed from a pattern of six horizontal lines. Once your hexagram(s) are determined, you go to the *Book of Changes* for its prophetic interpretations and advice.

The hexagrams are composed of 2 trigrams, which are formed by three lines which may be broken or solid, depending on the combinations and arrangements of the coins. A name is assigned to each trigram, which gives a meaning of its own to your family, your image, and other attributes in relation to the hexagrams themselves.

The art of the I Ching, like the rest of the occult sciences, rests upon the skill of the interpreter. The longer they have dedicated themselves to their respective area, the more likely you are to get an accurate reading. And like anything else, this area of study also requires years and years of learning and research, but above all application. Like the Tarot, there are now numerous books on the subject of the I Ching.

The Mystical Obi Ifa Divination

Obi, the mystical science of Ifa divination, like the other occult sciences, is ancient in origin. The Obi system of Cola nut casts originated in West Africa. The Cola (sometimes spelled Kola) nut is known as *Obi Abata*, and is considered to be a sacred and valuable nut. In fact, even today, students, who have to spend long hours of study, will chew on bits of the Cola nut to help keep them alert and awake. Because of the holy and divinatory qualities of the nut, its tree could not be cut down in an ordinary fashion.

According to Dr. Afolabi A. Epega, one of the foremost authorities on this subject, inside the pods produced by the Cola tree are four nuts. Two of the nuts are *Ako Meji*, or male, and the other two are *Abo Meji*, or female. This seemed to me very similar to the yin and yang (male-female) Oriental philosophy of the I Ching. The male nuts represent the forces of light and the female nuts represent the forces of dark. Diviners shake the nuts in their hands while repeating the question being asked, then cast them on the *Obon-Ifa* (divining board).

The top of the board denotes the spirit world; the bottom suggests rebirth. The direction the nuts fall in is also important. South indicates the element of Earth; east is Fire; west is Death; and north is Water. These represent the cycle of reincarnation in man and nature. According to Dr. Epega, there are two hundred and fifty-six ways of interpreting the divination, depending upon how the Cola nuts fall or arrange themselves.

There is a saying under this system that a thousand and one questions may be asked in a day, but never ask the same question twice, for the one asking the question will be deceived. Ifa divination, like the other branches of the occult, requires long years of study and dedication.

There are other occult systems, from reading playing cards to Phrenology (the study of size and shape of the head and the bumps on it). The purpose of this section was not to examine each area in depth, for each subject requires volumes. I simply hoped that, depending on your chemistry, you'd find your own niche, as I did. For me, it's Numerology, what's your choice?

Numerology and Astrology

What's your numerological sign? Over 90 percent of you know your astrological sign, yet less than 10 percent know your number sign. Numerology is the study of the mysterious and hidden influences of numbers and how they affect your life. Numbers are used every day of our lives in some way, but we often fail to understand the power and the wonderful secrets that they hold for us.

Before the day is over you will use a number or set of numbers to make decisions that will influence you. For instance, what is your address number? What number bus or train will you take to travel, shop, or work today? When you're at home this evening, what channel numbers on your TV will you watch? Numbers are interwoven in our everyday speech—"one of a kind," "a two timer," "working 9 to 5," "hitting the number" (jackpot), Friday the 13th, and so on. Numbers are all around us—in money (numbers expressed in dollars and cents), a paycheck, a Social Security card, even a zip code. They're expressed in every form imaginable.

Your character, strengths and weaknesses, mate, occupation, health and many other facets of your life are affected by numbers. Let's start with the numbers that rule your Zodiac sign, along with your best day. If you were born under the Zodiac sign of:

Your Zodiac Number

ARIES (March 21–April 20):

9 is your number and Tuesday is your day.

TAURUS (April 21–May 20):

6 is your number and Friday is your day.

GEMINI (May 21–June 20):

5 is your number and Wednesday is your day.

CANCER (June 21–July 20):

2 and 7 are your numbers and Monday is your day.

LEO (July 21–August 20):

1 and 4 are your numbers and Sunday is your day.

VIRGO (August 21–September 20):

5 is your number and Wednesday is your day.

LIBRA (September 21–October 20):

6 is your number and Friday is your day.

SCORPIO (October 21–November 21):

9 is your number and Tuesday is your day.

SAGITTARIUS (November 22–December 21):

3 is your number and Thursday is your day.

CAPRICORN (December 22–January 20):

8 is your number—there is no day.

AQUARIUS (January 21–February 19):

4 and 1 are your numbers and Sunday is your day.

PISCES (February 20–March 20):

3 is your number and Thursday is your day.

Astrological and Numerological Correspondences

Not only are Numerology and Astrology kissing cousins, but there's an amazing similarity between the numerological positions in your name and birth day and your astrological chart. For instance, we're all born under a Sun sign, which denotes one individuality and ego. In Numerology, The Expression number (the sum total of your name at birth) is the equivalent of your Sun Sign.

The Moon in your chart denotes your inner personality, dreams, goals, and desires. In Numerology this is equivalent to the Motivation Number—your heart's desire or soul urge—which is derived from the sum total of the vowels in your name.

Another important factor in Astrology is your Ascendant, or rising sign. It denotes the impression you make on others. It also gives clues to your physical appearance. Numerologically, this information is given in the sum total of the consonants in your name, and is known as the Appearance, or Quiescent, number. Let's take my name as an example:

6 7	1 7 6		= 27/9 Motivation (Moon)
L L O Y D	S T R A Y H O R N		= 8 Expression (Sun)
3 3 4	1 2 9 8 9 5		= 44/8 Appearance (Ascendant)

My Expression number, which is the sum total of all the numbers in my name, adds up to an 8. Ruled by Saturn, 8 governs the signs of Capricorn and Aquarius (my Sun sign), as well as the 8th sign of the Zodiac (Scorpio). In addition, it may indicate that your Sun sign may be found in or around the 8th House in your chart.

My Motivation number is a nine. Ruled by Mars, nine governs the signs of Aries and Scorpio (my Moon sign), as well as the 9th sign of the Zodiac (Sagittarius). It can also indicate that the Moon sign may be found in or around the 9th House of the chart.

My Appearance number is an 8, like my Expression number. Although this doesn't seem to apply to my Sun sign, Zodiac placement, or House position, my Virgo Ascendant does begin in the 8th month (late August through September).

There are two ways to analyze your name. The first is to use your original name given at birth. The second is to use the name you're presently known by. Remember, add up the total of the vowel numbers (a,e,i,o,u, and sometimes y) to find your possible Moon equivalent.

Next, add up the sum total of the consonants in your name to find your possible Ascendant equivalent. Finally, add up the sum total of all the numbers in your name to find your possible Sun sign equivalent.

If you're not certain of your Sun, Moon, or Ascendant, I recommend that you consult a professional astrologer or use an ephemeris to locate your planet positions.

Numbers and Their Astrological Correspondence

If your Expression, Motivation, or Appearance number is a:

1 The sign is likely Leo, or represents the 1st or 10th sign of the Zodiac, which are Aries and Capricorn respectively. The 1st or 10th House in your chart could be strongly aspected.

2 The sign suggests Cancer, or represents the 2nd or 11th sign of the Zodiac, Taurus and Aquarius respectively. The 2nd or 11th House in your chart may be aspected in some important way.

3 The sign may be Pisces or Sagittarius, or perhaps it indicates the 3rd and 12th sign of the Zodiac, which is Gemini followed by Pisces. Look at the 3rd and 12th Houses in your chart for possible confirmation.

4 The sign is likely Aquarius, or represents the 4th sign of the Zodiac, which is Cancer. Perhaps the 4th House in your chart matches this position.

5 The sign is likely Gemini or Virgo, or represents the 5th sign of the Zodiac, in this case Leo. The 5th House in your chart may be emphasized in some important way.

6 Taurus or Libra are the likely signs or perhaps the 6th sign of the Zodiac, which is Virgo. In addition, look to the 6th House in your chart for further clues.

7 Pisces or Cancer are suggested indicators. Libra, being the 7th sign in the Zodiac is a strong possibility. The 7th House in your chart may hold important aspects.

8 The signs are likely Capricorn or Aquarius, followed by the 8th sign of the Zodiac, which is Scorpio. Since the 8th House is a fateful one, it would be good to look at the aspects.

9 Aries or Scorpio may possibly be your sign, or perhaps the 9th sign in the Zodiac, which is Sagittarius. Look to the 9th House for further insight.

Biorhythms in Action

On April 6, 1987, the fight of the century took place in Las Vegas between Marvelous Marvin Hagler and Sugar Ray Leonard. Fight experts gave Hagler a 3-to-1 margin in favor of winning. In fact, the bout was expected to be a cakewalk for Hagler. However, despite all the odds, Sugar Ray Leonard won the championship fight by a split decision. Had Hagler's handlers and manager checked his biorhythm chart, I'm sure they would have chosen another date for the match.

Below are the biorhythm charts of both fighters on the day of the big fight. As you can see, all three of Hagler's biorhythm cycles were low. In fact, on the day of the fight—April 6th—his physical cycle (the most important in this game) was critical. Sugar Ray Leonard's physical biorhythm was higher. No wonder Leonard was able to defy the experts. Ironically, had the fight been scheduled for the next day—April 7th—it would have been a critical day for Leonard.

On the day President John F. Kennedy was assissinated in Dallas, Texas—November 22, 1963—his biorhythm chart was critical in the mental cycle. Although his physical and emotional cycles were high, the mental cycle, governing judgment and thinking, was at its weakest point.

```
COMPUTERIZED STUDY OF BIORHYTHMIC CURVES
SUBJECT: MARVELOUS MARVIN HAGLER
DATE OF STUDY: 870401—DURATION 30 DAYS
```

P = PHYSICAL*   E = EMOTIONAL*   M = MENTAL*

```
:      LOW             :         HIGH        :  DATE   :CRITICAL:
:    P   M     E       I                     :  870401 :
:    MP  E             I                     :  870402 :
:    M E  P            I                     :  870403 :
:    ME        P       I                     :  870404 :
:    EM            P   I                     :  870405 :
:     EM               I                     :  870406 :   P
:      E M             I   P                 :  870407 :
:       E M            I       P             :  870408 :
:          EM          I          P          :  870409 :
:           E M        I             P       :  870410 :
:              E       I               P     :  870411 :
:                      I                 P   :  870412 :  M E
:                      I             P       :  870413 :
:                      I   M E     P         :  870414 :
:                      I     MEP             :  870415 :
:                      I   P   M E           :  870416 :
:                      I P         M E       :  870417 :
:                P     I             ME       :  870418 :  P
:                      I              ME     :  870419 :
:             P        I             EM      :  870420 :
:          P           I           E M       :  870421 :
:    P                 I          E   M      :  870422 :
:    P                 I       E    M        :  870423 :
:    P                 I      E    M         :  870424 :
:     P                I    E   M            :  870425 :
:        P             I    M                :  870426 :   E
:           P      E   I   M                 :  870427 :
:            E  P      I M                   :  870428 :   M
:         E        M I                       :  870429 :   P
:     E         M      I   P                 :  870430 :
```

```
: HIGH        DAYS OF FULL VITALITY, EFFICIENCY, AND HIGH ENDURANCE:
: LOW         DAYS OF REDUCED EFFICIENCY, RECUPERATION, TIRE EASILY:
: CRITICAL    DAYS TO AVOID SITUATIONS THAT MIGHT LEAD TO TROUBLE   :
```

```
------------------------------------------------------------
COMPUTERIZED STUDY OF BIORHYTHMIC CURVES
SUBJECT: SUGAR RAY LEONARD
DATE OF STUDY: 870401 —DURATION 30 DAYS
------------------------------------------------------------
  P = PHYSICAL*     E = EMOTIONAL*      M = MENTAL*
------------------------------------------------------------
:      LOW        :         HIGH        :  DATE  :CRITICAL:
:       E   M     I              P      :  870401 :
:     E M         I         P           :  870402 :
:     EM          I  P                  :  870403 :
:     ME          P I                   :  870404 :   P
:     M E         P I                   :  870405 :
:      M E P        I                   :  870406 :
:       M P   E     I                   :  870407 :
:      P  M      E  I                   :  870408 :
:      P    M        E  I               :  870409 :
:      P       M       E I              :  870410 :   E
:       P           M   I  E            :  870411 :
:         P             M I     E       :  870412 :
:           P           I       E       :  870413 :   M
:             P         I  M         E  :  870414 :
:                       I    P    M    E:  870415 :   P
:                       I       P   M   E  870416 :
:                       I         P  M  E  870417 :
:                       I          PM  E   870418 :
:                       I              P   870419 :
:                       I         E  MP :  870420 :
:                       I        E    P :  870421 :
:                       I            PM :  870422 :
:                       I      E    P  M:  870423 :
:                       I          P   M:  870424 :   E
:              E    I   I     P    M    :  870425 :
:           E           I P        M    :  870426 :
:         E       P  `P I        M      :  870427 :   P
:      E    P           I   M           :  870428 :
:       E   P           I M             :  870429 :   M
:     E P           M   I               :  870430 :
------------------------------------------------------------
: HIGH       DAYS OF FULL VITALITY, EFFICIENCY, AND HIGH ENDURANCE:
: LOW        DAYS OF REDUCED EFFICIENCY, RECUPERATION, TIRE EASILY:
: CRITICAL   DAYS TO AVOID SITUATIONS THAT MIGHT LEAD TO TROUBLE  :
------------------------------------------------------------
```

In the case of President Ronald Reagan, on March 30, 1981, the day of his attempted assassination in Washington, D.C., he was going through a critical emotional

COMPUTERIZED STUDY OF BIORHYTHMIC CURVES
SUBJECT: JOHN F. KENNEDY—DALLAS
DATE OF STUDY: 631101—DURATION 30 DAYS

P = PHYSICAL*   E = EMOTIONAL*   M = MENTAL*

```
|     LOW        |          HIGH         |  DATE   |CRITICAL|
|        M  E       I              P     | 631101  |
|         E M       I             P      | 631102  |
|      E      M     I           P        | 631103  |
|      E         M  I         P          | 631104  |
|     E           M I     P              | 631105  |
|     E             I P                  | 631106  |   M
|      E         P  I  M                 | 631107  |   P
|        E     P    I      M             | 631108  |
|         PE        I       M            | 631109  |
|       P     E     I        M           | 631110  |
|     P           E I          M         | 631111  |
|     P             I            M       | 631112  |   E
|     P             I E          M       | 631113  |
|      P            I      E      M      | 631114  |
|        P          I        E    M      | 631115  |
|          P        I          E M       | 631116  |
|            P      I          ME        | 631117  |
|                   I      M  E          | 631118  |   P
|                   I P    M      E      | 631119  |
|                   I      MP     E      | 631120  |
|                   I  M      P E        | 631121  |
|                   I M       E P        | 631122  |   M
|              M I        E        P     | 631123  |
|            M      I    E         P     | 631124  |
|          M        I E            P     | 631125  |
|        M          I            P       | 631126  |   E
|       M      E    I           P        | 631127  |
|      M    E       I P                  | 631128  |
|    M  E          P I                   | 631129  |
|   M E            P I                   | 631130  |   P
```

HIGH	DAYS OF FULL VITALITY, EFFICIENCY, AND HIGH ENDURANCE
LOW	DAYS OF REDUCED EFFICIENCY, RECUPERATION, TIRE EASILY
CRITICAL	DAYS TO AVOID SITUATIONS THAT MIGHT LEAD TO TROUBLE

cycle. As you can see from his biorhythm chart, his physical as well as emotional cycles were low on that day.

```
COMPUTERIZED STUDY OF BIORHYTHMIC CURVES
SUBJECT: PRESIDENT RONALD REAGAN
DATE OF STUDY: 810301—DURATION 30 DAYS
-------------------------------------------------------------------
:  P=PHYSICAL*     E=EMOTIONAL*     M=MENTAL*
-------------------------------------------------------------------
 :      LOW        :        HIGH         :  DATE   :CRITICAL:
 :-----------------------------------------------------------------
 :      P         E  I M                 :  810301  :   M
 :       P           M I                 :  810302  :   E
 :      P            M I   E             :  810303  :
 :      P          M     I     E         :  810304  :
 :      P     M      I        E          :  810305  :
 :        P          I          E        :  810306  :
 :      M     P      I           E       :  810307  :
 :       M       P   I            E      :  810308  :
 :      M            I             E     :  810309  :   P
 :     M             I   P        E      :  810310  :
 :     M             I       P  E        :  810311  :
 :      M            I        PE         :  810312  :
 :       M           I    E      P       :  810313  :
 :        M          I   E         P     :  810314  :
 :          M        I  E           P    :  810315  :
 :           M       I            P      :  810316  :   E
 :         E     I   I             P     :  810317  :
 :        E          I        P          :  810318  :   M
 :      E            I M   P             :  810319  :
 :       E           I P  M              :  810320  :
 :        E       P  I        M          :  810321  :   P
 :      E      P     I          M        :  810322  :
 :     E    P        I           M       :  810323  :
 :     E P           I            M      :  810324  :
 :     PE            I             M     :  810325  :
 :     P  E          I             M     :  810326  :
 :     P       E     I              M    :  810327  :
 :      P       E    I             M     :  810328  :
 :       . P        E  I        M        :  810329  :
 :         P         I          M        :  810330  :   E
 :-----------------------------------------------------------------
 : HIGH       DAYS OF FULL VITALITY, EFFICIENCY, AND HIGH ENDURANCE:
 : LOW        DAYS OF REDUCED EFFICIENCY, RECUPERATION, TIRE EASILY:
 : CRITICAL   DAYS TO AVOID SITUATIONS THAT MIGHT LEAD TO TROUBLE  :
-------------------------------------------------------------------
```

The biorhythm cycles of lottery winners are most interesting. In our researches, fellow occultist Ken Dickkerson and I found that not only do lottery winners tend to win more under certain Zodiac signs, birth dates, and parts of the year—but they also win when their biorhythm cycles are in a certain position.

COMPUTERIZED STUDY OF BIORHYTHMIC CURVES
SUBJECT: FELIPE HASSELL—LOTTERY WINNER (6/14)
   $11 MILLION
DATE OF STUDY: 860601—DURATION 30 DAYS

P = PHYSICAL*   E = EMOTIONAL*   M = MENTAL*

LOW	HIGH	DATE	CRITICAL
P	M E	860601	
P	M E	860602	
P	E	860603	
P	E M	860604	
P	E M	860605	
P	E M	860606	
	M	860607	P
EP	M	860608	
P M P	860609	E
E	M P	860610	
E	M	860611	
E	M	860612	M
E M	P	860613	
E M	P	860614	
E M	P	860615	
E M	P	860616	
EM	P	860617	
EM	P	860618	
M E P	860619	P
M P E	860620	
M P	860621	
PM	860623	E
P M	E	860624	
P M	E	860625	
P M	E	860626	
P M	E	860627	
P	E	860628	
P	E	860629	M
M	E	860630	P

HIGH	DAYS OF FULL VITALITY, EFFICIENCY, AND HIGH ENDURANCE
LOW	DAYS OF REDUCED EFFICIENCY, RECUPERATION, TIRE EASILY
CRITICAL	DAYS TO AVOID SITUATIONS THAT MIGHT LEAD TO TROUBLE

Felipe Hassell's physical cycle was at its peak on the day of his $11 million win. Ken refers to the physical cycle as the money cycle.

COMPUTERIZED STUDY OF BIORHYTHMIC CURVES
SUBJECT: IRVING SCOTT—LOTTERY WINNER (6/23)
  $2.5 MILLION
DATE OF STUDY: 840601—DURATION 30 DAYS

```
: P = PHYSICAL*     E = EMOTIONAL*     M = MENTAL*

:       LOW          :          HIGH        :  DATE   :CRITICAL:
:        —           I       E          P   :  840601 :
:                    I     E          MP    :  840602 :
:                    I              M  P    :  840603 :      E
:              E     I           MP         :  840604 :
:          E     E   I        MP            :  840605 :
:         E          I      PM              :  840606 :
:       E            I  P  M                :  840607 :
:     E            P I M                    :  840608 :     M P
:    E          P    M I                    :  840609 :
:   E      P       M  I                     :  840610 :
:   E P         M     I                     :  840611 :
:  PE        M        I                     :  840612 :
:  P  EM              I                     :  840613 :
:  P  M   E           I                     :  840614 :
:  MP        E        I                     :  840615 :
:  M    P          E  I                     :  840616 :
:  M              P   I  E                  :  840617 :      E
:  M    —       P     I E                   :  840618 :
:    M              I   E                    :  840619 :      P
:     M             I    P   E              :  840620 :
:       M           I      P   E            :  840621 :
:         M         I         P  E          :  840622 :
:           M       I           PE          :  840623 :
:            M      I             P         :  840624 :
:                   I            EP         :  840625 :      M
:                   I M        EP           :  840626 :
:                   I     M     P           :  840627 :
:                   I      MEP              :  840628 :
:                   I    PE   M             :  840629 :
:                   I PE          M         :  840630 :

: HIGH      DAYS OF FULL VITALITY, EFFICIENCY, AND HIGH ENDURANCE:
: LOW       DAYS OF REDUCED EFFICIENCY, RECUPERATION, TIRE EASILY:
: CRITICAL  DAYS TO AVOID SITUATIONS THAT MIGHT LEAD TO TROUBLE   :
```

Irving Scott, born August 29th, won $2.5 million on a
day when both his physical and mental cycles were high.

COMPUTERIZED STUDY OF BIORHYTHMIC CURVES
SUBJECT: HENNY LIGHTY—LOTTERY WINNER (9/7)
   $6 MILLION
DATE OF STUDY: 860901—DURATION 30 DAYS

P = PHYSICAL*   E = EMOTIONAL*   M = MENTAL*

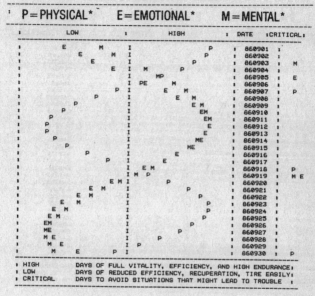

Interestingly, on the day Henny Lighty, born March 17th, won $6 million, although his physical (money) cycle was marked critical, it was still on the high side of his chart, as were his mental and emotional cycles.

COMPUTERIZED STUDY OF BIORHYTHMIC CURVES
SUBJECT: CAROLINE FORTE—LOTTERY WINNER (2/6)
  $5.9 MILLION
DATE OF STUDY: 840201—DURATION 30 DAYS

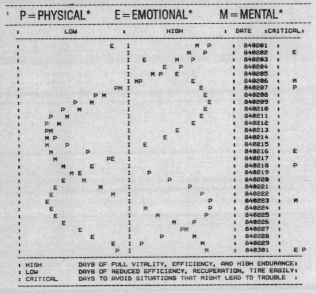

```
:  P = PHYSICAL*      E = EMOTIONAL*      M = MENTAL*

'          LOW            '         HIGH        '  DATE   'CRITICAL'
'                    E    I               M  P   '  840201 '
'                         I               M  P   '  840202 '    E
'                         I   E       M    P      '  840203 '
'                         I      E P            '  840204 '
'                         I    M P  E           '  840205 '
'                     I MP          E           '  840206 '    M
'               PM  I                  E        '  840207 '    P
'          P  M     I                    E      '  840208 '
'          P  M     I                     E     '  840209 '
'        P    M     I                      E    '  840210 '
'      P    M       I                      E    '  840211 '
'      P  M         I                     E     '  840212 '
'      PM           I                  E        '  840213 '
'      M P          I               E           '  840214 '
'      M    P       I       E                   '  840215 '
'      M        P   I                           '  840216 '    E
'       M       PE  I                           '  840217 '
'        M E        I        P                  '  840218 '    P
'         M E       I     P                     '  840219 '
'       E    M      I         P                 '  840220 '
'        E       M  I            P              '  840221 '
'       E        M  I              P            '  840222 '
'       E           I                 P         '  840223 '    M
'        E          I    M            P         '  840224 '
'         E         I        M      P           '  840225 '
'          E        I          M  P            '  840226 '
'           E       I         PM               '  840227 '
'            E      I      P       M           '  840228 '
'               E   I P              M         '  840229 '
'                 P I                 M        '  840301 '  E P

' HIGH      DAYS OF FULL VITALITY, EFFICIENCY, AND HIGH ENDURANCE'
' LOW       DAYS OF REDUCED EFFICIENCY, RECUPERATION, TIRE EASILY'
: CRITICAL  DAYS TO AVOID SITUATIONS THAT MIGHT LEAD TO TROUBLE  :
```

Caroline Forte, born November 22nd, had the good fortune to win $5.9 million on the day her physical, mental, and emotional cycles were high, although it was still a mentally critical day.

COMPUTERIZED STUDY OF BIORHYTHMIC CURVES
SUBJECT: GEORGE BENT—LOTTERY WINNER (2/26)
  $2 MILLION
DATE OF STUDY: 860201—DURATION 30 DAYS

: P = PHYSICAL*   E = EMOTIONAL*   M = MENTAL*

	LOW			HIGH		DATE	CRITICAL
	E		I		MP		860201	
	E		I		M P		860202	
	E		I		M P		860203	
	E		I		MP		860204	
	E		I		PM		860205	
	E		I		P M		860206	
			I		P M		860207	E
		I	E P		M		860208	
		I P	E	M		860209	
	P	I		E		860210	P
	P	I	M	E		860211	
	P	I	M		E		860212	
	P	I M			E		860213	M
	P	M I			E		860214	
	P	M	I		E		860215	
	P	M	I		E		860216	
	P	M	I		E		860217	
	P	I		E		860218	
	M	P	I	E		860219	
	M		P	I E		860220	
	M		I			860221	E P
	M	E	I	P		860222	
	M		I	P		860223	
	M	E	I		P		860224	
		E	I		P		860225	
	E M		I		P		860226	
	E	M	I		P		860227	
	E		M I		P		860228	
	E		M I		P		860301	
	E		I		P		860302	M

: HIGH   DAYS OF FULL VITALITY, EFFICIENCY, AND HIGH ENDURANCE:
: LOW   DAYS OF REDUCED EFFICIENCY, RECUPERATION, TIRE EASILY:
: CRITICAL   DAYS TO AVOID SITUATIONS THAT MIGHT LEAD TO TROUBLE   :

Both George Bent, born August 8th, and Joseph Urban, born February 10th, won over a million dollars when their physical cycles were at their peak.

COMPUTERIZED STUDY OF BIORHYTHMIC CURVES
SUBJECT: JOSEPH URBAN—LOTTERY WINNER (2/6)
  $1.7 MILLION
DATE OF STUDY: 840201—DURATION 30 DAYS

: P = PHYSICAL*   E = EMOTIONAL*   M = MENTAL*

```
:        LOW          :         HIGH          :  DATE   :CRITICAL :
:      E        M     I         P             :  840201 :
:       E     M       I            P          :  840202 :
:        M  E         I              P        :  840203 :
:     M     E         I               P       :  840204 :
:      M         E    I               P       :  840205 :
:     M               I               P       :  840206 :    E
:     M               I    E       P          :  840207 :
:     M               I      E   E            :  840208 :
:     M               I      P  E             :  840209 :
:      M              I  P           E        :  840210 :
:       M        P    I               E       :  840211 :    P
:        M    P       I               E       :  840212 :
:      P M        M   I               E       :  840213 :
:      P        M     I              E        :  840214 :
:          M          I             E         :  840215 :
:      P              I           E           :  840216 :    M
:      P              I    M   E              :  840217 :
:      P              I    M E                :  840218 :
:        P            I  E    M               :  840219 :
:          P          I         M             :  840220 :    E
:            PE       I          M            :  840221 :
:         E           I           M           :  840222 :    P
:       E             I            M          :  840223 :
:      E              I     P      M          :  840224 :
:      E              I       P    M          :  840225 :
:      E              I           PM          :  840226 :
:      E              I        M  P           :  840227 :
:      E              I       M    P          :  840228 :
:       E             I            P          :  840229 :
:        E            I      M     P          :  840301 :
```

```
: HIGH       DAYS OF FULL VITALITY, EFFICIENCY, AND HIGH ENDURANCE:
: LOW        DAYS OF REDUCED EFFICIENCY, RECUPERATION, TIRE EASILY:
: CRITICAL   DAYS TO AVOID SITUATIONS THAT MIGHT LEAD TO TROUBLE  :
```

In the case of 5-million-dollar winner, Curtis Sharp, born April 30th, although his physical (money) cycle was low the day he won, both his emotional and mental cycles were high.

COMPUTERIZED STUDY OF BIORHYTHMIC CURVES
SUBJECT: CURTIS SHARP—LOTTERY WINNER (11/27)
  $5 MILLION
DATE OF STUDY: 821101—DURATION 30 DAYS

```
P = PHYSICAL*      E = EMOTIONAL*      M = MENTAL*

:         LOW         :         HIGH         : DATE   :CRITICAL:
:     P      M  E     I                      : 821101 :
:       P  M  E       I                      : 821102 :
:         MEP         I                      : 821103 :
:       ME      P     I                      : 821104 :
:       ME            P  I                   : 821105 :
:     E               I                      : 821106 :    P
:     E               I     P                : 821107 :
:      E              I        P             : 821108 :
:        E            I           P          : 821109 :
:         M E         I              P       : 821110 :
:          M E        I               P      : 821111 :
:            M  E     I                P     : 821112 :
:             M       I                 P    : 821113 :    E
:                     I    E        P        : 821114 :    M
:                     I   M    E   P         : 821115 :
:                     I   MP   E             : 821116 :
:                     I  P    M    E         : 821117 :
:               P     I        M     E       : 821118 :    P
:                     I          M E         : 821119 :
:            P        I            M E       : 821120 :
:          P          I              E       : 821121 :
:         P           I             E  M     : 821122 :
:         P           I            E   M     : 821123 :
:         P           I          E     M     : 821124 :
:          P          I        E      M      : 821125 :
:           P         I      E      M        : 821126 :
:         P           I    E      M          : 821127 :    E
:              PE     I       M              : 821128 :
:           E         I    M                 : 821129 :    P
:       E             I  M  P                 : 821130 :    M

: HIGH        DAYS OF FULL VITALITY, EFFICIENCY, AND HIGH ENDURANCE:
: LOW         DAYS OF REDUCED EFFICIENCY, RECUPERATION, TIRE EASILY:
: CRITICAL    DAYS TO AVOID SITUATIONS THAT MIGHT LEAD TO TROUBLE   :
```

The next time you play any game of chance, check your biorhythm cycles, especially the physical curve. It could make all the difference in the world.

Lucky Colors, Gems, and Metals

Colors affect your moods and feelings to a very large extent. The right use of colors can not only soothe and relax you, it can aid in the attraction of good luck and favorable vibrations. Have you ever noticed how wearing certain colors makes you feel at ease and relaxed, while other colors may cause you to feel tense and irritable, not quite yourself? Colors can even make you look slim or fat—ask any woman.

Suppose, for example, you have a very important job interview coming up, or you're going out on a first date. Choosing the right colors in harmony with your date of birth will help insure favorable vibrations for your plans. The right use of colors in your home, such as the bedroom, will have a wonderfully soothing affect on your nerves.

In addition to the right use of colors, precious stones and metals, especially when worn next to the skin, also have a magical influence in human affairs. Precious stones and metals, like colors, also have a definite affect upon your health and state of mind. Wearing man-made (synthetic) stones has no affect at all, only the precious stones produced by nature will be beneficial. While the use of colors, gems, and metals for healing and attracting good luck is an entire field of study in itself, the following list suggests which colors, stones, and metals are most harmonious with your date of birth.

Compatible Colors, Gems, and Metals

NUMBER 1 PERSON

Born on the 1st, 10th, 19th, or 28th, or in the months of February, April, and August, your colors are: all shades of gold, yellow, orange, and golden browns; second choices are: green, blue, and crimson. Gems: ruby, topaz, amber, and yellow diamond. Metal: gold.

NUMBER 2 PERSON

If you were born on the 2nd, 11th, 20th, or 29th, or in the months of May and July, your colors are: all shades of creams, whites, and greens; second choice: blue and yellow. Gems: moonstones, pearls, jade, and cat's-eyes. Metal: silver.

NUMBER 3 PERSON

For those born on the 3rd, 12th, 21st, or 30th, or in the months of March and December, your colors are: all shades of purple, lilac, mauve, and violet; second choice: blues and crimson. Gems: amethyst, and all purple or violet-colored stones. Metal: tin.

NUMBER 4 PERSON

If you were born on the 4th, 13th, 22nd, or 31st, or in the months of February and August, your colors are: the electric shades of all colors, as well as blues, greys, plaids, and half-tones; second choice: yellow, red, and orange. Gems: sapphire and topaz. Metal: uranium.*

NUMBER 5 PERSON

Born on the 5th, 14th, or 23rd, or in the months of June and September, your colors are: all light colors and glistening materials; second choice: silver and grey.

Gems: diamonds and yellow sapphires. Metal: quick-silver.*

NUMBER 6 PERSON

For those born on the 6th, 15th, or 24th, or in the months of May and October, your colors are: all shades of blue, from the lightest to the darkest; second choice: rose, pink, and red. Gems: turquoise and emeralds. Metal: copper.

NUMBER 7 PERSON

If you were born on the 7th, 16th, or 25th, or in the months of February, July, and August, your colors are: all pastel colors, particularly creams, greens, and whites; second choice: silver and orange. Gems: green jade, pearls, moonstones, and cat's-eyes. Metal: uranium.

NUMBER 8 PERSON

For those born on the 8th, 17th, or 26th, or in the months of January and October, your best colors are: dark colors such as black and blue-black, and the darker shades of violet and purple; second choice: dark greys and blues. Gems: black pearls and black diamonds. Metal: lead.

NUMBER 9 PERSON

Born on the 9th, 18th, or 27th, or in the months of April and November, your colors are: all shades of red, crimson, and rose, from the lightest to the darkest; second choice: blue, mauve, and pink. Gems: ruby, garnet, and bloodstone. Metal: iron.

*Note: Uranium and quicksilver (mercury) are not safe to wear on the physical body.

III.

Your Personal Numbers

Birth Numbers and Their Meanings

Your most immediate and important number, which always remains constant, comes from the day of the month on which you were born. This date of birth number offers amazing insights into your character, personality, and individuality. Before we go into the meaning of your birth number, just think for a moment of friends you know. Have you ever noticed how one person may be strong and forceful, yet another person be just the opposite—shy and gentle? This is because each number has its own individual nature, quality, and personal vibration. A person born on the 13th of July, for instance, has the number 4 (1+3=4) as their most important number. Someone born on the 24th of June is a number 6 (2+4=6). (Those with double numbers in their birth date must remember to add the two numbers together to get one single digit.)

Your Birth Numbers

NUMBER 1 PERSON

If you were born on the 1st, 10th, 19th, or 28th of the month, you are by nature, determined, forceful, and daring, with a strong desire to be at the head of things. You are original, creative, inventive, and very definite in your points of view. As a number 1 person, you generally don't like second-place positions of any kind. You prefer to lead or take charge of the situation. This is why you'd make an excellent manager, director, president, supervisor, or head of a department. As a 1 person you can be direct and straightforward in dealing with others, probably because you respond more to will and logic than feelings and emotions. The number 1 as your birth date is ruled by the Sun, and therefore you'd get along well with those born in February, April, and August. Sunday is your best day of the week.

NUMBER 2 PERSON

You're a number 2 person if your date of birth is the 2nd, 11th, 20th, or 29th of the month. You're just the opposite of your number 1 counterpart—gentle, imaginative, considerate, persuasive, and romantic. Because you're basically sensitive and receptive to people, situations, and surroundings, you should choose your friends and living environment with the greatest of care. You have a love of music, poetry, painting, dance, drama, and acting. If you had a motto to hang over your door, it would probably say, "Love, Peace, and Harmony." Your birth number is ruled by the Moon and therefore you tend to get along with those born in the months of May and July. Of all the days in the week, Monday is your best day.

NUMBER 3 PERSON

If you were born on the 3rd, 12th, 21st, or 30th of the month, you are a number 3 person. You're generally proud of yourself, ambitious, very independent and don't like restraints by anyone. You're not afraid to put in the necessary hours to get the job done. You prefer to be in authority over others, rather than being dictated to. You're basically conscientious and respected, and have a desire to rise to the top wherever you go. For this reason, you generally excel in areas related to the arts, government, or religion. You love a good name or reputation and are usually considered "popular," sociable, or the life of the party. Since your birth number is ruled by Jupiter, you get along easily with those born in March and December. Of the seven days in the week, Thursday is your best choice.

NUMBER 4 PERSON

Born on the 4th, 13th, 22nd, or 31st of the month, you like to think of yourself as different in some way from the rest. You have a sense of accomplishment, a sense of purpose and vision. Although you are cautious and deliberate in nature, in the heat of an argument, you tend to take the side opposite popular opinion. This may lead to secret enemies or opposition. You have a mechanical, mathematical, and inventive turn of mind. Your birth number also suggests a moody personality, and a tendency for your feelings to be easily wounded. Another aspect of your birth number is to attract those outside your own social background. You have a strong attraction for the odd and unusual and love to be different from others. This may explain your inner urge to rebel against rules and regulations. Uranus is the planet of your birth number, and Sunday is your best choice of the week.

NUMBER 5 PERSON

If you are born on the 5th, 14th, or 23rd of the month, you make friends easily and may have more friends than most. You love change, travel, variety, and above all— your personal freedom. Your philosophy is to be free and unattached. This may explain why you have a need to be on the go. You have an intellectual nature, and usually dislike hard manual labor, preferring to make your living through your brain power. You're adaptable and seem to actually thrive under stress or crisis conditions. Because of your flexible, adaptable personality, choose your friends and surroundings with care. Guard against impulsiveness, in word and deed. Mercury is your ruling birth planet, which would explain the attraction you have with those born in June and September. Wednesday is your best day.

NUMBER 6 PERSON

If you were born on the 6th, 15th, or 24th of the month you have a love of all things beautiful, esthetic, and comforting, such as art, rich colors and fabrics, music, and a beautiful home or apartment. Because of your loving nature, you dislike jealousy and discord of any kind. You like making others happy and at home. You're likely to be known for your magnetic personality and your ability to read people and situations very accurately. You respond to love, praise, and appreciation. You have a strong sense of justice and of right and wrong; along with a belief in duty, responsibility, and fighting for what you believe. Your birth number is ruled by Venus, which attracts those born in May, July, and October. Friday is your best day.

NUMBER 7 PERSON

Born on the 7th, 16th, or 25th of the month, you're basically quiet, reserved, and low key when first approached. You're independent in your own way and have a unique individuality. This may explain why you prefer to be your own best company. You're analytical, knowledgeable, usually well read, and continually search for the causes and effects underlying a situation. You'd love to travel across large bodies of water to far-off places and exotic islands. Your intuitive nature may lead to prophetic or lucid dreams, or a feeling of *déjà vu* in certain situations. Although you may say very little you observe a great deal since you have a need to inspect and analyze. You have a natural gift for writing, research, computers, science, and the occult. Neptune is the planetary ruler of your birth number, which attracts those born under Pisces and Cancer. Monday is your best day of the week.

NUMBER 8 PERSON

If you were born on the 8th, 17th, or 26th of the month, you have a deep, intense personality and will often exhibit a maturity beyond your biological years. You're basically serious-minded and philosophical in your approach to life. Your ambitious nature could lead to success in public life. You're not afraid to involve yourself in work or projects that require personal sacrifice. Of all the birth numbers, yours tends to be misunderstood the most. This may account for the loneliness and isolation you feel from time to time. Deep down, however, you're really warm and caring once others get to know you. Your birth number is ruled by Saturn drawing you to people born in the months of January and October. Saturday is your best day out of seven.

NUMBER 9 PERSON

If you were born on the 9th, 18th, or 27th of the month, you tend to be a fighter in all matters of life. Although the early stages of childhood, adolescence, and young adulthood, may be filled with strife and opposition, your strong will, grit, and determination will help you succeed in the end. Your character is bold and courageous, backed by a very good opinion of yourself—regardless of what others may say or think. You have an equally strong desire to be in charge of your life; to be the master of your fate. On the other hand, you have to control impulsiveness, a hasty temper, and a tendency to leap before you look. If you make the attempt, you have a gift for leadership and organization and the ability to inspire others. Mars is the planet assigned to your birth number, attracting those born in the months of April and November. Tuesday is your best day.

The Life Cycles

There are three major phases or cycles that each of us must pass through in life. These cycles are determined from your month, day, and year of birth.

Your first cycle is calculated from your birth month and represents your formative years—childhood, family, education, friends, early environment, etc. Growth, development, and personal relationships will dominate your birth month cycle from ages 1 to 28 as a rule.

Your second major cycle is calculated from your day of birth. This cycle represents your productive years. It governs your adulthood, your maturity, career, marriage, children, goals, and objectives. This period greatly influences the direction of your life from the ages of 28 to 56.

Your third major cycle is calculated from your birth year and represents the harvest or setting Sun of your life, generally from age 56 to the end. This final cycle denotes the direction, influence, and contributions you're likely to pass on to benefit others.

Let's take an example:

Bill Cosby, Born July 12, 1937:

1st Cycle (month number—July): 7.
2nd Cycle (date number—12th; $1 + 2 = 3$): 3.
3rd Cycle (year number—1937; $1 + 9 + 3 + 7 = 20$; $2 + 0 = 2$): 2.

Bill Cosby's first cycle is ruled by the number 7; his second cycle by the number 3; and his final cycle by the number 2. Ideally, your cycle numbers—from the month to the year—should progress numerically upward. For example, a person born January 25, 1962, would have progressive cycles of 1 (January), 7 (2+5=7), and 9 (1+9+6+2=18; 1+8=9). If your cycle numbers progress downward, the theory is you may have to work a little harder than most.

Some birth dates have cycles of high and low, such as a person born April 8, 1972 (expressed as 4, 8, and 2). In this case, the month cycle starts at 4, then jumps to a date cycle of 8, finally ending with a year cycle that jumps back to 2. A cycle pattern of this nature usually indicates drastic, or marked changes relating to the early, middle and latter stages of this person's life.

Finally, there's yet another birthday pattern where each cycle number is exactly the same. Let's say someone was born July 16, 1978. In this case, the month (7th), the day (16th; 1+6=7) and the year (1978; 1+9+7+8=25; 2+5=7) are exactly the same. It's been my experience that those with the same cycle numbers across the board are consistent in relationship and environment. They may still associate or have some contact with their childhood friends. I've found this pattern to occur where such adults still live in or near the area of their birth.

Determine your cycle numbers from your birth month, day, and year, then read below. After you've read the definitions for your particular cycles, look to see if they progress upward, downward, up and down, or are the same across the board.

Life Cycles

1 CYCLE

The number 1 *in the first cycle* governs those born in January and October. This first period of your life deals with family, childhood experiences, and social and environmental influences. Until your 28th birthday, this period of your life should be one of self-reliance, activity, changes, new beginnings and new directions. Almost always, this first stage of your life will force you to stand on your own, make decisions, and assume early responsibility. Those born in January may encounter more difficulties and misunderstandings than those born in October.

The number 1 *as a second cycle* governs those of you born on the 1st, 10th, 19th, or 28th of the month. As you enter your 28th birthday, this period of your life becomes more productive. By the 31st year of your life, you should begin to assume some position of leadership or authority over others, if you haven't done so already. Your desire to lead, take charge, command, and direct is strong during this phase of your life. This period, between your 28th and 56th birthday attracts those born in the months of February, April, and August, as well as those born on dates adding up to the numbers 1, 2, 4, and 7.

The number 1 *in the third cycle* governs your year of birth, such as $1963(1+9+6+3=19; 1+9=10; 1+0=1)$. This phase of your life begins about your 55th birthday. It's a period of your life that could find you in a position of authority over others. On the other hand, this final stage of your life may force you to stand on your own two feet, not depending on anyone or anything. You have to rely more on your own resources, hopefully saved and accumulated from past years. In this period of life, guard against high blood pressure, heart problems, and irregular blood circulation; there may be problems with the lungs as well as with the eyes.

2 CYCLE

The number 2 *in the first cycle* governs those born in February and November. As this stage of life relates to the personal self, those of you born in February may be inclined to be more sensitive and emotional, and more influenced by females in the family. The ages of 11 and/ or 20 should prove important to you in some way. They could be of a transitory nature, such as moving from one location to another. Those of you born in February are more likely to be misunderstood during this stage than your November counterparts. Those born in November seem to have a better chance of early success.

The number 2 *in the second cycle* governs those of you born on the 2nd, 11th, 20th, or 29th of the month. An important turn of events for the better should come your way beginning with your 29th birthday up to 56. During this time, choose your friends and surroundings with care. You'll find the fields of poetry, computers, and electronics, among others, are your doors to success. This cycle of your life will draw those born in May, July, and October more than any other; this also includes those whose birth dates add up to 2, 7, 1, or 4.

The number 2 *as a third cycle* governs those born in a year totaling 2, such as $1973(1+9+7+3=20; 2+0=2)$. As you enter this final cycle of life about your 56th year, love, relationships, and companionship will be important to you. There may be times when you seem uncertain and unsettled about what you really want at this point in your life. As a result, carefully pick and choose your associates, living conditions, and physical surroundings. As for your health, guard against stomach and digestive orders of all kinds, watch out for hemorrhoids, diabetes, tumors, ulcers, ptomaine poisoning, and the like.

3 CYCLE

The number 3 *in the first cycle* governs those of you born in March and December. You're likely to be influenced by a third party other than a family member, during this early stage of life. Your 21st and 24th years should prove important in some way. There will be a pronounced need to express the self through words, music, and art. This usually occurs at an early age. If December is your birth month, you're likely to have a better chance at getting started in life than those born in

March. If your birthday is in March, you're more likely to be affected by emotions in the beginning.

The number 3 *in the second cycle* governs those of you born on the 3rd, 12th, 21st, or 30th of the month. Under this cycle, pride, ambition, independence, and a desire not be restrained by anyone will dominate your attitude. By your 30th birthday, lasting until age 57, you're likely to pursue careers closely related to the arts, religion, or government. This productive cycle will draw people into your life who were born in the months of March and December, followed by April and November. This also includes those born on dates adding up to 3, 6, or 9.

The number 3 *in the third cycle* governs those born in a year adding up to 3, such as 1983 $(1+9+8+3=21;$ $2+1=3)$. As you enter your 57th birthday, this final stage should prove to be sociable, entertaining, and enjoyable, especially if you've played your cards right during your previous cycle. On the positive side, you can end your days with a good reputation, prestige, and money. On the reverse, you could end up living for the moment, drinking to excess, and being extremely boastful. Guard the health against overstrained nerves, low blood pressure, neuritis, and skin and foot problems of all kinds.

4 CYCLE

The number 4 *in the first cycle* governs those of you born in April. Since this cycle rules early childhood, family, and environmental stages, there may have been limitations or severe restrictions in this regard. Hard work, misunderstandings, and circumstances out of your control, will be more pronounced. The ages of 19, 22, as well as 28, are likely to be important in some way. A practical approach to life will be the theme of things.

The number 4 *in the second cycle* governs your life if you happen to be born on the 4th, 13th, 22nd, or 31st of the month. Generally, the first 31 years of your life may be your most difficult. But around your 31st birthday or just afterward, circumstances and events should come under your control. You are cautious and deliberate by nature and inclined to view most things contrary to how others see them. Occupations, careers, friends, and associates that are considered odd and unusual will be attractive during this cycle. You'll find those born in the months of February, June, and August drawn to you; also those born on dates adding up to 1, 2, 5, and 7.

The number 4 *in the final cycle* governs those born in a year adding up to the number 4, such as 1975 ($1+9+7+5=22$; $2+2=4$). This stage of your life should be carefully set, since the 4 is associated with hard work, ups and downs, the unexpected, and misunderstandings. As a result, financial security should be arranged during your second cycle. Structure your life and follow a plan as much as possible during this harvest cycle. If you prepare carefully, you may have one final chance to build lasting things. Your health may be affected through moodiness, periods of depression, or mental disorders, as well as sudden and mysterious illnesses and accidents.

5 CYCLE

The number 5 *in the first cycle* governs those of you born in May. During this first stage, you're likely to experience a number of changes, travels, relocations, and involvements with people and public activity. Generally, a packed suitcase is the theme during this cycle, allowing you to move at a moment's notice. Ages 14 and 23 should prove important in some way. Since the number 5 represents mental qualities, a good education is of utmost importance at this stage in your cycles.

The number 5 *in a second cycle* governs those of you born on the 5th, 14th, or 23rd of the month. By age 32, you will experience some degree of freedom, change, variety, and travel among other things. Since this cycle stage affects your career, occupations related to business, science, and the literary field would be excellent to pursue. At this stage in your life, you'll draw to you those born in the months of May, June, September, and

October. This also includes those born on dates adding up to 5 and 6.

The number 5 *in the third cycle* governs those born in a year adding up to a 5, such as $1967(1+9+6+7=23; 2+3=5)$. Since this cycle represents the final stage of things, you can expect a full, active life as a result. Public involvement of some sort should be pronounced, if not dominant. In this case, there's no need to get out your wheelchair—you don't have time. Be on guard, however, against overstraining the nervous system, mental breakdowns, nervous tension, paralysis, and insomnia.

6 CYCLE

The number 6 *in the first cycle* governs those of you born in the month of June. Since 6 also governs love, family, duty, and commitments, this is likely to be the theme of your life until your 28th birthday. Chances are strong that you'll be popular in your peer group. Because this cycle represents your formative, growing, and emotional years, there may be a tendency to put the people and things you love up on a pedestal. Establish a balance if you can. Women ruled by 6 in this period usually experience an early or late marriage. A good education is of utmost importance. Your 21st and 24th year of life should prove to be eventful in some way.

The number 6 *in the second cycle* governs your birth date if it happens to be on the 6th, 15th, or 24th of the month. The rays of the 6 in your productive cycle should commence about your 24th birthday and reach full steam by age 33. You'll exhibit a distinct love for all things beautiful and esthetic, such as an artistic home, rich colors and décor, music, and art. You have a deep love and respect for education and learning. Careers that offer comfort, council, and advice to others, such as nursing, teaching, law, and coaching, to name a few, should bring you a lot of personal satisfaction. During this stage of your life, your friends, acquaintances, and others will tend to be born in the months of March, May,

July, October, and December. The same is true for those born on dates adding up to 6, 3, and 2.

The number 6 *in the third cycle* affects those of you born in a year adding up to this number, such as 1968 $(1+9+6+8=24; 2+4=6)$. This final stage of life may find a late marriage or romance starting to blossom around your 51st birthday. Depending on the progress of your second cycle, you should be able to establish a comfortable home for yourself and your loved ones. Guard against irregular blood circulation, overweight, heart disease, sinus problems, and all conditions generally affecting the nose, throat, or upper part of the lungs.

7 CYCLE

The number 7 *in the first cycle* governs those born in July. As 7 is an inward number, there may be periods in this stage of life where emotions are held inside instead of expressed in the normal way. The tendency is to be alone—to study, to search for truth, and to understand the mysteries of life. During this cycle, your 16th and 25th birthdays should prove important or at least eventful. The pattern is for you to be more of a spectator than a participator.

The number 7 *in the second cycle* governs your birthday if you were born on the 7th, 16th, or 25th of the month. Beginning around age 25, you should begin to develop an independent nature, originality, and above all, a strongly marked individuality. You'll have a desire to travel to faraway places, and to learn all you can about inner truth and wisdom. Careers related to writing, music, analysis, research, technology, and mysticism will be dominant. Those born in March, May, July, and August will be drawn to you; also those born on dates adding up to 1, 2, 4, 6, or 7.

The number 7 *in the third cycle* governs those born in a year totaling this number, for instance, 1951 $(1+9+5+1=16; 1+6=7)$. At this final stage of life, there's likely to be a strong desire to get away from stress and noise, away from the hustle and bustle of life. Religious and spiritual interests are usually heightened when in this stage of your life. Avoid becoming a recluse or withdrawn. As far as your health is concerned, watch out for excessive worry, annoyance, and mental aggravation, digestive disorders, and night sweats; try not to imagine the worst.

8 CYCLE

The number 8 *in the first cycle* governs those of you born in the month of August. This beginning stage of your life gives you a chance to assume authority over others at an early age. Things of a material and tangible nature will come under this influence as well. Your 17th and 26th birthdays will prove important in some way. At this early stage of life, you're mentally mature far beyond your biological years, which draws older people into your life. You may be a victim of circumstances and misunderstanding until the ages of 31, at the earliest, or age 33 at the latest.

The number 8 *in the second cycle* governs your life if you were born on the 8th, 17th, or 26th of the month. According to this cycle stage, you may not feel in control of your affairs until about your 35th birthday. During this time in your life, you're likely to develop a deep, intense personality, having a mind of your own. A strong concentration of purpose as well as a philosophical approach to life should be the dominant theme until about your 58th birthday. Anything connected with the public, banking, real estate, or working for the government could easily lead to financial success. Persons born in January, May, and October will be drawn to you, as well as those born on dates adding up to 8, 6, or 3.

The number 8 *in the third cycle* governs those born in a year adding to an 8, such as 1979 $(1+9+7+9=26;$ $2+6=8)$. Beginning around age 53 and lasting until the end of your life, your attitude may be a philosophical acceptance of your fate and your role on life's stage. Rest from labor, or some form of retirement, will be the theme. There's is an even stronger possibility of material things gained through effort, hard work, and determination. As for health, guard against headaches, depression, feelings of intense loneliness, constipation, and blood poisoning, as well as problems with the knees, teeth, and bones.

9 CYCLE

The number 9 *in the first cycle* governs your life if you were born in the month of September. Because the 9 is a broad and impersonal number, this may be some cause for concern, since this stage of life governs your formative, impressionable, and emotional years. Your 18th and 27th birthdays should prove important. Your life at this point will very likely be influenced by distant travels and meeting outstanding personalities, as well as a broad range of contacts.

The number 9 *in the second cycle* governs your date of birth, if it happens to be on the 9th, 18th, or 27th of the month. As you enter your 27th birthday, opportunities should begin to open up for you. You will begin to experience a strong desire to be in control of your affairs, to become the captain of your ship. Your will and determination are the basic ingredients of your success. Careers in law, the military, medicine, art, and religion generally open your door to success. Persons born in April, August, and November are often drawn to you, and the same holds true for those with a birth date adding up to 9, 3, or 1.

The number 9 *in the third cycle* governs your last years if you were born in a year adding up to a 9, such as 1971 $(1+9+7+1=18; 1+8=9)$. The rays of this influence on your life should begin to be felt by your 54th birthday. This last stage of your life should be filled with constant activity, meeting outstanding celebrities and personalities, as well as traveling the globe. At this stage of your life guard against bumps and bruises, arguments, cuts, burns, auto accidents, dangers from machinery and firearms, fevers, and high temperatures.

A Rosicrucian Approach to the Life Cycles

In our last chapter we examined the major cycles found in your month, day, and year of birth that affect you over a long period of time. However, there's another type of cycle that affects you more immediately—from year to year. This cycle goes from birthday to birthday and is broken into seven phases, or periods, of 52 days each. Let's take someone born on December 7th of any year. Start with December 7th as day number 1. Next, count forward 51 days to cover your first 52-day period. In this case, it spans the period from December 7th to January 25th. Now, count forward another 52 days, starting with January 25th. In our example, this second period covers January 25th to March 17th. Then count 51 days again, starting with March 17th, to get period number three, and so on until you have determined your seven yearly periods of 52 days each.

This cycle system of seven periods from birthday to birthday, has long been understood and applied by the ancient and mystic Rosicrucian Order (AMORC). The following list from each of the seven periods is only a small synopsis of the wisdom and practical experience that men and women in the Rosicrucian Order have accumulated. The purpose of this yearly birthday-to-birthday cycle is to guide you in an intelligent manner about what to do and not do in your everyday life. It enables you to live in harmony with the laws of nature and the universe, as well as with yourself. It also enables you to understand the role that cosmic forces play in the divine scheme of things. With a calendar, start from your day of birth (considered day one), then count 52 days forward until you have done so seven times to find your seven cycles.

FIRST CYCLE OF 52 DAYS (Reputation Period)

- Seek favors from persons in high positions, promotions, loans, and career advancements.
- Good for advancing personal self-interests and for building up your personal credit.
- Good for dealing with government and public officials.
- Good for promoting your name and personal reputation.

SECOND CYCLE OF 52 DAYS (Journey Period)

- Good for journey by train and water.
- Good for moving into a new home or new location.
- Not a good time to loan or borrow money.
- Long-term contracts should not be started or completed in this period.

THIRD CYCLE OF 52 DAYS (Energy Period)

- Good period for physical energy, effort, endurance, and determination.
- Good period to deal with rivals and competitors.
- Good for salespersons and speakers who must use persuasion.
- Bad period to argue, especially over contracts, documents, or other legal matters.

FOURTH CYCLE OF 52 DAYS (Mental Period)

- Good period for writing, creative thoughts, new ideas, and the study of special interests.
- Good for following impulses, hunches, intuition, and inspiration.

- Good for literary matters, artists, bookkeepers, reporters, and the like.
- Greatest period to beware of fraud and deception by others.

FIFTH CYCLE OF 52 DAYS (Success Period)

- Good period for the successful termination of things.
- Good time to expand, prosper, and grow in personal and intimate affairs.
- Good time to collect, speculate, and borrow money.

SIXTH CYCLE OF 52 DAYS (Vacation Period)

- Good for pleasure, amusement, entertainment, and other fun things.
- Good for long or short visits of a relaxing nature.
- Good for renewing friendships, and for men dealing with women.
- Not good for long travels by water.

SEVENTH CYCLE OF 52 DAYS (Critical Period)

- Good time for dealing with the elderly.
- Good for dealing with real estate, mines, and things of the Earth.
- Good for finishing or ending things.
- Sudden travels, long or short, especially by sea or overland should be avoided.

For more details on this fascinating study of the birthday-to-birthday cycles, I recommend reading, *Life Mastery and the Cycles of Fate*, by Dr. H. Lewis Spencer.

Your Personal Destiny Number

Why was I born? What am I here for? What is my destiny? Are these familiar questions? Whether you know it or not, you're here on this physical Earth for a reason, a purpose. You are here to learn what must be mastered in order to be successful in this life. As in any school, but especially the school of life, we must learn the basic lessons we need to move from grade to grade. In Numerology, the grades go from 1 to 9. Again, as in any school, if you fail to learn the lessons or fail to pass the tests that must eventually be taken, you will be left back until you master the fundamentals or make up the lessons.

To find out what lessons you have to learn, and what grade you have attained in this physical life, the rule of thumb is to add up all the numbers of your birthday. For instance, let's take someone born February 15, 1948:

$$
\begin{array}{rl}
2 & \text{(Birth Month)} \\
15 & \text{(Birth Date)} \\
\underline{1948} & \text{(Birth Year)} \\
1965 & = 21 \ (2+1=3) \ \text{3 is the Destiny} \\
& \text{Number}
\end{array}
$$

This person's destiny number, or grade, in this life is the number 3. Also, consider the day on which you were born as additional information on your destiny. In our example the birth date is the 15th, which adds up to 6 $(1+5=6)$. This means the number 6 plays an equally important part in this person's destiny.

Add up your birthday numbers in this manner, as well as those of your family members, loved ones, and friends, to find the destiny number. Once you've found it, study what lessons are required of you for personal happiness and success. Next, consider your birth date number to gain further insight. Don't forget, if you fail to learn the required lessons, you may get left back in the school of life. If you're not prepared, this could be a crushing blow.

Listed below are the lessons to be learned from your destiny number. Also listed are the things you must learn NOT TO DO.

Lessons of the Destiny Numbers

DESTINY NUMBER 1

You must learn to be: original, creative, forceful, determined, ambitious, bold, self-controlled, and self-confident.

Learn NOT to be: bossy, selfish, limited, egotistical, weak-minded, arrogant, a bully, domineering.

DESTINY NUMBER 2

You must learn to be: loving, peaceful, considerate, kind, understanding, persuasive, patient, and gentle.

Learn NOT to be: overly sensitive, easily swayed by others, moody, impressionable, indecisive, or petty.

DESTINY NUMBER 3

You must learn to be: cheerful and optimistic, sociable, confident, conscientious, proud, creative, and articulate.

Learn NOT to be: superficial, dictatorial, vain, boastful, pessimistic, extravagant, gossiping.

DESTINY NUMBER 4

You must learn to be: practical, methodical, studious, serious, down to earth, disciplined, honest, loyal, punctual and trustworthy.

Learn NOT to be: fearful of change, rigid, dogmatic, stubborn, melancholy, dull, boring, or slow.

DESTINY NUMBER 5

You must learn to be: enthusiastic, clever, adaptable, an adventurer, expressive in writing and speech, curious, scientific, crisis oriented.

Learn NOT to be: careless, vulgar, indifferent, overindulgent in sensual pleasures, a wanderer, irritable, wasteful, callous.

DESTINY NUMBER 6

You must learn to be: responsible, magnetic, dependable, kind, affectionate, artistic, friendly, a helper to those in need.

Learn NOT to be: stubborn, obstinate, slow to decide, irresponsible, interfering, and unyielding.

DESTINY NUMBER 7

You must learn to be: spiritual, analytical, intuitive, faithful, original, independent, professional, silent, knowledgeable, truthful.

Learn NOT to be: skeptical, pessimistic, cold and aloof, fault finding with others, afraid, nervous.

DESTINY NUMBER 8

You must learn to be: authoritative, determined, in control, successful, persevering, thorough, philosophical, a leader.

Learn NOT to be: hungry for power, money, or material possessions, fatalistic in outlook, domineering, oppressive, a schemer, bullying, or misunderstood.

DESTINY NUMBER 9

You must learn to be: inspirational, energetic, an organizer, strong willed, forceful, artistic, humane, and generous.

Learn NOT to be: emotional, narrow in outlook, an influence for bad, hasty in temper, impulsive, bitter, quick to fight.

The Master Numbers

Do you have the master numbers in your birth date, birth path, or name? Do you know what the master numbers are, what they mean and why? There are basically two master numbers, the 11 and the 22. These two numbers, under modern Numerology, possess certain powers and should never be reduced to the single numbers of 2 or 4. Persons born on the 11th or 22nd of the month possess the qualities of leadership and inspiration. If the master numbers are not found on the 11th or 22nd of the month, these numbers may be found in the entire birth date when it is laid out in the following manner:

1. person born 3/31/1975

3 (Birth Month)
31 (Birth Date)
<u>1975</u> (Birth Year)
add 2009 = 11 master number

2. person born 2/11/1935

2 (Birth Month)
11 (Birth Date)
<u>1935</u> (Birth Year)
add 1948 = 22 master number

In example number 2, both master numbers are present not only in the birth path (the sum total of a person's month, day, and year of birth) but in the birth date itself.

The final place to look for the master numbers, if they weren't found in the birth path or birth date, is in the name. For instance:

L   O   U   I   S
$3 + 6 + 3 + 9 + 1 = 22$ master number name

Now that you have examples of how to find a possible master number, let's begin to deal briefly with each of the master numbers separately.

The Master Number 11

The 11 is a magnetic number. Those who have it are usually considered visionary, inventive, idealistic, and inspirational. The master number 11 vibrates with revelation, abstract impressions, and with things from On High. In Astrology, the master number 11 is assigned to the Zodiac signs of Leo and Aquarius.

In order for those carrying the 11 vibration in their name or date of birth to realize and maintain its power, they must strive to raise themselves to the highest possible levels of human understanding and wisdom. Love, peace, harmony, justice, and equality are strongly associated with the number 11.

One of the callings of an 11 person is to light the world through lofty ideas; it can also mean tests of determination or aggressiveness. The 11 is composed of two 1s. The number 1 by itself represents the Sun—it is powerful, authoritative, and independent. However, when you add the two 1s together, you get the single number of 2, which represents all things gentle, artistic, and imaginative.

Although the 11 under modern Numerology is a master number and represents the highest qualities, the original meaning of this compound number under the Chaldean system of numbers is different. In the Chaldean, or mystic, system, the 11 offers a warning to occultists. It denotes hidden dangers and great trials and difficulties.

The Master Number 22

The master number 22 is somewhat similar to the 11 in that both are magnetic and powerful. However, where the 11 deals with the mental plane, the 22 deals more directly with the physical plane. Perhaps this is why the 22 is often referred to as the "master builder." In modern Numerology, the 22 is all powerful and far reaching in its influence. Under this number, master achievements become quite possible. It has the power to make or break, depending on the person holding this number. In Astrology, the master number 22 is governed by the Zodiac sign of Aquarius, the water bearer.

Those carrying the 22 in their names or birth dates must learn the right use of its power, for the 22 can tear down and destroy as well as build. Precision, accuracy, analysis, and determination are strongly associated with the number 22. A 22 person usually has a strong mechanical turn of mind and the power to succeed in whatever areas of interest are the strongest.

The 22 is composed of two 2s. The 2 by itself represents the Moon and is inventive, artistic, and imaginative. However, when you add up $2 + 2$, you get the single number 4. This represents the planet Uranus, which governs odd and unusual things, social questions of all kind, new schools of thought, and the like.

Although the 22 under modern Numerology is a master number, the original meaning of this compound number under the Chaldean system is different. There, the 22 shows us a good man, blinded by the follies of others, carrying a knapsack on his back filled with errors. It is a number that warns us against illusions and delusions caused by the false judgments of others.

You now have a brief description of the numbers 11 and 22. Because these are considered master numbers, holding the potential of power and dominion, everyone wants to own one. On the other hand, you may not want to pay the price that is often required of these numbers.

Your Personal Year Forecast

Each year, we and our environment move through different sets of conditions known as the "universal" and "personal" year cycles. The universal cycle is very easy to determine. You simply add up the numbers of any year; this makes it simple to find the numerical influence for any year, be it past, present, or future. Let's take a year in the past, 1978. It adds up to a 7 $(1+9+7+8=25; 2+5=7)$. Taking 2016, a year in the future, this adds up to a 9 universal year $(2+0+1+6=9)$. The universal cycle affects all of us.

The personal year cycle, however, affects us individually in a more personal or intimate way. I classify the personal year cycles into four general categories:

- Mental outlook, mood, and way of thinking.
- The environment or conditions of things around you.
- The attraction or assistance you're likely to encounter.
- The health or physical well-being that may speed or hinder your progress.

To find your very own personal year number, take your month and day of birth and add it to the present year. Taking someone born April 13th:

4 (Birth Month)
13 (Birth Date)
1988 (Present Year)
_____
2005 = 7 personal year for this
particular person in 1988.

Determine your own personal year cycle in this manner. Don't forget, add your month and day of birth to any year you wish to know about.

The 1 Personal Year

THEME:

Independence, new opportunities, planting seeds.

DESCRIPTION:

In a 1 personal cycle you have a chance to symbolically begin life over again. This should be a year for all things new as well as new opportunities and personal experiences. If you were born on the 1st, 10th, 19th, or 28th of the month, or under the sign of Leo or Aries, this year should be all the more important. In this cycle, it's best for you to strike out on your own in some way, to take the lead wherever required. It's no accident that most people start their own businesses or launch important projects and long-range plans under this cycle. The 1 year represents planting, laying the groundwork for the next nine years ahead. So choose and plant your seeds very carefully.

LOVE/RELATIONSHIPS:

In this particular cycle, whether the relationship is personal, business, or otherwise, it's an excellent time to get involved with someone new, authoritative, or perhaps younger than yourself. If you already have an established relationship, a renewal of some kind may be just what you need—take a second honeymoon, or renew your vows. In matters of romance or business, you'll find those born under the signs of Leo, Aries, and Aquarius entering your life, as well as those born on the 1st, 4th, 9th, 10th, 13th, 18th, 19th, 22nd, 27th, 28th, and 31st of the month. The months of January, May, July, and October are likely to bring these persons into your life and plans. Your colors of attraction are gold, yellow, orange and golden brown.

HEALTH:

The emphasis during this cycle is on the eyes, such as problems with astigmatism; the lungs, and the heart, as well as irregular circulation or heart palpitations. It's best to start this cycle with a medical checkup. Begin a new physical fitness program to meet the busy year. The months to keep an eye on your own health as well as the health of others are March, May, and August.

CAREER:

If you've been wanting to make a break, to go for something completely new in your career, this is certainly the year for it. More major changes, improvements, or job independence take place under this cycle than any other. Aggressiveness, decision-making, ability, leadership qualities, and the will to win impress others and gain their assistance. If you're looking for work or making career moves, Tuesday and Monday are your best days (in that order). These are also good days to ask for a raise or promotion. Job or career changes are likely to be more noticeable during April, May, July and September.

TRAVEL:

The travel opportunities that come your way are likely to be new, different, and exciting compared with the past. This year, travel may be strongly connected with your career in some way, or simply offer a change of scenery, a way to start life anew. January, April, August, September, and October hold the strongest possibilities for travel.

The 2 Personal Year

THEME:

Patience, companionship, harmony, and teamwork.

DESCRIPTION:

The major focus of a 2 personal cycle is on tact, cooperation, and understanding. Whatever seeds you planted last year are now in the germination stage. Changes are likely to be slow rather than rapid. Gradually, but with purpose, changes take place in the environment—you might move from one location to another, even to another city. Changes also occur in the home or in relationships with the opposite sex. This is an excellent year to get what you want by asking for favors rather than by forcing yourself on others. If you were born under the signs of Cancer or Taurus, or if your birthday falls on the 2nd, 11th, 20th, or 29th of the month, this year is all the more important.

LOVE/RELATIONSHIPS:

Love, friends, and partnerships of some sort seem to be a necessity. Members of the opposite sex tend to get more involved in your life than normal. Engagements, marriages, even pregnancies and births are strongly indicated for you or those close to you under this cycle. The cosmic, intuitive, nurturing side of your nature is likely to emerge. Since this is a very emotional cycle, deeply influenced by the Moon, you may be extra sensitive to remarks or suggestions. You're likely to find those under Cancer, Taurus, and Libra coming into your life more. This also includes those born on the 2nd, 6th, 7th, 11th, 15th, 16th, 20th, 24th, 25th, or 29th of the month. Romantic and domestic events are especially strong during April, June, and September. The colors of attraction are cream, green, white, and blue.

HEALTH:

This personal cycle generally brings concerns with the stomach and gastric problems of all kind. Women may have female problems during this period. Be selective when eating out, to avoid possible ptomaine poisoning. In addition, tumors, and ulcers due to emotional stress could develop. Start off the year with a proper diet program focusing on nutrition rather than weight gain or loss. Your weight should adjust itself naturally if you eat properly. The months of February, April, July especially and November may show health changes in some way.

CAREER:

Internal rather than external changes are likely in the workplace when passing through this cycle. For example, you may find your work area moving from one floor to another, or even relocating to another building or area. You may also be assigned another task in addition to your present responsibilities. Should you be in search of work this year, schedule your appointments for Monday and Friday. These are also excellent days to ask for a raise, promotion, or transfer. The months of March, April, June, August, and December are important for job moves or advances.

TRAVEL:

An excellent year for short trips up to a few days or of a temporary nature. Trips by water or across water are also strongly indicated. It's also possible that your geographical setting will be changed or altered in some way before the year is over. You can expect to take advantage of travel opportunities during the months of March, July, August, and December.

The 3 Personal Year

THEME:

Imagination, expansion, self-improvement, and creation.

DESCRIPTION:

Happiness, growth, artistic and social developments, along with a desire for self-improvement are among the many highlights in store for you. Improving your image or reputation will add to your popularity with others and the public. Doing something creative, such as writing, painting, or making music, will add much to your personal self-satisfaction. Be positive in attitude and action as much as possible. The seeds you planted two years ago are likely to bear fruit. If you were born under the sign of Pisces or Sagittarius, or if your birthday falls on the 3rd, 12th, 21st, or 30th of the month, this year should be all the more important.

LOVE/RELATIONSHIPS:

Love and romance are fanciful and flirty rather than serious. Under this aspect, love relationships may be more fun and passing fancy than domestic. You're likely to find relationships developing with those younger than yourself. This also includes those born under the signs of Pisces and Sagittarius, and those born on dates that add up to 3, 6, or 9. During this particular cycle, the best months to develop relationships are March, May, August, and December.

HEALTH:

Out of the fun of it all, may come the strain of it all—especially if carried to excess. Health during this cycle may be stressed by overwork, nervous strain, emotional outbursts and upsets. There may be skin problems, low blood pressure or anemia, as well as foot problems. The best medicine is not to overwork the mind and body through too much work or play. Stay alert to health concerns during January, March, June, and October.

CAREER:

Three is the number of expansion and personal growth, therefore your career outlook should be bright. Develop a more positive, ambitious attitude. Take a conscientious approach to your job responsibilities. If you're looking for the right time to advance yourself, or to ask for a raise or promotion, take interviews or tests, select Thursday and Friday as your best days. Look for the months of February, March, May, July, and November to bring better opportunities.

TRAVEL:

Trips and travel during this cycle year are likely to be short, and more in connection with fun and entertainment. On the other side of the coin, however, chances are excellent for traveling to foreign lands. Travel months strongly indicated this year are February, June, July, and November.

The 4 Personal Year

THEME:

Foundation, organization, structure, work.

DESCRIPTION:

This cycle year, have a plan, a road map, or schedule for your personal and business dealings. More may be required of you, which may give you the feeling of being boxed-in, burdened, or pressured in some way. This cycle generally suggests limitations, whether it's emotional, physical, psychological, or economic. On the other hand, you now have a chance to get yourself organized and to build a solid and secure foundation for yourself. This year, be sure to ask, "who, what, where, when, why and how" about any activity, project, or plan you wish to undertake. If you're an Aquarius, Leo, or Gemini, or born on the 4th, 13th, 22nd, or 31st of any month, this personal year cycle will be all the more important.

LOVE/RELATIONSHIPS:

Persons who are considered unconventional, odd, or unusual are likely to be drawn to you in this cycle. Interestingly, those from the past, someone older, or outside of your own ethnic, social, or religious background may be drawn to you as well. A romance out of left field is also indicated. Gemini, Leo, and Aquarius are the likely favorites, as well as anyone whose birth number is 1, 4, 5, or 7. The best months for romance are February, April, July, and November. Electric colors attract during this cycle, as do pastels and halftones.

HEALTH:

Of all the personal year cycles, this one generally puts the most stress on your physical well-being and psychological attitude. Unpredictable and unexplainable behavior may occur during this cycle. Odd or mysterious illnesses may develop, which could lead to misdiagnoses, wrong medical treatment, even the wrong drug prescription. Watch for changes in moods, mental attitudes, or health during February, May, September, and November.

CAREER:

Since this cycle tends to bring the unexpected and extreme, this may also happen in your job or career. For instance, one week you may be happy and secure—then the following week, quite unexpectedly, you find yourself out of work, in a panic, looking for another place of employment. Or you may be in a lull at work with nothing developing, then suddenly you're pushed to the top. Life is strange in a 4 cycle year. This cycle also tends to bring additional burdens or responsibilities. Don't shun them, for there's a lesson to be learned that will pay dividends later. When setting up interviews or approaching your boss about a raise or promotion, make it Monday or Wednesday for best results. January, February, April, October, and November are the months to stay alert for job changes and opportunities.

TRAVEL:

You may not get much of an opportunity to travel, at least the first two-thirds of the year. Travel this year comes about under two conditions: an illness of someone close, or a sudden opportunity out of the blue. Travel indicators are strong for January, May, June, and October.

The 5 Personal Year

THEME:

Dramatic changes, freedom, public activity, and travel.

DESCRIPTION:

If you didn't get an opportunity to get things off the ground several years ago, you'll get a second chance now. You'll sense a change for the better in all your affairs. You're likely to see more of your activities coming before the public. Life's lessons will seem easier to learn, and you'll find yourself more mentally and physically alert to your environment than ever before. If you're a Gemini or Virgo, or were born on the 5th, 14th, or 23rd of the month, this will prove to be an important cycle indeed.

LOVE/RELATIONSHIPS:

Since 5 is the number of sexual attraction, you're likely to experience a number of relationships with members of the opposite sex. Through no fault of your own, your sex appeal will increase during this and next year's cycle. The tendency here is to attract persons younger than yourself. Look for those born under Taurus, Gemini, Virgo, and Libra, as well as those whose birth date adds up to 5 or 6. Wear bright, shimmering colors during the months of January, March, June, October, and December.

HEALTH:

There may be problems connected with insomnia, nervous disorders, mental irritability, or exhaustion, even dizziness. Slow down! Rest and relaxing sleep will do more for you than anything else. Since 5 is a very active cycle, a heavy schedule of activities on your cosmic calendar may be at the root of these difficulties. Avoid excess, especially with alcohol, drugs, sex, gambling, and high-risk adventures. During January, April, August, and October guard the health.

CAREER:

This is considered one of the best cycles for making changes or improving your job or career prospects. It should be quite easy to sell your ideas, as well as to push your talents, skills, and expertise. Pass your résumé around, for out there in the world someone will be aware of what you can really do. Wednesday and Friday are the best days to look for employment, set up interviews, or ask for a raise, promotion, or transfer. Look for March, May, September, October, and December to be significant for job opportunities and advancements.

TRAVEL:

As 5 is a number long associated with movement, you're likely to have more than your share of trips and travel of a personal and business nature this year. These will prove refreshing as well as beneficial. Travel indications are especially strong during April, May, and September.

The 6 Personal Year

THEME:

Duty, domestic activity, family life, and responsibility.

DESCRIPTION:

When entering a 6 personal year cycle, activities will center around the home, family, loved ones, and romantic episodes. Esthetic appreciation will run high toward anything beautiful, with a strong appeal to the eye. In matters of the home, there are strong indications that you may move out of one and into another. Going back to school, graduating, or taking additional educational courses may also be in store. You'll receive many invitations to social functions, galas, art openings, festivities, and the like. Attend these functions, since opportunities for advancement are evident. If you were born on the 6th, 15th, or 24th of the month, or should your sign be Taurus, Libra, or Cancer, this is a very important year cycle.

LOVE/RELATIONSHIPS:

The 6 is the top cycle for matters of love and romance. This is the year for love, engagement, marriage, separation, divorce, pregnancy, birth, abortion, or a change in an existing relationship. Those born under the signs of Taurus, Cancer, and Libra are slated to play more of a key role, as well as those born on dates adding up to 6, 3, and 2. The outstanding months of this cycle are February, May, September, and November. Wear all shades of blue for attraction and assistance.

HEALTH:

The emphasis during this cycle is on the upper part of the body. The nose, throat, tonsils, upper part of the lungs, breasts, or heart top the list. Depending on your present physical condition (6 has a tendency to put on weight later in life), problems could develop with irregular blood circulation or heart palpitations. Plenty of sunlight, fresh air, and outdoor physical activity should offset much of the above. This year, keep an eye on things during March, July, September, and December.

CAREER:

Recognition, promotions, or improvements in your job or career should come into play. Your financial rewards will come through fulfilling your obligations and commitments to the letter. There's praise in store for you. Should you be looking for work, setting up an important interview, or simply asking for job advancement, your best days are Friday, Thursday, and Monday, in that order. As for longer range indicators, opportunities are equally strong during February, April, August, September, and November.

TRAVEL:

As this is a domestic, home-loving cycle, trips and travel may be limited in scope. Whatever travel comes into the picture this year will center around family reunions, family illness, funerals, births, marriages, graduations, or perhaps a social function of some sort. Look for these events to manifest themselves during the months of March, April, August, and December.

The 7 Personal Year

THEME:

Inner growth, sabbatical, self-awareness, self-discovery.

DESCRIPTION:

In a 7 personal year cycle you have a chance to place special emphasis on your personal life and well-being. You'll find yourself analyzing your past motives and actions, and developing an intense need to be alone to give more time and attention to your own personal needs, goals, and desires. There will be a need to get away from all the noise and confusion. If you visualize what you want this year, you're likely to get it. This is much better than chasing after what you want. Secrets about yourself and others generally surface in a 7 year. If you were born under the signs of Pisces or Cancer, or on the 7th, 16th, or 25th of the month, this year will be all the more important.

LOVE/RELATIONSHIPS:

This is not the best personal year for love and romance since 7 is generally a loner cycle. As the 7 is a more spiritual indicator than an emotional or material one, any romance that develops this year may not be of a long or permanent nature. Possibly the best way of getting what you want romantically is to put it in your mind's eye, to visualize your ideal romantic mate. Whatever romantic interests do come along this year will be with those born on dates adding up to 2, 7, or 4, as well as those born under Cancer and Pisces. Watch for possible romantic hints during January, April, August, and October.

HEALTH:

Since you're transiting a rather quiet, somber year, any irritations or changes of the health may come through worry or annoyances. It's important to maintain a calm, meditative state of mind for best results. If not, you may create problems for yourself by imagining the worst. Find time alone to energize and restore your cosmic cells. Health changes are indicated for February, June, August, and November.

CAREER:

When passing through this cycle, two things tend to happen: a retirement or a slowing down by taking a leave of absence or a sabbatical from work; and you will also develop a deeper awareness about your skills and occupational expertise—an understanding of your true role and purpose comes to light. Perhaps more than any other cycle other than the 1, inner discoveries and long-sought secrets are finally unearthed. Therefore it's best to have an investigative and exploratory attitude toward your work. Schedule Monday and Friday for interviews and job hunting or for seeking a raise, promotion, or unveiling a new discovery. January, March, July, August, October, and December are favorable for such job matters.

TRAVEL:

You'll find frequent trips to the countryside or to the sea soothing and refreshing to the mind, body, and spirit. In traveling this year, you may develop a strong interest in the customs and cultures of other nations. Exotic, faraway places and islands will have a magnetic, mysterious appeal at this time. Travel is indicated this year during the months of February, April, June, and November.

The 8 Personal Year

THEME:

Achievement, career, major moves, power, recognition.

DESCRIPTION:

Consider this your "power year" cycle—the chance to do and achieve something big in your life. If you were born on the 8th, 17th, or 26th of the month, or come under the sign of Capricorn, pay more attention to this cycle year. You should develop maturity and a deeper sense of destiny or faith in yourself and in events about to happen. Not only is this cycle year associated with money and career, but debts out of the past. For instance, an old debt or responsibility avoided in the past may appear. But whatever you do this cycle year, aim for the Sun—think positive, think large, think success!

LOVE/RELATIONSHIPS:

This personal year cycle is strongly associated with marriage, divorce, and pregnancy. Romantically, those who are older than yourself or someone of influence or wealth should be very appealing. This cycle puts you in touch with those you know from the past—a long-lost relative, a romance from long ago, or even an old school friend. You'll find no problems romantically this year with Capricorns or Librans, or with those whose dates of birth add up to 8, 6, or 3. Wear deep blues, black, and other dark colors for attraction. Romance is likely to develop during March, July, September, and December.

HEALTH:

This is the cycle that usually brings on headaches, constipation, problems connected with the liver, blood, and excretory parts of the system. In addition, there may be concerns with the knees, teeth, and bones. Deep moods of despondency and feelings of intense loneliness emerge in this cycle. Furthermore, there's a likelihood of receiving the wrong drug prescription or medical treatment during surgery. Be careful of your diet and maintain a positive mental attitude for balance. Watch your health during January, May, July, and October.

CAREER:

This cycle is considered the best when it comes to making money, getting a big raise, or achieving authority over others. This is your year for recognition as a result of your work efforts. And since 8 is an executive number, act the part for your own financial success. Set large goals for yourself this year, you'll be surprised how close you come. Looking for work? Setting an interview? Want to ask your boss for a raise? Save Saturday, Thursday, and Friday for such matters. Watch for job or career opportunities during February, June, July, September, and November.

TRAVEL:

As 8 is considered an Earth number, travel overland would perhaps be best this year. As a rule, 8 is not a travel number, so journeys are more likely to occur in connection with property, legacies, or funerals. On the other hand, there could be travel related to business, or to receiving an award, plaque, or certificate. Look for these occurrences during the months of January, February, June, October, and November.

The 9 Personal Year

THEME:

Completions, dreams fulfilled, endings, inspiration, long trips.

DESCRIPTION:

With the exception of the master number cycles of 11 and 22, the 9 cycle is the highest you can go. The 9 year generally symbolizes a completion of sorts, either in your personal or business affairs. Your capacity to let go of persons, habits, negative circumstances, or conditions that you've outgrown will be strong. During this cycle, develop the humanitarian side of your nature, learn to give more of yourself to others without expecting payment in return. Cosmically, you'll be rewarded if you do. If you're an Aries or a Scorpio, or born on the 9th, 18th, or 27th of the month, this should be a significant year cycle.

LOVE/RELATIONSHIPS:

The 9 cycle is universal in influence and appeal. As a result, getting involved with the opposite sex outside your own religious, cultural, or ethnic group may be indicated. This is because the 9 relates to humanity, and it overshadows prejudice and ignorance. Cosmically, Aries, Leo, and Scorpio are likely to be more involved in your domestic affairs, as well as those whose birth dates add up to 9, 3, and 1. For help and attraction, wear all shades of red, from pink to deep crimson. February, June, August, and November will be more eventful from a romantic point of view.

HEALTH:

During this cycle, the rule is to avoid accidents at all costs, as well as altercations and arguments with others. Be careful how you drive, and how you handle knives, scissors, and other sharp instruments—even guns. The 9 is a fire number, so be careful of anything to do with fire—even smoking in bed. This cycle also brings on inflammations and fevers. Rash, impulsive statements or actions can equally undermine your physical health and mental well-being. Patience will reward you with fewer injuries, arguments, and accidents. Be especially careful during April, June, and September.

CAREER:

Since this is a fulfillment cycle, most of your dreams in terms of career goals and innermost plans are likely to come true. Yet, at the same time, this is also an indicator of career termination, retirement, or job loss. However, for overall success this is an excellent period for marketing your professional skills or expertise on a broader, more universal scale. Cooperating and sharing more with your co-workers will also accelerate your career. Tuesday and Thursday are your best days if you're in the process of looking for work, setting up an interview, or asking your present employer for that well-deserved raise. Job changes take on significance during January, May, June, August, and October.

TRAVEL:

If you've been wanting to take a long trip, go off to a distant land, this is your year. As 9 is a long-distance and travel number, getting away this year should be quite easy. If you don't get to travel this year, chances are someone from afar will visit you or get in touch. This cycle number also brings you in contact with famous personalities. Travel indicators are strong during January, May, September, and October.

The 11 Personal Year

THEME:

Abstract impressions, revelations, spiritual awakening.

DESCRIPTION:

This is a special cycle year because it doesn't come often. You'll have a deeper sense of mission and purpose, more inspiration and initiative in wanting to help others by lighting the way. If you were born on the 11th of any month, or come under the signs of Leo and Aquarius, this year will be all the more important. Ideas and hunches will come with lightning speed. Write them down immediately or quickly put them into action. Your sense of idealism and human understanding will take on a deeper meaning. You will be compassionate and forgiving about the flaws, faults, and frailties of your fellow human beings.

LOVE/RELATIONSHIPS:

Since this is considered a more spiritual, idealistic, and visionary cycle, love or romance is likely to follow suit. By attending religious, philosophical, or metaphysical events or meetings, you will likely meet someone who feels and thinks as you do. In matters of love and romance, you'll find Aquarius and Leo persons drawn to you more. This also holds true for those born on the 11th or 22nd of any month. The colors of cream, green, and white should be included in your wardrobe. Relationships are likely to bloom during April, June, September, and November.

HEALTH:

The eyes may tend to be a little out of focus or astigmatic when passing through this master number cycle. Problems with high blood pressure or heart disorders and diseases (depending on your age and physical condition) may arise, followed by lung or stomach problems. Try not to let the pessimism and negativity of others get the best of you emotionally. Remember, this is your mission year. Being around positive people and surroundings will keep you in good health. However, be careful during February, April, July, and November.

CAREER:

The master number 11 is usually associated with fame. Therefore, fame, fortune, and friends could be a part of your career package in this cycle. Being part of the team, coaching and encouraging others on the job, will put a feather in your cap. The secret of your success will be to act with leadership, with vision, and above all, with humanity and humility. Should you be looking for work or thinking of approaching your boss about a promotion, select Monday and Friday to do so. Watch for job developments during March, April, June, August, and December.

TRAVEL:

This cycle generally denotes travel for the purpose of enlightening others—or, perhaps, becoming enlightened yourself. As a result, your travels may cover large expanses of water or land—there's likely to be a learning experience on both sides. Expect such travel during March, July, August, and December.

The 22 Personal Year

THEME:

Foundation building, large undertakings, mastership, and the achievement of power.

DESCRIPTION:

Like the 11 master year cycle, the 22 master year cycle doesn't come often. When it does, it means exceptional opportunities to do exceptional things. You're given a chance to take your plans and ideas off the drawing board and put them into some concrete form. This is truly your cycle of power—the power to do things on a grand scale with lasting results. There may be an equally strong desire to reach out and help humanity in some way. If you were born on the 11th or 22nd of any month, especially under the sign of Aquarius, this year will be all the more important for you.

LOVE/RELATIONSHIPS:

The cycle of the 22 master vibration calls for a more impersonal type of love, rather than an emotional one. The reason is that this cycle requires you to share your love, vision, and power to succeed on a more global scale. However, the love that does come into your personal life will likely be affected by Aquarians more than anyone else this year. Also those born on the 11th and 22nd could come into your romantic circle as well. The best months for love and universal sharing will be March, May, August, and December. Wear all shades of electric blues and greys.

HEALTH:

Under this master number cycle, the tendency is to attempt to move mountains or push one's physical and mental endurance to the limits. Since this is your power year for large accomplishments, you'll find that pacing yourself and getting large projects done in small stages, will minimize any premature ills. The health stresses that do develop this year may come in connection with the digestive system, ulcers, or tumors, followed by mental breakdowns, moodiness, delusions of grandeur, even physical violence. So stay alert to health matters during February, May, September, and November.

CAREER:

This cycle year gives you the opportunity to leave a lasting mark. You're in a special cycle that should allow you to make the most of your business and financial standing. As a result this puts you on a more solid and secure footing. For interviews, seeking employment, or simply asking for a raise on your present job, Wednesday and Monday are your best days to do so. Think of yourself this year as the "master builder." You should forge ahead during the months of January, February, April, October, and November.

TRAVEL:

Travel by air and by land this year should be broad and expansive—if time and money permit. Think of your travels and encounters as stepping stones, experiences to be shared later with the world. Under this master cycle number, your travels should help you gain a deeper, more universal understanding. Travel is strongly indicated for January, May, June, and October.

Your Personal Month Forecast

The universal cycle is very easy to determine. For instance, to find the univeral year for 1987, you simply add up the four numbers: $1+9+8+7=25$; $2+5=7$. This 7 cycle will affect the world at large, but what about you personally? How will you be affected this year in a more intimate personal way? By simply adding your month and day of birth to the present year you can determine not only your personal year cycle, but your own personal month cycle as well. Take, for example, a person born on March 11:

$$
\begin{array}{ll}
3 & \text{(Birth Month)} \\
11 & \text{(Birth Date)} \\
\underline{1987} & \text{(Present Year)} \\
2001 & =2+0+0+1=3
\end{array}
$$

This person is passing through a 3 personal year for 1987. To arrive at the personal month number in our example, go to the 3 personal year column in the chart below. Next, run the finger down the number 3 personal year column to the month you wish to know about, present or future. The chart below will determine your personal month number:

Personal Year Numbers:	1	2	3	4	5	6	7	8	9
Personal Month Numbers:									
January	2	3	4	5	6	7	8	9	1
February	3	4	5	6	7	8	9	1	2
March	4	5	6	7	8	9	1	2	3
April	5	6	7	8	9	1	2	3	4
May	6	7	8	9	1	2	3	4	5
June	7	8	9	1	2	3	4	5	6
July	8	9	1	2	3	4	5	6	7
August	9	1	2	3	4	5	6	7	8
September	1	2	3	4	5	6	7	8	9
October	2	3	4	5	6	7	8	9	1
November	3	4	5	6	7	8	9	1	2
December	4	5	6	7	8	9	1	2	3

Don't forget you need to know your personal year number to use this chart accurately.

1 Personal Month

THEME:

Independence, new opportunities.

DESCRIPTION:

This is a month for getting a fresh start, for all things new, innovative, bold, and forceful. If you're a Leo or Aries, or born on a date adding to a 1, this month is all the more important. Strike out on your own in some way.

LOVE:

Excellent cycle month to meet or get involved with someone new, perhaps younger than yourself. Those born in the months of February, April, and August have the best chance with you.

CAREER:

Take charge, act with confidence during this cycle. Deal with those in positions of authority as much as you can. The 8th to the 14th hold the best chance for advancement.

2 Personal Month

THEME:

Companionship, teamwork.

DESCRIPTION:

A month of transitions related to the home, a relationship, or the work place. This is the time for tact, coupled with an attitude of cooperation, understanding, and patience. If your birthday adds up to a 2, or should you be a Cancer or Taurus, this is an important month.

LOVE:

Love, family, and friends seem a necessity. Generally during this cycle, news related to engagements, marriage, births, or pregnancies is even more pronounced. Persons born in May, July, or October may be both helpful and attracted to you.

CAREER:

Changes in the work place become evident in some small way. Use a soft, easy approach rather than a demanding one. Opportunities are strongest just after the 14th.

3 Personal Month

THEME:

Imagination, self-expression.

DESCRIPTION:

A time for personal happiness, self-improvement, or taking a more positive approach to life. Get into something creative to bring out your best. This is an excellent period if you happen to be a Pisces, Sagittarius, or have a 3 birth number.

LOVE:

Love and business relationships are likely to be connected with fun and passing fancy rather than being a more serious type of commitment. Romance is enhanced with those born in the months of March, May, and December.

CAREER:

This is your cycle for expansion, especially for promotions, money, or making a name for yourself. Think of enhancing your present position now, particularly from the 8th of the month until the 20th.

4 Personal Month

THEME:

Foundation, organization.

DESCRIPTION:

This is the cycle where it's best to have a plan rather than doing things in a helter-skelter fashion. This cycle also brings about limitations or restrictions in some way. If your sign is Aquarius, or your birth numbers add up to 4, this cycle is all the more important.

LOVE:

During this time you're likely to fall into relationships considered unconventional by normal standards. Someone from the past may make a reappearance. Look for those born in February, June, and August.

CAREER:

Watch for unexpected opportunities and personal advances in the work place. The weeks between the 1st and 7th, followed by the 22nd to the end of the month, offer the best possibilities.

5 Personal Month

THEME:

Freedom, dramatic changes.

DESCRIPTION:

This is the cycle of constant movement, activities, and travel. This is an excellent period to turn yourself around, both mentally and physically. If your birth number adds up to 5, or your sign happens to be Gemini or Virgo, there should be considerable gains.

LOVE:

5 is the number of sexual attraction, and you may attract many members of the opposite sex. The chances are equally strong that they're likely to be younger, especially if they were born in the months of February, May, June, and September.

CAREER:

This is considered one of the best cycles for important changes on the career front. A good period for getting your name, skills, and abilities before others who can help advance you to the next step. This should be more pronounced during the third week.

6 Personal Month

THEME:

Domestic matters, responsibilities.

DESCRIPTION:

If your sign is Taurus or Libra, or your birth number is 6 or 3, this cycle focuses on matters of love, home, family, duty, and commitments. Social functions such as weddings, exhibits, fairs, and educational settings should be pronounced.

LOVE:

The 6 places more emphasis on engagements, marriages, pregnancies, and births than any other cycle number—if not for you directly, then for someone very close to you, especially if their birth month happens to be May, July, or October.

CAREER:

This is generally the cycle of promotions, graduations, and recognition. Rewards are likely to come by fulfilling obligations and commitments to the letter. Stay alert to such matters just after the 7th, and again toward the end of the month.

7 Personal Month

THEME:

Self-awareness, inner growth.

DESCRIPTION:

This is a month of introspection and self-analysis. The tendency is to spend more time alone in order to make assessments about your past actions, present conditions, and future direction. If your date of birth adds up to 7, or if you're a Pisces or Cancer, this cycle should be very important in some special way.

LOVE:

This isn't the best cycle for matters of love and romance since the 7 is spiritual in nature. Visualizing the type of relationship you want to have for yourself is your best approach. Look for those born in the months of March, May, July, and October to play a part in your emotional life.

CAREER:

A 7 cycle usually suggests a retirement or temporary leave of absence in some manner. You're likely to sense a deeper awareness and understanding about your job or your expertise. The first week in this cycle, as well as the third week, hold the best possibilities for advancement.

8 Personal Month

THEME:

Personal achievement, recognition.

DESCRIPTION:

This is considered your power cycle—the best period for making major moves of a financial or romantic nature. This is your chance to do something big in life. You're likely to develop a deeper sense of destiny about your life. If you're a Capricorn, or your birth number is 8, this cycle is even more meaningful.

LOVE:

An 8 month is usually associated with marriages, pregnancies, and births, even divorce. Romantic attractions arise from the past; someone much older or perhaps of financial means is likely to enter your life. Those born in January, March, May, and October may be attracted to you more.

CAREER:

This is certainly the time for making money, getting a big boost, or that important raise. And since this is an executive number, you should act the part. Set large goals for yourself. Aim high. The 8th to the 14th is the best period for advancement.

9 Personal Month

THEME:

Endings, fulfillment of dreams.

DESCRIPTION:

This cycle symbolizes completion or letting go of persons, places, or things that you've outgrown. This is a good period for inspiration, making dreams come true, taking long trips, or facing the competition. If your birth number adds up to 9, or your sign is Aries or Scorpio, this cycle is for you.

LOVE:

Since 9 is universal in nature, it tends to overshadow prejudice on all levels. Romance and other related matters could occur outside of your own religious, cultural, or ethnic background. The attraction should be especially strong with those born in April, May, October, and November.

CAREER:

This is a cycle generally denoting fulfillment of one's career goals. Yet, at the same time, it also means possible job termination or retirement. It is an excellent time for marketing your professional skills and expertise on a broader, more universal scale. The first and third weeks of the month are likely to stand out in some important way.

Your Personal Week Forecast: A New Concept

One day in late 1980, a close personal friend, Louis Wheeler, called me to check on his personal cycle numbers. In the course of our conversation, we reviewed his personal year cycle, personal month, as well as his personal day cycle. He then asked, "What about my personal week cycle?" I told him there was no such thing. His response was: "Why not?"

I didn't have an answer, but it started me thinking—if there's a personal year, month, and day cycle, why not a weekly cycle? In checking over my extensive collection of books on Numerology, only one book mentioned a personal week cycle. However it didn't give me what I was looking for.

So, pondering the question further, I came up with what I feel is a simple, yet entirely new concept. On average, there are four weeks in a month. I surmised that just as you add your personal year number to a particular month of the year to get your personal month number, why not use the same principal of applying the personal month number to the four weeks in the month. The results were quite gratifying, and should prove useful for those busy individuals who plan ahead on their weekly calendar, as well as their daily or monthly calendars.

In the laws of numbers, the 7 seems to indicate a natural division—there are 7 days in the week, 52 weeks in a year $(5 + 2 = 7)$; the Moon goes through seven phases, and so on. In the West, there's an average of 30 to 31 days to the month, with the exception of February which has 28 days (4×7).

Using 7 as a divider, I made the first seven days of the month Week Number 1. The second seven-day period (the 8th to the 14th) became week number 2. The third seven-day period (the 15th to the 21st) was week number 3. Finally the last seven-day period (the 22nd to 28th, or to the end of the month) was week number 4. This principal also holds true for finding the universal week.

My next step was to learn how to interpret the personal week—not in the traditional way of reading the number for each week, but taking it one step further. For example: to arrive at your personal week number, you must first know your personal year, as well as your personal month number. A person born February 7th may be in a number 9 personal year (you find the personal year number by adding your month and date of birth to the present year, or any year you wish to know about). Next, this person wants to know his personal month number for July of that year. July is the 7th calendar month, and so 7 is added to his personal year number of 9, which adds up to 7 $(9 + 7 = 16; 1 + 6 = 7)$. A person born on February 7th, in a 9 personal year, will be passing thru a 7 personal month for July.

Normally, the next step in Numerology would be finding the personal day. This is where the new concept of the personal week comes into play. If you are in a 7 personal month, you add a 7 to the first week in the month, and you get an 8 personal week $(7 + 1st week = 8)$ Add 7 to the second week in the month, and you get a 9 personal week $(7 + 2 = 9)$. Add 7 to the third calender week and it equals a 1 personal week—it's just that simple.

How to Read the Personal Week

There are two ways to read the personal week. The first is the traditional way, that is, reading the number symbols for the month and the weeks within the month. In our example, the person going through a 7 personal month should find himself in a reflective period. The first week, which in this case is an 8 personal week, could mean reflecting on money or financial matters. The second week, a 9 personal week, could be reflective about endings, the fulfillment of dreams, long trips, etc. The third week, which is a 1 personal week in this case, may represent reflections on new beginnings or on self-determination. The fourth and final week for this person is a 2 personal week, and is likely to find him in a reflective period concerning partnerships as well as personal relationships. Naturally, there can be several interpretations for these numbers.

My second way of interpreting the personal week is totally unique. In Numerology each number represents a particular day and date as well. Taking our example of February 7th again, the first week, being an 8 personal week, means the first Saturday in the month (8 rules Saturday), or the period around the 8th, is likely to be very important. As for the second week, which is a 9 personal week, the second Tuesday in the month (9 rules Tuesday), or around the 9th, is likely to be significant. The third week, in our example, would find this person in a 1 personal week, which means the third Sunday (1 rules Sunday), or the 19th ($1 + 9 = 10$; $1 + 0 = 1$), should be important in some way. The final week, in our example, represents a 2 personal week, simply means the last Monday in the month (2 rules Monday), or around the 29th ($2 + 9 = 11$; $1 + 1 = 2$) of the month will probably be important in some way.

Numerological Equivalents
for Days of the Week

Sunday = 1, 4
Monday = 2, 7
Tuesday = 9
Wednesday = 5
Thursday = 3
Friday = 6
Saturday = 8

After experimenting with this concept over the last five years or so, it's proven to be of great value, but more importantly, very accurate in its meaning.

Personal Changes in Your Life

All human beings undergo physiological and mental changes every seven years, beginning at birth. For example, are you now the same person in appearance and way of thinking that you were 14 years ago? In this country the legal age is 21, which is simply 3 × 7. In Astrology, the first basic change in a person's life occurs at age 28 (first lunar return), or 4 × 7.

It's been observed since antiquity that not only are you affected basically in some way every 7 years but that these events are influenced by your date of birth. Through the fascinating science of Numerology, you can get an accurate indication as to what ages and years of changes and events are likely to be important during your life. What do I mean by important changes and events? These simply refer to the milestones we all go through in life—birth, marriage, children, job, travel, winning an award or contest, death. Below are some of the general areas of importance that are likely to affect you in some way.

1. Good Fortune
2. Births
3. Deaths
4. Pregnancy
5. Separation
6. Marriage
7. New Love
8. Divorce
9. Graduations
10. New Job
11. Promotions
12. A Legacy
13. Trips and Travel
14. New Residence/ Locations
15. Accidents or Health Changes

Listed below, you will find the ages and years of important events related to you and your loved ones. Next, look at the list above to see which of these events apply to you, past or present. You'll be amazed at what you discover.

Personal Changes

NUMBER 1

If you were born on the 1st, 10th, 19th, or 28th of any month:

Ages: 10, 13, 19, 28, 31, 37, 40, 46, 55, 58, 64, 67, 73, 76, 82, 85, 91, 94.
Years: 1963, 1966, 1972, 1975, 1981, 1984, 1990, 1993, 1999, 2002, 2008, 2011, 2017.

NUMBER 2

If you were born on the 2nd, 11th, 20th, or 29th of any month:

Ages: 11, 16, 20, 25, 29, 34, 38, 43, 47, 52, 56, 61, 65, 70, 74, 83, 88, 92, 97.
Years: 1964, 1969, 1973, 1978, 1982, 1987, 1991, 1996, 2000, 2005, 2009, 2014, 2018.

NUMBER 3

If you were born on the 3rd, 12th, 21st, or 30th of the month:

Ages: 12, 18, 21, 27, 30, 36, 39, 45, 48, 54, 57, 63, 66, 72, 75, 81, 84, 90, 93, 99.
Years: 1965, 1968, 1971, 1974, 1977, 1980, 1982, 1986, 1989, 1992, 1995, 1998, 2001, 2004, 2007, 2010, 2013, 2016, 2019.

NUMBER 4

If your were born on the 4th, 13th, 22nd, or 31st of the month:

Ages: 13, 17, 19, 22, 26, 28, 31, 35, 37, 40, 44, 46, 49, 53, 55, 58, 62, 64, 67, 71, 73, 76, 80, 82, 85, 89, 91, 94, 98.
Years: 1963, 1966, 1970, 1972, 1975, 1979, 1981, 1984, 1988, 1990, 1993, 1997, 1999, 2002, 2006, 2008, 2011, 2015, 2017.

NUMBER 5

If you were born on the 5th, 14th or 23rd of the month:

Ages: 14, 15, 23, 24, 32, 33, 41, 42, 50, 51, 59, 60, 68, 69, 77, 78, 86, 87, 95, 96.
Years: 1967, 1968, 1976, 1977, 1985, 1986, 1994, 1995, 2003, 2004, 2012, 2013.

NUMBER 6

If you were born on the 6th, 15th, or 24th of the month:

Ages: 15, 20, 21, 24, 29, 30, 33, 38, 39, 42, 42, 47, 48, 51, 56, 57, 60, 65, 66, 69, 74, 75, 78, 83, 84, 87, 92, 93, 96.
Years: 1964, 1965, 1973, 1974, 1977, 1982, 1983, 1986, 1991, 1992, 1995, 2000, 2001, 2004, 2009, 2010, 2013, 2018.

NUMBER 7

If you were born on the 7th, 16th, or 25th of the month:

Ages: 11, 16, 20, 25, 29, 34, 38, 43, 47, 52, 56, 61, 65, 70, 74, 79, 83, 88, 92, 97.
Years: 1964, 1969, 1973, 1978, 1982, 1987, 1991, 1996, 2000, 2005, 2009, 2014, 2018.

NUMBER 8

If you were born on the 8th, 17th, or 26th of the month:

Ages: 13, 15, 17, 22, 24, 26, 31, 33, 35, 40, 42, 44, 49, 51, 53, 58, 60, 61, 67, 69, 71, 76, 78, 80, 85, 87, 89, 94, 96, 98.

Years: 1966, 1968, 1970, 1975, 1977, 1979, 1984, 1986, 1988, 1993, 1995, 1997, 2002, 2004, 2006, 2011, 2013, 2015.

NUMBER 9

If you were born on the 9th, 18th, or 27th of the month:

Ages: 12, 18, 19, 21, 28, 30, 36, 37, 39, 45, 46, 48, 54, 55, 57, 63, 64, 66, 72, 73, 75, 81, 82, 84, 90, 91, 93, 99.
Years: 1965, 1971, 1972, 1974, 1980, 1981, 1983, 1989, 1990, 1992, 1998, 1999, 2001, 2007, 2008, 2010, 2016, 2017.

What Day of the Week Were You Born?

What day of the week were you born? Knowing what day you were born can add further understanding to knowing yourself better. Let's say for example you were born August 26, 1959, and you have a friend who was born August 26, 1963. Although both you and your friend were born the same month and day, but in different years, you do not share the same day of birth. August 26 in 1959 occurred on a Wednesday, whereas August 26 in 1963 occurred on a Monday.

The day of your birth modifies your character. In some societies, a person's day of birth is held sacred and special. In some cases, a person is called by a name representing his or her day of birth. Folklore has given us various sayings on the days of the week. Perhaps you remember this popular verse:

> *Sunday's child is full of grace,*
> *Monday's child is full in the face,*
> *Tuesday's child is solemn and sad,*
> *Wednesday's child is merry and glad,*
> *Thursday's child is inclined to thieving,*
> *Friday's child is free in giving,*
> *Saturday's child works hard for a living.*

Or perhaps you've heard this variation:

Monday's child is fair of face,
Tuesday's child is full of grace,
Wednesday's child is full of woe,
Thursday's child has far to go,
Friday's child is loving and giving,
Saturday's child works hard for its living,
But a child that's born on the Sabbath Day
Is handsome and wise, and loving, and gay.

Interestingly enough, my experience has been that women tend to know intuitively their best days of the week. This even includes the day they were born on. You can easily determine your day of birth by checking a perpetual calendar (see Appendix).

Days of Birth

SUNDAY

If Sunday is the day of your birth the Sun has a lot of influence over your character and profile. Let's say you were born under the sensitive sign of Cancer. The fact that your day of birth is a Sunday adds another dimension to your sign. Develop a more cheerful, optimistic attitude toward life. You have everything to gain.

MONDAY

If you were born on a Monday your personality is greatly influenced by the Moon. Even if you're a Leo, typically known for an aggressive attitude, because of your day of birth, your sign would be interwoven with sensitivity and emotional expression. It would be wise to cultivate a common-sense approach to life and to use your imagination to the fullest.

TUESDAY

If you were born on Tuesday, you very likely have an aggressive, forthright personality. Mars, the active planet, adds force and energy to your Zodiac sign. If you were born under a fire sign, however, this could add more fuel and lead to excessive fights, arguments, and accidents. Develop a stronger sense of self-determination.

WEDNESDAY

If you were born on a Wednesday, as I was, Mercury enters your personal expression and ways of doing things. Interestingly, I always taught classes on Wednesdays, but never thought about it until years later. Mercury adds mental quickness to your Zodiac sign, along with agility and good reaction time—especially in crisis situations.

THURSDAY

If Thursday happens to be your day of birth, you are under the influence of planet Jupiter. This may explain your ever-present desire to undertake ambitious projects, and to achieve great accomplishments. Depending on your birth sign, you probably have to stay on guard against going to extremes and overindulging. Being born on this day adds youthfulness to your personality.

FRIDAY

Is Friday your day of birth? If so, you are ruled by the planet Venus, the planet of love, beauty, and affection. Perhaps this may explain why you need to be surrounded by rich colors, music, flowers, and anything else that your nature finds esthetic. Being born on this day gives you excellent insight into others.

SATURDAY

If Saturday is your day of birth, Saturn adds a somewhat melancholy, yet mature approach to your life and surroundings. You may feel destined to do something special with your life that can't be explained to everyone. Develop a more positive attitude to keep you in balance.

Careers and Occupations

What kind of work do you do? Are you happy with it? Is there a future for you? Men and women enjoying what they do for a living are hard to find nowadays. Yet, it's a known fact that the happier you are at your job, the more productive you are. You put in more time, energy, effort, and enthusiasm as a result. Numerology is a very helpful guide for this important area of your life. Each of us is different, with different skills, different ways of doing things, and different preferences for a wide variety of job pursuits. We all have our place in the scheme of things, this is why one person may be a leader and another a follower. Look to your date of birth or Zodiac sign for your best occupational clues.

Choosing a Career

NUMBER 1 PERSON

Born on the 1st, 10th, 19th, or 28th, or if you're a Leo or Aries, you'll find success in work as an administrator, athlete, businessperson, director, doctor, explorer, judge, instructor, inventor, lawyer, military officer, politician, president, salesperson, scientist, supervisor, writer, or union leader. Your best days for job interviews are Tuesdays and Mondays. Over and above job experiences, sell your interviewer on the fact that you can take the initiative, make decisions, and get things done on your own.

NUMBER 2 PERSON

If you were born on the 2nd, 11th, 20th, or 29th, or if you happen to be a Cancer, you'd do well to pursue a career as an actor, artist, bank teller, caterer, collector, computer expert, cook, dancer, diplomat, editor, homemaker, mediator, musician, nutritionist, poet, psychiatrist, psychologist, sailor, secretary, statistician, or teacher. Your best days for the job interviews or for asking for a raise are Monday and Friday. Beyond your job experience, let it be known that you're teamwork oriented, patient enough to learn the ropes, and that you like cooperating with others for a common cause.

NUMBER 3 PERSON

Born on the 3rd, 12th, 21st, 30th, or under the signs of Pisces or Sagittarius, success generally comes your way as an actor, artist, administrator, entertainer, fashion designer, government official, horse trainer, illustrator, jeweler, judge, lawyer, minister, photographer, publisher, religious offical, socialite, writer, veterinarian, or youth counselor. Your best interview days are Thursday and Friday. In selling yourself, let the interviewer know that you're conscientious and hard working, that you don't mind putting in long hours, and that you're creative and optimistic when it comes to solving problems and getting things done.

NUMBER 4 PERSON

If you were born on the 4th, 13th, 22nd, 31st, or if you're an Aquarius, you'll find unusual success in careers as an accountant, aviator, computer expert, electrician, inventor, investigator, machinist, manufacturer, mathematician, mechanic, motorman, musician, occultist, plumber, printer, radio personality, radiologist, reformer, sculptor, or TV personality. Your best interview days are Wednesday and Monday. In an interview, emphasize your love of detail, that you like to be punctual (if you sincerely mean it), and that you're excellent at coming up with different or unique ways of doing things.

NUMBER 5 PERSON

Born on the 5th, 14th, or 23rd, or if you're a Gemini or Virgo, you find personal satisfaction as an astrologer, aviator, broker, crisis expert, detective, editor, gambler, importer/exporter, medical technician, musician, public official, promoter, racing driver, salesperson, scientist, speculator, travel agent, wholesaler, or writer. Wednesday and Friday are your best interview days. Stress the fact you're a fast learner and generally quick on your feet, as well as the fact that you're flexible and can easily adjust to new situations.

NUMBER 6 PERSON

If you were born on the 6th, 15th, or 24th, or you happen to be a Taurus or Libra, look for fields of endeavor as an advisor, artist, athlete, barber, beautician, cashier, civil servant, counselor, designer, dentist, doctor, educator, homemaker, host or hostess, lawyer, musician, nurse, professor, realtor, singer, social worker, surgeon, teacher, or waiter. Your best interview days are Friday and Thursday. Let your interviewer know you're dependable and responsible and not afraid to take on the burdens that go with those traits. You have a sense of justice and fair play, and know the difference between right and wrong.

NUMBER 7 PERSON

If you were born on the 7th, 16th, or 25th, or if you're a Pisces or Cancer, you're likely to find career enjoyment as an accountant, analyst, astrologer, actor, artist (the spiritual kind), as an expert on a specialized subject, healer, historian, librarian, minister, navigator, occultist, photographer, poet, psychiatrist, researcher, sailor, secret agent, scientist, technician, underwater explorer, or writer. Your best interview days are Monday and Friday. During your interview, emphasize the fact that you're discriminating and discreet; that you can do a task or assignment without being told or prodded, that you can easily work alone if you have to.

NUMBER 8 PERSON

Those born on the 8th, 17th, or 26th, or under Capricorn, can be a success as an authority, banker, boxer, builder, cemetery worker, church official, composer, controller, corporate lawyer, criminal expert, financial expert, government official, farmer, mathematician, miner, minister, organizer, police officer, philosopher, public official, realtor, or repairman. Your best interview days are Thursdays and Fridays. Aside from your past work experience, you're serious-minded, loyal, determined, and respected by others. Remember, in your case, others need a little warm up time before they really appreciate you.

NUMBER 9 PERSON

If you were born on the 9th, 18th or 27th, or if you're an Aries or Scorpio, you can find personal success in jobs and careers as an athlete, barber, ballistics expert, construction worker, explosives expert, fireman, gun collector, international personality, ironworker, lawyer, leader, marksman, metalworker, military officer, organizer, politician, publisher, steelworker, or surgeon. Your best interview days are Tuesdays and Thursdays. Let it be known that you have self-confidence (not egotistism), and an ability to inspire others and to get along with everyone you meet.

Your Home and Office

Numbers play an important part in all aspects of your life, even down to the address where you live or work. Before you finish this chapter, you'll discover a connection between your key number or numbers and where you live. For instance, I'm a birth date number 7 person. Just after my marriage, I lived in a particular building on the 7th floor for 7 years. Our next location was on 7th avenue. In a majority of cases, your date of birth number may be closely associated in some way with your residence. I have a client born on April 20th, which adds up to 2. His address was 650 Lenox Avenue($6 + 5 + 0 = 11$; $1 + 1 = 2$), a building number matching his own.

The numerical rule for finding harmony and happiness in your residence is to have it match your date of birth. This is especially true if you're moving into a new home or apartment. As a second-best choice, select the residence according to your Zodiac sign (see section on "Numerology and Astrology"). Below are some basic questions to help you search for yours.

- What are the numbers in your present address? (Don't forget to add up all the numbers to get the single digit.)
- What were the numbers in your previous address? How many years did you live there?

- What floor do you live on now? What about your previous address?
- What's your apartment number?
- What number street or avenue do you live on or near?
- What's your zip code number?
- What month number did you move into your residence? For instance, if you moved in July, that's the 7th calendar month. (This happened in my case.)
- What does your rent or mortgage payment add up to?
- If you live in a project or complex with a number of buildings, is your building assigned a number other than the address number? If so, what?
- What number bus, subway, or other form of transit is closest to your address?
- What about your place of work? Ask all the questions above, but apply them to where you work. What month did you start your job? Does your salary match your birth date number? Does it match your office number; office floor; number of co-workers, and so on.

There are a few rules of thumb. If your birth number is a 4 or 8, YOU SHOULD NOT use all of the above rules. Because of the peculiarities of your birth number, an alternative number should be used. For example, if you're a 4 person, you should not live in an 8 house, and vice versa. A 4 person should choose an address that adds up to a 1 or 5, such as 100 or 2300 (adding up to 1 and 5 respectively) XYZ lane. If you're an 8 person, you'd do best picking a residence number that adds up to 3 or 6.

Those of you with a mid-sized or large family choose a number 6 residence, for 6 rules the home and family. If you're a single person, however, the 6 rules residence selection even more. Not too long ago, the residents in a fashionable part of California were changing their house numbers to match their dates of births. However, this created monstrous confusion in the Post Office, for the numbers were not in sequence to deliver mail properly.

In a case like this, where your residence number

doesn't match your birth date, simply add a letter to the house number. Let's say you're a number 6 person and your house address is 130 ABC Avenue. This adds up to a 4, which is in direct opposition. What you could do is attach the letter B to 130, making the address 130B ABC Avenue. The letter B has the numerical value of 2, so 130B (2) adds up to $1+3+0+2(B) = 6$, which now matches your birth number. As a test, check the birth numbers of your family members and friends in the same manner.

The Best Place to Live

The city or town you live in can have a profound affect on your health, success, happiness, and wealth. You can have all the talents, skills, and abilities to be successful, but if you live in the wrong city or town, which adds a negative vibration to your own, you may find it difficult to get your plans off the ground.

Those who travel frequently from city to city—salespeople, politicians, airline personnel—will tell you that in certain places, for some reason, they don't like the surroundings and want to leave quickly. Then, there are other cities or towns they'd like to return to again and again.

Take the case of a client who called me wanting to know about a particular city she wished to move to. Born August 31st, a birth number adding up to 4 (3 + 1 = 4), it just so happened that the particular city that interested her added up to 31, matching her birth number exactly. She was overjoyed hearing the news. She had been visiting someone in this city, and while there, she was not only offered a wonderful, well-paying job but an automobile as well. No wonder she called me.

Choosing Where to Live

NUMBER 1 PERSON

Born on the 1st, 10th, 19th, or 28th, choose Alexandria, Atlanta, Birmingham, Boston, Houston, Knoxville, New York, Providence, Reno, or Shelby. Also select any city that adds up to 2, 4, 7, or 9 to harmonize with as a second choice.

Be CAREFUL in cities such as Buffalo, Cleveland, Dallas, Jersey City, Kansas City, and San Francisco.

NUMBER 2 PERSON

If you were born on the 2nd, 11th, 20th, or 29th, your selection should be Austin, Baltimore, Bridgeport, Brooklyn, Charleston, Cincinnati, Harlem, Los Angeles, Miami, or Raleigh. The same applies to other cities and towns totaling 1, 4, 6, or 7, as a second choice.

Be CAREFUL in Denver, Detroit, Philadelphia Phoenix, St. Louis, and Tampa.

NUMBER 3 PERSON

Those born on the 3rd, 12th, 21st, or 30th should be productive in Andover, the Bronx, Kingston, Manhattan, Memphis, Montclair, Red Bank, San Antonio, Staten Island, and Toledo. Same also applies to places adding up to 6 or 9.

Be CAREFUL in cities such as Attica, Chicago, Greensboro, Hicksville, Nashville, and Trenton.

NUMBER 4 PERSON

If you were born on the 4th, 13th, 22nd, or 31st, you should find harmony in Atlantic City, Dayton, Jackson, Mobile, Princeton, Richmond, Salt Lake City, Saratoga, or Washington, D.C. Cities under the numbers 1, 2, 7, and 5 are a good second choice.

Be CAREFUL in cities such as Akron, Buffalo, Cleveland, Dallas, Montgomery, or San Francisco.

NUMBER 5 PERSON

Those born on the 5th, 14th, or 23rd, and who may travel frequently, would do well in Asheville, Attica, Chicago, Greensboro, Hicksville, Nashville, Oakland, Palm Beach, Santa Cruz, and Trenton. Because you're the most adaptable, you can live in almost any city or town with the exception of those places totaling 3 or 8.

Be CAREFUL in Akron, Buffalo, Cleveland, Kingston, Manhattan, and Staten Island.

NUMBER 6 PERSON

Born on the 6th, 15th, or 24th, you'd do well in Amherst, Augusta, Baton Rouge, Dallas, Dover, Hartford, Kansas City, Milwaukee, New Orleans, and San Francisco. Second choice would be cities under the numbers of 3, 9, and 2.

Be CAREFUL visiting or living in Atlanta, Atlantic City, Boston, Dayton, New York, Richmond, and Washington.

NUMBER 7 PERSON

If you were born on the 7th, 16th, or 25th, you're likely to feel at home in Annapolis, Canton, Columbus, Hollywood, Little Rock, Norfolk, Queens, Paramus, Tallahassee, and Teaneck. As a second choice, select cities under the numbers 2, 4, or 1.

Be CAREFUL in Akron, Buffalo, Detroit, Jersey City, Tampa, and St. Louis.

NUMBER 8 PERSON

Born on the 8th, 17th, or 26th, you'd do well in such cities as Akron, Bloomfield, Buffalo, Cleveland, Delta, Fairfax, Jersey City, Rye, Sacramento and Tulsa. Also pick cities under the numbers 3 or 6 as a second choice.

Be CAREFUL in Atlanta, Atlantic City, Boston, Chicago, New York, Richmond, and Washington.

NUMBER 9 PERSON

Those born on the 9th, 18th, or 27th should really feel energized in Boise, Denver, Detroit, Forth Worth, Philadelphia, Phoenix, Savannah, Silver Springs, St. Louis and Tampa. Next, select an alternative city adding up to 3, 9, 6, or 1.

Be CAREFUL in Austin, Baltimore, Cincinnati, Los Angeles, Miami, and Raleigh.

Vacation Spots

Choosing a place out of harmony with yourself can ruin valuable vacation time and money. After all, the purpose of a vacation is to rest and relax, to travel when possible, to broaden your horizons, and then to return to your daily work refreshed.

Always go to your date of birth for the answers. For instance, if your birth number adds up to 7, you can be sure you'd have a better time and more fun and enjoyment at places ruled by this number.

Add up your date of birth number and look below for the vacation places where you're likely to have more fun. We've listed the major vacation spots in the United States and around the world.

Choosing Your Vacation Spots

NUMBER 1 PERSON

Those born on the 1st, 10th, 19th, or 28th, or in April and August, will enjoy vacationing in Accra, Addis Ababa, Alexandria, Atlanta, Boston, Dakar, Dar es Salaam, Havana, Guatemala, Nairobi, Nassau, Negril, New York, Reno, St. Kitts, and Tunis. Persons born under numbers adding up to 2, 4, or 7 will also find harmony with number 1 vacation places.

NUMBER 2 PERSON

Those born on the 2nd, 11th, 20th, or 29th, or in May and July, will love traveling to Austin, Baltimore, Barcelona, Caicos Islands, Harlem, Leningrad, Los Angeles, Miami, Panama, St. Thomas, St. Vincent, and Timbuktu. Persons born under numbers adding up to 1, 4, and 7 will also find harmony with number 2 vacation places.

NUMBER 3 PERSON

Those born on the 3rd, 12th, 21st, or 30th, or in March and December, will vibrate to such vacation places as Antigua, Aruba, Cuba, Gambia, Grenada, Guadeloupe, Haiti, Jamaica, Kingston, Manhattan, Martinique, Montego Bay, Moscow, Sierra Leone. Persons born under numbers adding up to 6 and 9 will also find harmony with number 3 places.

NUMBER 4 PERSON

Those born on the 4th, 13th, 22nd, or 31st, or in February and August, can look forward to unusual enjoyment in Atlantic City, Barbados, Buenos Aires, Jackson, Khartoum, London, Mobile, Richmond, Surinam, Trinidad, and Washington. Persons born under numbers adding up to 1, 2, and 7 can also find harmony and fun here.

NUMBER 5 PERSON

Those born on the 5th, 14th, or 23rd, or in June and September, will find much variety and fun while vacationing in Acapulco, Anguilla, Athens, Belize, Bimini, Cairo, Caracas, Chicago, Curaçao, Freeport, Hamburg, Nicaragua, Rio de Janeiro, St. Croix, St. John, or Vienna. Persons born under the number 5 are adaptable to almost any vacation place except those under the numbers 3 or 8.

NUMBER 6 PERSON

Those born on the 6th, 15th, or 24th, or in May and October, will feel a romantic air vacationing in Bermuda, Bogota, Dallas, El Salvador, Hawaii, Honolulu, Lucaya, Munich, New Orleans, Paradise Island, Paris, San Francisco, and Santo Domingo. Persons born under numbers adding up to 3 and 9 can also find harmony at number 6 places.

NUMBER 7 PERSON

Those born on the 7th, 16th, or 25th, or in March and July, should try vacationing in Barcelona, Brazil, Columbus, Costa Rica, Istanbul, Lusaka, Madrid, Mexico, Naples, Norfolk, Santiago, Senegal, and Zaire. Persons born under numbers adding up to 1, 2, and 4 will also find harmony in number 7 places.

NUMBER 8 PERSON

Those born on the 8th, 17th, or 26th, or in January and October, can seriously consider the Bahamas, Bombay, Cayman Islands, Cuba, Gambia, Guyana, Haiti, Jamaica, Lagos, Montego Bay, Ocho Rios, Sacramento, and Tulsa. Persons born under 8 would also do best selecting number 3 and 6 places to vacation.

NUMBER 9 PERSON

Those born on the 9th, 18th, or 27th, or in April and November, will find much excitement, vacationing in Algiers, Antigua, Beijing, Columbia, Cuba, Denver, Dominica, Fort Worth, Philadelphia, Puerto Rico, Rome, San Salvador, and Tampa. Persons born under the numbers 3 and 6 will also find harmony in number 9 places.

Happy Vacationing!

IV.

Your Family

Tracing Your Roots

Thanks to the age-old science of Numerology, I've been able to trace the numerical and astrological roots of my clients. Just as a doctor can make determinations regarding hereditary diseases or illnesses by analyzing a family's medical history, I, as a numerologist, have been able to determine the dates of a person's birth and/or zodiac sign from the birth dates and signs of family members. For example, I have a client born March 2nd whose family displays a strong numerological relationship as shown in the recurring numbers in their dates of birth.

Client's Date of Birth	March 2nd = $\underline{2}$
Mother's Date of Birth	August 29 (2 + 9 = 11;
	1 + 1 = 2)$\underline{2}$
Father's Date of Birth	June 20 (2 + 0 = 2) $\underline{2}$

This evaluation process started one day when a woman came to me with a question about her husband. She wasn't sure whether he was born on the 23rd or 24th of the month. Just as a doctor would do, I began to take a numerical family history. She had three children, and I asked their dates of birth. Their oldest child was born on the 23rd, and their second child was also born on the 23rd. The birth date of their third child, however, was closer to the mother's.

I then went into the area of health (see chapter on "Health and Illness"). For numbers also have dominion over diseases and different parts of the body. Her husband's general health picture and illnesses over the previous years fitted the description of the number 5 (23rd or $2+3=5$), or a person under its influence. After she answered other numerical questions, I was able to conclude quite comfortably that her husband had been born on the 23rd of the month.

Take the case of another client I know who was born on the 29th of the month $(2+9=11; 1+1=2)$, which adds up to a 2). Her mother was born on the 2nd of the month, and her dad on the 20th (both dates, like her own, adding up to a 2).

Take my own personal life. My wife was born under a number 6. Two of our children were also born under a 6; and they look just like her. I was born under a number 7, and so was our daughter. Guess what—we look just alike. From years of research, and working with many, many clients, I was able to determine unknown months or dates of birth (oftentimes both) of clients' parents and children, even friends and business associates. From this I could tell who would get along with who in the family and why. I could determine which child would be closest to the parent (see chapter on "Parenting")—even which one was likely to fall from grace.

Over the years, I have found this subject consistent and fascinating, and to my knowledge, I've never seen this concept presented in this way. To trace your numerical roots, use your date of birth number. For instance, someone born on June 17 would be a number 8 person $(1+7=8)$. Then check below to see the likely months and dates when your parents, siblings, children, loved ones, friends, and others were born.

Root Numbers

NUMBER 1

If you were born on the 1st, 10th, 19th, or 28th of the month, you're likely to have those close to you born in late January through February, late March through April, and late July through August. The same for those born on the 1st, 4th, 9th, 10th, 13th, 18th, 19th, 22nd, 27th, 28th, and 31st of the month.

NUMBER 2

If you were born on the 2nd, 11th, 20th, or 29th of the month, your family and friends were born in late February through March, late April through May, late June through July, and late September through October. The same rule applies for those born on the 2nd, 6th, 7th, 11th, 15th, 16th, 20th, 24th, 25th, and 29th of any month.

NUMBER 3

If you were born on the 3rd, 12th, 21st, or 30th of the month, the chances are very strong that one or both of your parents or other close relative was born in late February through March, late March through April and May; then late September through October, followed by November into December. This is also true of those whose birth dates are the 3rd, 6th, 18th, 12th, 15th, 18th, 21st, 24th, 27th, or 30th of the month.

NUMBER 4

If you were born on the 4th, 13th, or 22nd, you're most likely to have loved ones and relatives born in late December through January into February; late May through June, and late July into August. This is the same for those with birth dates on the 1st, 4th, 8th, 10th, 13th, 17th, 19th, 22nd, 26th, 28th, and 31st of the month.

NUMBER 5

If you were born on the 5th, 14th, or 23rd, your relatives and associates were born in late January through February, late April through May into June; and late September into October. For those born on the 5th, 6th, 14th, 15th, 23rd, or 24th, the same applies.

NUMBER 6

If you were born on the 6th, 15th or 24th, those related to you are likely to have been born in late February through March, late April through May, late June through July, late September through October, and finally, late November through December. This holds true for those born on the 2nd, 3rd, 6th, 11th, 12th, 15th, 20th, 21st, 24th, 29th, and 30th of the month.

NUMBER 7

If you were born on the 7th, 16th, or 25th, the chances are good that someone you know was born in late February through March, late April through May, late June through July, followed by August. Relatives and friends are also likely to have been born on the 2nd, 6th, 7th, 11th, 15th, 16th, 20th, 24th, 25th, and 29th of the month.

NUMBER 8

If you were born on the 8th, 17th or 24th, parents and others close to you were born in late December through January, and into February, late July through August, followed by late September into October. The same is true for those born on the 4th, 8th, 13th, 17th, 22nd, 26th, and 31st of any month.

NUMBER 9

If you were born on the 9th, 18th, or 27th of the month, look for those close and important in your life to have been born in late February through March, going into April, late July through August, and late October through November, followed by December. The same applies to those born on the 1st, 3rd, 9th, 10th, 12th, 18th, 19th, 21st, 27th, 28th, and 30th of the month.

A majority of you should have been able to find some birth date or month that matched your numerical makeup and those of your loved ones and friends. If these clues did not seem to apply in your case, here's another tip. Check your year of birth. I had a client who was born in the year of the 9 (1962 = 18 = 9). His father was born in the period of late March through April, which matched his birth year number. In most cases, however, the root numbers are mainly determined from your date of birth.

Attraction and Compatibility

Why is it you're strongly attracted to a person—or they to you? What makes for compatibility on the one hand, and turns you off on the other? This question of attraction, compatibility, and harmony is about as old as the attraction between Adam and Eve. As an individual, you may respond to love, sex, passion, feelings, and emotions totally differently from your mate or others close to you. But that's the beauty of God's creation. Life would be pretty boring if we all responded in the same way, at the same time, and on the same level.

Thanks to Numerology, however, much of the mystery that surrounds the harmony and disharmony in personal, business, and intimate relations can be easily answered. Numerology covers the wide variety of differences between you and others. Just taking the time to know yourself and others numerically may well explain why you may be attracted to those born under certain months and dates and not to others.

Choosing Compatible Partners

NUMBER 1 PERSON

Born on the 1st, 10th, 19th, or 28th of the month, you are "mentally" attracted to people in matters of love, romance, and business. As a 1 person, your way of expressing love is more intellectual than emotional. Because of your Numerical nature, you respond more on the plane of will and logic. You'll do better in relationships where you can take the lead, or at least have a say. As a rule, you don't like playing second fiddle to anyone or anything and should be treated accordingly. You tend to be more harmonious with those born in the months of April, August, and February, and those born on dates adding up to 2, 4, 7, and 9. Persons born in the months of January, May, and October are likely to cause you more than your share of problems and opposition. The same is true with those born on dates adding up to 6 and 8.

NUMBER 2 PERSON

If you were born on the 2nd, 11th, 20th, or 29th of the month, you express your feelings and love more from the emotional side of your nature. Love, friends, companions, and partnerships are very important to you. Your inner being yearns to love, to feel with great sensitivity and emotion. You must have companionship in order to be happy. However, you should avoid an early marriage, especially if you were born on the 29th of the month. Part of your attraction for others is that you're a natural listener to anyone with problems or anyone who needs a helping hand. This is the reason you have to be more discriminating in your selection of friends, mates, and lovers. When you pay careful attention, you tend to harmonize best with those born in the months of March, May, July, August, and October, and those whose birth dates add up to 1, 4, 6, or 7. Just the reverse is true for persons born in January, April, and November, as well as those with a birth date that adds up to a 9 or 8.

NUMBER 3 PERSON

Being born on the 3rd, 12th, 21st, or 30th of the month suggests that you express love from the emotional and active side of your nature. Love and romantic relations may at times be elusive for you. You'd like to rise to be somebody in life, to make a name for yourself. In fact, a proud and ambitious nature would also be a requirement in your relationships. You expect others close to you to be conscientious in everything they do. But from their point of view, you're likely to seem dictatorial. When it comes to matters of love you prefer your mate to have a name, status, or a high position in life. If not, you prefer that he or she at least have a goal or objective in life. Another aspect that must be considered is that you are more career than domestically oriented. You attract and harmonize with those born in the months of March, December, April, November, and May, and with those born on dates adding up to 3, 6, and 9. You'll have to be careful around persons born in February, June, August, and September to avoid unnecessary stress. The same goes for those born on dates adding up to 4 and 5.

NUMBER 4 PERSON

If you were born on the 4th, 13th, 22nd, or 31st, you basically express your love and emotional feelings from the physical and intellectual side of things. You're likely to experience ups and downs, or involvements in odd and unusual affairs. Your relationships—intimate or otherwise—usually come from outside your own ethnic, social, or religious background. There'll be times when those you feel close to will let you down; as a result, love and romance may come out of left field. You're positive, but at the same time easily wounded in your feelings, and loved ones have to keep this in mind. Those born in February, August, and June, as well as those whose birth dates add up to 1, 2, 5 or 7 are closely related to you. However, those born in January, May, and October are likely to be the cause of emotional concerns. This is also true of those with birth dates adding up to 6 or 8.

NUMBER 5 PERSON

Being born on the 5th, 14th, or 23rd means you express your love and desires in a more physical or sensual ways. Sex is your middle name with this birth number. You may be known for your attractiveness or good looks, which constantly draw others to you. While you may not feel that you're attractive, from the viewpoint of others, you give off a strong animal magnetism. Ask TV personality Johnny Carson—born on the 23rd. You love your freedom and independence, as well as travel and variety. The one who figures that out will probably land you first. For best results, guard against an early marriage, as it may take you awhile to settle down. Romantically or otherwise, you attract those born in February, May, June, September, and October, or those having a birth date that adds up to a 1, 4, 6, 7, or 9. Care and caution may have to be used when it comes to someone born in January, March, and December.

NUMBER 6 PERSON

If you were born on the 6th, 15th, or 24th, you can express deep and loving feelings. Love, family, friends, and being appreciated goes along way in your book. By temperament, you basically have more mother love for close ones, than physical. As a rule, like your number 5 counterpart, your birth number has dominion over physical beauty and/or a pleasing personality. This may explain why the opposite sex is constantly attracted to you. If possible, you should avoid marriage until a certain level of maturity is reached. You're likely to find personal and business attraction with those born in the months of March, May, July, October, and December, also those with a birth date adding up to 2, 3, 6, or 9. Prudence and reservation should be the rule with those born in January, February and August. The same applies for those born on dates totaling 4 and 8.

NUMBER 7 PERSON

Born on the 7th, 16th, or 25th, you tend to express your love and feelings from a spiritual base. You love family life and appreciate affectionate gestures, yet you may have difficulty expressing the same in return—you can easily be misunderstood. Because of your spiritual and intuitive chemistry, you may hold emotions and feelings inside rather than sharing these thoughts with your loved ones. Moreover, if you continue to keep your emotions bottled up, you may experience rough times later on in marriage and partnerships. After all, you really prefer to be your own best company. You have a quiet, low-key way of going about attracting and harmonizing with others. Once you find the right person, you rarely go off course. Look for more promising relationships with those born in February, May, July, and August; or those with a 1, 2, 4, 5 or 6 birth date. Take care with those born in January, April, and November, and those born on Tuesdays, Saturdays, and under the numbers 8, 9, 17, 18, 26, and 27.

NUMBER 8 PERSON

If you were born on the 8th, 17th, or 26th, you express your love from a more mental and logical level. And because of your deep and intense nature, others on first approach may feel that you're cold. This can lead to misunderstandings in the early phases of a relationship. However, those who may feel you are uncaring and lack affection, are in for a surprise as you're really very warm, kind-hearted, and generous. Because of your more serious and mature way of thinking and behaving, you're likely to get involved with those much older than yourself. Ironically, when it comes to love with passion, intensity, and warmth—you win the prize. You're likely to attract those born in January, March, May, and October, also those with 3, 6, or 8 birth dates. On the other hand, exercise more discretion in the beginning with persons born in February, August, June, and September, as well as those born on dates that add up to a 4, 1, or 5.

NUMBER 9 PERSON

Being born on the 9th, 18th, or 27th of the month strongly suggests that you want an active and somewhat aggressive type of relationship. You pride yourself on being energetic, courageous, and dynamic, and may feel these traits should be a part of your mate's characteristics as well. Whatever you do or whoever you get involved with, you like to do it with gusto. Yet, ironically, you can be easily manipulated once your heartstrings have been plucked. Since you're somewhat hasty in temper and blunt with words, you need to control these tendencies to keep relationships in balance. You'll find your best relationships with those born in the months of March through May, July, followed by October through December, or with those whose birth dates add up to 9, 3, 6, and 1. Be sure to pay special attention in all your personal and business dealings with those born in the months of January and July, especially if their birth date adds up to 2, 7, or 8.

Numerology and Marriage

Marriage, or the union between man and woman, is one of the oldest institutions in the world. Marriage requires love, harmony, and above all, consideration and understanding. However, the timing of such an important event is as important as the marriage itself.

The divorce rate in this country is extremely high, and so is the number of separations. I have found after extensive study that those who married in their "good" period had healthier, longer marriages. Those who married in their opposition period experienced the opposite results. I have had clients who married on their opposition day tell me of their difficult experiences on the day of the wedding, just prior to the ceremony or afterward. They often experienced disagreements, delays, or other problems surrounding the day of the event. For example:

- One client had her period on her wedding day.
- Another told me that on the day of the wedding it snowed like crazy, although snow wasn't in the forecast.
- An ill-fated groom confided that a stolen car battery made him late to his own wedding.

The purpose of this section is to help guide you in making the right decision for lasting happiness. Simply

follow your birth number, then select the month and date
that best fit you.

Guide to Selecting Wedding Dates

NUMBER 1 PERSON

Born on the 1st, 10th, 19th, or 28th, you'd do best to
select either late January through February, late March
through April, or late July through August for blissful
matrimony. Or, select a date in the month adding to a 1,
4, or 9. If possible, avoid the months of January, May,
and October. This also includes dates adding up to
6 or 8.

NUMBER 2 PERSON

Born on the 2nd, 11th, 20th, or 29th of the month,
choose late February through March, late April through
May, late June through July, or late September through
October for nuptial relations. Also, try to choose a date
adding up to 2, 7, or 6. If possible, avoid the months of
January, April, and November; the same applies to dates
adding up to 9 or 8.

NUMBER 3 PERSON

Born on the 3rd, 12th, 21st, or 30th of the month, you
should enter into matrimony during late February
through March, late April through May, late September
through October, as well as late November through December. This includes any date that adds up to 3, 6, or 9.
Save the months of February, June, August, and September for things other than marriage, also any date that
adds up to a 4 or 5.

NUMBER 4 PERSON

Born on the 4th, 13th, 22nd, or 31st of the month, you
should select a time for going down the aisle in late Jan-

uary through February, late May through June, and mid July through August. Dates that add up to a 4, 1, or 5 would be equally good. Let the months of January, May, and October pass before putting such a decision into action; this also means avoiding dates adding up to a 6 or 8.

NUMBER 5 PERSON

Born on the 5th, 14th, or 23rd, your best time to settle down should be late April through May and June, followed by late August through September, spilling over into October. As for a choice of dates, select one adding up to a 5 or 6. Forget the months of January, March, and December for this kind of decision, or any date that adds up to a 3 or 8.

NUMBER 6 PERSON

Born on the 6th, 15th or 24th, you tend to take to marriage like a fish to water. You would do best to marry in late February through March, late April through May, late June through July, and late September through October. Next, choose a date adding up to 6, 3, or 2. On the flip side, avoid January, February, and August for entering into blissful arrangements, or any date that adds up to 4, 1, or 8.

NUMBER 7 PERSON

Born on the 7th, 16th, or 25th of the month, you may be the last to marry, as you tend to shy away from such things because of your need to be alone. When the time does come, however, select a date in late February through March, late June through July, and late July through August. Or choose a date that adds up to 2, 7, 1, or 4. On the other hand, the months of January, April, and November may prove to be difficult; this also applies to dates totaling 8 or 9.

NUMBER 8 PERSON

Born on the 8th, 17th, or 26th of the month, you would do well to marry in late December through January, late February through March, late April through May, and late September through October. If you can't, then choose a date adding up to an 8, 3, or 6. If possible, avoid the months of February, June, August, and September, as well as any date adding up to 4, 1, or 5.

NUMBER 9 PERSON

Born on the 9th, 18th, or 27th, of the month, you can expect Cupid to bless your marriage if you select a time in late February through March and April, followed by late July through August, late October through November and December. Next, select a date adding up to 9, 3, 6, or 1. Where possible, avoid January and July for such matters, and those dates totaling 8, 2, or 7.

Numerology and Sex

Without a doubt, sex is a fundamental human drive. After all, how did we get here? On one level, sex represents life—the perpetuation of humankind to avoid extinction. When you look at your parents, yourself, your children—and their future children—you can see yourself as a part of the sexual process in the evolution of life.

On another level, sex represents sensual pleasure of the highest order. The total senses are involved to arouse and express your passions and emotions. Advertisers, books, magazines, television and movies aim at this level of your sexuality to sell products, services, and ideas. Oftentimes there's an attractive woman holding or caressing an item. She's made to look inviting, ready to respond at the snap of a finger. These selling techniques are "subliminal," aimed at your subconscious mind. Experts in the field of buyer motivation and behavior know that sex is important to everyone.

Yet, there are differences in sexual preferences. For instance, one person may want to indulge frequently, whereas another may not. I've had couples as clients who loved each other, but who had totally different modes of sexual expression. This area alone has been a leading cause of breakups, separations and divorces.

Perhaps the highest level of sex is action and energy

exchange. This force could best be described as drive, or desires. This energy is also a means to an end. It can be used for problem solving and goal setting. For instance, before an important fight, a boxer trains hard and usually refrains from sexual relations. This allows him to channel his sexual expression into physical energy in order to beat his opponent. This rule also seems to apply in other areas of sports.

Once you understand the different levels, you need to know when your sexual energy is high or low, and how to use it to accomplish what you want. These periods of peaks and valleys are determined from your day of birth.

Sexual Peaks and Valleys

NUMBER 1 PERSON

Born on the 1st, 10th, 19th, or 28th, you're usually quick and direct when it comes to sexual expression. You pride yourself on endurance and stamina in this area of your life. You'd do best directing your energies for work or pleasure on Sunday and Tuesday, and during the months of February, April, and August. Conserve sexual energy on Saturday and Friday, especially during January, May, and October.

NUMBER 2 PERSON

If you were born on the 2nd, 11th, 20th, or 29th, you're likely to prefer the slow and subtle approach to sex. No rushing or quickies, thank you. You like taking your time, enjoying yourself bit by bit, letting emotions and passions build to a crescendo. Your best days and months for this side of your life are Monday and Friday, particularly in the months of March, May, July, and October. On the reverse side of this matter, avoid draining yourself on Tuesday and Saturday and in the months of January, April, and November.

NUMBER 3 PERSON

With a birth date on the 3rd, 12th, 21st, or 30th, you can be flashy or flamboyant, particularly if you feel you have the type of body worth looking at. This is because of your youthful quality that slows your aging process. You have tremendous energy, and whether it's sex or something else, you enjoy what you do. It's best to direct your energies toward Thursday and Friday, and toward March, May, October, and December. Control your sexual urges more on Wednesday and Sunday, as well as in February, June, and September.

NUMBER 4 PERSON

If you were born on the 4th, 13th, 22nd, or 31st of the month, you like to express yourself sexually in unusual erotic or exotic ways. This approach may completely surprise your mate, because you appear to be a "sleeper" until you're aroused—then watch out! Whatever you do, you like to do it differently. Sunday and Wednesday are your best days, and the months of February, June, July, and August. Reserve yourself, however, on Saturday and Friday, and in January, May, and October.

NUMBER 5 PERSON

Born on the 5th, 14th, or 23rd, of the month, sex is your middle name. Since one of the attributes of sex is the ability to attract, this may explain why members of the opposite sex are continually drawn to you, even if you're married. You're active, day and night—no matter what time it is, you're ready for sexual expression. You're generally at your best in this regard on Wednesday and Friday, and in May, June, September, and October. Conversely, you'll have to stay more on your toes on Thursday and Saturday, and in the months of January, March, and December.

NUMBER 6 PERSON

Like the Number 5 person, if you were born on the 6th, 15th, or 24th, you will attract many people to you sexually and romantically during your life. Your charm and beauty have a lot to do with this. Sexually, you're loving, but conservative; enticing, yet somewhat distant, depending upon your mate or the emotional relationship. When in love, you love deeply. Your best days and months for sensual matters are Friday, Thursday, and Monday, and in the months of March, May, July, October, and December. Use a somewhat cautious approach on Saturday and Sunday, and in January, February, and August.

NUMBER 7 PERSON

If you were born on the 7th, 16th, and 26th, you have a low-key, discriminating approach when it comes to sex. Like a Number 4 person, others tend to underrate you until they get intimately involved. Because of your inward, imaginative nature, be more open, tell your mate what you want out of sex, rather than keeping it to yourself. Sexually, you tend to be at your best on Monday and Sunday, and in the months of February, March, May, July, and August. Just the reverse is true for Saturday and Tuesday, and in January, April and November.

NUMBER 8 PERSON

Born on the 8th, 17th, or 26th, you may at first be wrongfully accused of lacking passion. However, nothing could be further from the truth. Because of your mental approach to things, a little warm-up time may first be required. But when aroused—they'd better be ready. You best express this area of life on Saturday and Friday, and during January, March, May, and October. Just the reverse is the case if it's on a Sunday or Wednesday, especially during February, June, August, and September.

NUMBER 9 PERSON

If you were born on the 9th, 18th, or 27th, you're known as the one with "body heat" when it comes to sensual side. Because you're active and energetic, mates can't quickly fulfill themselves and you don't. You pride yourself on being long lasting when it comes to this area of your intimate life, and rightfully so. It's best to exhibit your prowess on Tuesday and Sunday, and in the months of April, August, and November. On the other hand, you tend not to come up to par on Monday and Saturday, or during January and July.

Parenting

Being a parent is an art as well as a full-time career. An international survey on the treatment of children found that the United States ranked one of the lowest in child-rearing practices. Simply because a person can make a baby, or have a baby, does not automatically make them a good parent. Perhaps parenting should be a required course in school. It would make life a lot easier and happier for the little ones. The fact that thousands of children are abused physically, psychologically, and emotionally across socioeconomic lines really needs to be looked at.

Among the "lower forms" of the animal kingdom, offspring are nurtured, raised quickly, and sent off on their own. This is not the case with humans. Years—18 to 21 of them, sometimes more—as well as money, have to be invested before a child, hopefully, becomes a successful adult.

In many of my personal consultations, the questions ultimately get around to loved ones—especially children. I'm often asked, "Why is it we can't get along?" After devoting a number of years to this area of study, I've found that Numerology offers quick, simple, and logical explanations to the problem of disharmony in a parent/child relationship.

Take the case of a number 9 father. Men today have

been taught to be strong and masculine, and not to cry. This philosophy is often passed on to their sons. If our number 9 father has a number 2 son, the two of them have opposite natures, as number 2 children are generally described as "crybabies." They're sensitive, emotional, and easily wounded. If a number 9 father doesn't understand this, he may constantly demand that his son behave according to society's rules.

To give a real life example, I have a client who was born on the 20th of the month, making her a number 2 person (2 + 0 = 2). Her mother was born on the 29th, another 2 person (2 + 9 = 11; 1 + 1 = 2). Furthermore, her father was born on the 2nd of the month, amazingly, another 2 person. The last family member was her brother, born on the 9th of the month. I explained that the common number running in the family line was 2, and that her brother, broke the pattern by having a 9—a direct opposition number to theirs. She confirmed this was true. Not only was he different and rebellious (a 9 attribute), but he had died at age 20 (2 + 0 = 2) from an injury (another 9 trait).

Parenting Numbers

NUMBER 1 PARENT

If you were born on the 1st, 10th, 19th, or 28th of the month, being a good parent in your eyes is making sure you keep a roof over everyone's head. But children are often emotional by nature. Since you tend to be more mental, don't forget to express emotions in return. If your children were born on dates adding up to a 1, 4, or 9, chances are you'll have harmony. Children born on 6 or 8 dates cause you concern because they tend to be emotional and practical in nature rather than mental like yourself.

NUMBER 2 PARENT

Those born on the 2nd, 11th, 20th, and 29th of the month are generally described as nurturing mothers and fathers because of the Moon's influence. Children born on dates adding up to 2, 7, or 6 are generally more harmonious. The reverse is true if your children were born on dates adding up to a 9. Keep in mind that the nature of the 9 is to be aggressive, not gentle. Children born under the number 8 come in a close second.

NUMBER 3 PARENTS

If you were born on the 3rd, 12th, 21st and 30th of the month, you're considered a 3 parent. Any children born under 3, 6, or 9 generally come closest to your heart. Since you're generally ambitious you may find yourself trying to juggle your time between work and your family. If you have a child born on a 4 or 5 date, more time, attention, and understanding may be required. The 4 or 5 child may rub you the wrong way sometimes, but part of being a good parent is patience and understanding.

NUMBER 4 PARENT

If you were born on either the 4th, 13th, 22nd, or 31st of the month, those children born on dates adding up to 4, 1, or 5 are the ones you tend to scold less. Because you may be easily swayed by moods, your offspring may not understand you. Those times when you're in a good mood, take the initiative and explain to your children how you feel about them—they will certainly appreciate it. If you have a child or two born under a 6 or 8, a greater effort may have to be made to establish a balance of love and harmony between you. Ironically, the 6 child and 4 parent are somewhat alike—stubborn and slow to move, among other things. Because you're inclined to see the negative reality of life, try not to discourage your 6 and 8 children before they have their time to grow.

NUMBER 5 PARENT

Born on the 5th, 14th, or 23rd, you're usually adaptable when it comes to dealing with children. Those who were born on the 5th, 14th, and 23rd may look like you, walk like you, and act like you. Children with birth numbers adding up to 6 or 9 come a close second. However, the children born under a 3 or 8 may create a generation gap. Make a greater effort to understand them more. After all, they belong to you too, and you have just as much responsibility to give them love, affection, and understanding as the rest.

NUMBER 6 PARENT

If your date of birth is the 6th, 15th, or 24th of the month, you're a 6 parent. Like the number 2 parent, you take easily to nurturing others. You easily adjust to whatever birth day children may have, especially those born on dates that add up to 6, 2, or 3. Children born under 4 or 1 may sometimes puzzle you. A 4 child is usually difficult to know. Many times they can't explain their actions and behavior with others. You shouldn't expect them to be as outgoing or gregarious as yourself, but do encourage 4 or 1 children to make the best of themselves now to prepare for adulthood later.

NUMBER 7 PARENT

Were you born on the 7th, 16th, or 25th of the month? If so, you may find parenting somewhat stressful since the 7 by nature loves peace and quiet. However, there seems to be better harmony as your children get older and more settled. If you have a 7, 2, or 6 child, you may find yourself helping them more, and perhaps ignoring the rest. Those born under 8 or 9 may cause you greater worry. Because you tend to be more inward in feelings and affections, definitely take the time to tell your children how important they are to you. But more importantly—really mean it.

NUMBER 8 PARENT

Born on the 8th, 17th, or 26th, you would be a number 8 parent. The 8 has often been described as cold and distant in nature. If this is true in your case, be careful not to let it rub off on your children. There really is a tender, loving side to your nature that the higher forces really understand. Children born on dates adding up to 8, 3, or 6 tend to look or act like you. As a result, you tend to share more with them, and give them more time. The reverse may be true with 4, 5, and 1 children. They may cause you more melancholy than any of the rest. But remember they're yours too, and they need equal time and attention. It will pay off later on when you need their help.

NUMBER 9 PARENT

Born on the 9th, 18th, or 27th of the month, you have a courageous nature—and you may expect the same of your children. You may tell them, "Why don't you fight back? Why don't you stand up for yourself?" If any of your children share a 9 birth date, or are a number 1 or 3, you may not have a problem. But remember, every child is different and has to be treated accordingly. Your children may not be strong now, but they'll prove their merit later on—just give them a chance. If your child was born on a 2 or 7 date, don't expect a macho type of mentality, especially if they're boys. Let them develop at their own speed—under Divine Creation, each of us has our own timetable.

Numerology and Childbirth

Numerology plays an important role in childbirth. For some of you, childbirth may have been easy, all things considered. But for others, it may have been long or difficult. I had the good fortune of seeing the miracle of the births of each of my children. In fact, it was their births that led to this original research.

I observed that a majority of women who gave birth in what I call their "caution" or "opposition" periods almost always experienced some degree of difficulty. Births, in this case, were often premature, induced, breached, toxemic, or cesarean. In some cases during their opposition birth periods, there was also emotional stress at home or in some other area of their lives. On the other hand, women giving birth in their strong or best periods basically had a much easier, normal delivery without any added complications. Therefore, this section is for all childbearing women, present and future.

Best Childbearing Periods

1 MOTHER

If you were born on the 1st, 10th, 19th, or 28th, or in the sign of Leo or Aries, your best childbearing periods are late January through February, late March through

April or late July through August. There may be complications during late December through January, late April through May, or late September through October.

2 MOTHER

If you were born on the 2nd, 11th, 20th, 29th or under Cancer, Taurus, or Libra, your best childbearing periods are late February through March, late April through May, late June through July, and late September through October. Complications, even of a minor nature could prove stressful during late December through January, late March through April, and late October through November.

3 MOTHER

If you were born on the 3rd, 12th, 21st, or 30th, or come under the signs of Pisces, Taurus, Libra, or Sagittarius, you're likely to find bearing children easiest from late February through March, late April through May, late September through October, and late November through December. However, care and caution has to be exercised from late January through February, late May through June, and late July through August, going into September.

4 MOTHER

If you were born on the 4th, 13th, 22nd, or 31st, or under signs of Aquarius, Gemini, or Leo, your best childbearing periods are late January through February, and late May through June, July, and August. There could be unusual conditions related to births in late December through January, late April through May, and late September through October.

5 MOTHER

If you were born on the 5th, 14th, or 23rd, or your sign is Gemini or Virgo, you'll do well if you can bear

your children in late January through February, late
April through May, going into June; and late August
through September, as well as in October. Just the opposite might be true if the birth occurs in late December
into January, late February through March, or late November through December.

6 MOTHER

If you were born on the 6th, 15th, or 24th, or you're a
Taurus, Libra, or Cancer, your best childbearing periods
are late February through March, late April through
May, late June through July, late September through October, and late November through December. Births
could be a problem during late December through January, and into February; also late July through August.

7 MOTHER

If you were born on the 7th, 16th, or 25th, or come
under Pisces or Cancer, your best childbearing periods
are in late February into March, late April through May,
and late June through July, going into August. There may
be complications, however if the event occurs in late
December through January, late March through April, or
late October through November.

8 MOTHER

If you were born on the 8th, 17th, or 26th, or under
the sign of Capricorn, your best time is late December
into January, late February through March, late April
into May, and late September through October. The reverse is usually true should the birth occur in late January into February, late May through June, late July
through August and into September.

9 MOTHER

If you were born on the 9th, 18th, or 27th, or under
the sign of Aries or Scorpio, your best time is in late
March through May, followed by late September through

most of December. On the other hand, you may have some difficulties in late December through January, and especially late June through July.

You must remember these are simply numerical ideas. In my experience, Mother Nature is still the best judge. No matter what your child's birth period, give love and attention—it'll be worth all the time you've invested. Take care of your health and diet.

One final note of interest: Look to see if your child's birth number matches your own, or the other parent's.

Your Child

One of the most important things you can do as a parent or guardian is to understand your child. Since a child learns by watching you, the way you show love and compassion will usually be in direct proportion to the way you feel about yourself. A child, like an adult, has an individual nature and personality made up of strengths and weaknesses. If you observe closely, children will tell you a lot about themselves through their actions. In group situations, one child may take the lead, whereas another child will follow. Still another child may fight all the time, while another cries. Before they are molded into adults, children are basically free and innocent, giving us a truer picture of their nature. It's no accident that you are where you are today because of some childhood experience. As a parent (see chapter on "Parenting"), the better you understand your children, and give them direction, the better off they're likely to be as adults. By using Numerology, you may find helpful insights.

Knowing Your Child

1 CHILD

A number 1 child, born on the 1st, 10th, 19th, or 28th, is usually one of the leaders in the group. These children are basically forceful and determined, and like to have their own way. Because of their leadership potential, they should be encouraged to make decisions early. It also helps to develop the logical side of their mind. A 1 child is original in thought, independent, and direct with others. They like to win, to be "first," or to head a group. Bring out their self-confidence, and teach them that anything can be accomplished with the right use of will. Anything new or different attracts them; however, for this reason they should be encouraged to finish what they start. Number 1 children generally grow up to be writers, lawyers, inventors, administrators, supervisors, or explorers. They also make friends easily with those born in February, April, and August, or dates that add up to 2, 4, 7, and 9.

2 CHILD

A number 2 child, born on the 2nd, 11th, 20th, or 29th, is usually one of the followers in the group. The 2 child is shy, gentle, imaginative, and very sensitive to others and their surroundings. They can't stand harshness or cruelty. They thrive on love, companionship, and personal closeness. In their early stages, 2 children may be crybabies, but if they're nurtured with genuine love, warmth, and tenderness, they eventually come into their own. So try not to be too harsh or forceful with them. Number 2 children develop into psychics, artists, poets, dancers, food or health store owners, and computer and electronics experts. Their best friends tend to be born in the months of May, July, and October, or on dates that add up to a 1, 4, 6, or 7.

3 CHILD

A number 3 child, born on the 3rd, 12th, 21st or 30th, is also one of the leaders in the group. They are expressive, ambitious, and generally popular among their peers. The 3 child is usually known to be cheerful, quick to smile, and likes to be part of the crowd. Parents need to encourage them to be conscientious in their duties, but also instill the belief that they can rise as far as their imaginations can take them. Never discourage the 3 child, instead, help give them the confidence they'll need to make it in this world. They grow into excellent artists and writers, entertainers, heads of enterprises, jewelers, pediatricians, veterinarians, and photographers. Many of their friends are born in the months of March, May, October, and December, as well as anyone with a birth date adding up to a 3, 6, or 9.

4 CHILD

A number 4 child, born on the 4th, 13th, 22nd, or 31st, is best described as the different one in the group. At first, they may appear to be antisocial or rebellious since 4 children like to do things just opposite of others. If a group of kids want to go one way, the 4 child usually wants to go in the other direction. Their nature is slow and deliberate, cautious and methodical. They're usually high-strung, and their feelings are easily bruised. They may go through periods or moods that will be hard to shake, doing things that are contrary and unconventional. Encourage the 4 child to have a more positive outlook on life. They grow to be successful as aviators, mathematicians, mechanics, reformers, radio/TV personalities, occultists, and inventors, etc. Their friends are likely to be born in the months of February, June, July, and August, or have birth dates adding up to 1, 2, 5, or 7.

5 CHILD

Number 5 children, born on the 5th, 14th, or 23rd, are the fast learners in the group. Because of their mental gifts, they usually become the first to talk, read, and write. They make friends easily, and generally have more friends than most. The 5 child loves travel and being outdoors. Since they also love freedom and noncommitment, they need to be taught to be responsible. They also like crowds and public activities. Number 5 children think quickly and can be impulsive; they should be encouraged to stick to one thing at a time before going on to the next. And because of their adaptability, encourage them to choose their friends and surroundings carefully. They grow up to be writers, communicators, scientists, business persons, entrepreneurs, racers, travel agents, sales and PR persons. Although 5 children get along with almost everyone, they're especially drawn to those with birth dates adding up to a 5 or 6.

6 CHILD

Number 6 children, born on the 6th, 15th, or 24th, are the charmers in the group. A 6 child often turns out to be a crowd pleaser or the teacher's pet. They generally like beautiful things such as colors, music, paintings, and are athletically inclined. As they have a pleasing and magnetic personality, others often seek their advice. Encourage them to handle and accept duty and responsibility. Above all, a 6 child needs to be shown love, praise, affection, and appreciation. They posses a wonderful ability to " read" people and often know intuitively how things are likely to turn out. They grow up to be social workers, politicians, singers and dancers, doctors, nurses, lawyers, teachers, and community leaders. Their friends are likely to have been born in the months of March, May, July, October, and December; this also includes those born on dates adding up to 6, 3, 2, and 9.

7 CHILD

A number 7 child, born on the 7th, 14th, or 25th, is the quiet, reserved one in the group. They appear to be loners, keeping to themselves, but it's only because they're shy. They're more observant and analytical than other children—perhaps this is why they prefer their own company. They have strong personalities and an air of mystery. A 7 child is one of the first to read, and they express themselves through music, poetry, writing, and painting. Although they say very little, much is being seen and analyzed. They should be encouraged to express their inner feelings and emotions. Also encourage the 7 child to have a positive outlook on life and not to worry so much. As adults, 7 children make excellent researchers, investigators, mystics, accountants, religious officials, travelers, scientists, and analysts. Their friends are generally born in the months of February, March, May, July, and August or have birth dates that add up to 1, 2, 4, or 7.

8 CHILD

The number 8 child, born on the 8th, 17th, or 26th, is the serious-minded one in the group. They seem, from the beginning, to have an old person's head on their shoulders. Because they mature faster than other children, this may explain their attraction to older people. The 8 child has an intense personality and a strong sense of purpose. Of all the children, the 8 child is the most misunderstood. If no effort is made to correct this, it could lead to serious problems when they reach adulthood. They should be encouraged to take an open, positive approach to life. This is very important as they seem to be affected by stressful circumstances more than anything else. They grow up to be authority figures, bankers, realtors, government officials, managers, corporate lawyers, and heads of business. Their friends tend to be born in the months of January, February, July, and October, or dates that add up to 3, 4, 6, and 8.

9 CHILD

The number 9 child, born on the 9th, 18th, or 27th, is the fighter in the group. By nature they're forceful, energetic, and want to take the lead in group situations. A 9 child may be known at times as the one with the hot temper, but actually they're bold and courageous, and if provoked will fight. Unlike most children, you don't have to worry about their self-confidence—they seem to have a good opinion of themselves instinctively. They should be encouraged to control their tempers, as well as impulsive actions and words. However, never discourage them, as it retards their leadership potential. Encourage 9 children to be the masters of their fate. They grow up to become military officers, construction workers, firefighters, media personalities, politicians, publishers, artists, surgeons, and machinists. Their friends are generally born in April, August, November, and December, or have a birth date adding up to 9, 3, 6, or 1.

In addition to looking at your child's birth date, study his or her name as well. A number or numbers repeated many times in the child's name could shift the interpretation. For instance, if your child is a number 2, described as sensitive, emotional, and the crybaby in the group, but also has a lot of 9s the name, this will add courage, confidence, and a fighting spirit.

V.

Your Health

Health and Illnesses

All the money, power, glory, and fame in the world cannot buy back your health once you've lost it. Not only is it important to maintain good health, but to know the possible illnesses that are likely to affect you, your loved ones, and friends. This is determined by paying attention to your date of birth. Let's say you know someone ill, and they were born on the 17th of the month. This is an 8 person (1 + 7 = 8) and may likely have an illness related to those areas of health assigned to their birth number.

Health Concerns

NUMBER 1 PERSON

Born on the 1st, 10th, 19th, or 28th, or under the sign of Aries or Leo, you're likely to suffer from eye problems of all kinds, especially astigmatism, and from exposure to bright and direct sunlight. There may also be lung trouble, high blood pressure, irregular blood circulation, and heart palpitations. Be especially careful of your health during January, May, and October.

NUMBER 2 PERSON

If you were born on the 2nd, 11th, 20th, or 29th, or under the signs of Cancer or Taurus, you're likely to suffer with stomach and digestive troubles of all kinds. Watch out for ptomaine poisoning, internal growths, hemorrhoids, tumors, cancer, or diabetes. If you're a number 2 woman, you may have added health concerns connected with the reproductive organs. Be extra careful during January, April, and November.

NUMBER 3 PERSON

Those born on the 3rd, 12th, 21st, or 30th, or under Pisces or Sagittarius, may have health concern around emotional upsets, strained nerves brought on by overwork, low blood pressure, skin problems of all kinds, foot problems, kidney disorders, inflamed nerves, and jaundice. Be careful during February, June, August, and September.

NUMBER 4 PERSON

If you were born on the 4th, 13th, 22nd, or 31st, or under the sign of Aquarius, you're likely to suffer from odd and unusual types of illnesses that are hard to pinpoint or diagnose. There might be freak accidents and unexplainable injuries, moodiness, mental and emotional disorders, self-inflicted wounds, or suicides. Take special care of your health during January, May, and October.

NUMBER 5 PERSON

Those born on the 5th, 14th, or 23rd, or under Gemini or Virgo, will likely suffer from overstrained nerves, mental exhaustion or breakdowns, insomnia, nervous tension, amnesia, paralysis, vertigo, stammering, twitching in some part of the face, and lung problems. Care must be exercised during January, March, and December.

NUMBER 6 PERSON

Born on the 6th, 15th, or 24th, or under Libra or Taurus you tend to have problems with the nose, throat, sinuses and upper part of the lungs, hay fever, irregular blood circulation and/or heart palpitations, bronchitis, and asthma. If you're a woman, you may have to deal with additional problems concerning your breasts. Be careful during January, February, April, and August.

NUMBER 7 PERSON

If you were born on the 7th, 14th, 25th, or under the sign of Cancer or Pisces, you tend to suffer with worry, annoyance, and mental aggravation more than anything else. In addition, you tend to let your imagination get out of control by thinking the worst. There may also be skin problems and night sweats, as well as minor stomach concerns. Be careful during January, April, and August.

NUMBER 8 PERSON

Those born on the 8th, 17th, or 26th, or under the sign of Capricorn, may fall ill because of deep moods of despondency and intense feelings of loneliness. Also watch out for rheumatism, blood diseases, and a tendency to receive the wrong medical treatment or wrong drug prescription. In addition, there could be concerns with the liver, bile, and excretory system, as well as problems with the knees, teeth, and bones. Exercise the utmost care during February, June, August, and September.

NUMBER 9 PERSON

Born on the 9th, 18th, or 27th, or if you're an Aries or Scorpio, you may find yourself the victim of accidents, cuts, and bruises, more than illnesses. You have to be careful of fires, explosives, guns, knives, cuts from sharp instruments, machinery or car accidents, as well as fevers. Care has to be exercised during January, May, July, and October.

Herbs and Fruits: A Natural Way to Eat

How did early man survive and maintain his health? There were no hospitals then, no doctors, no emergency rooms for a toothache and certainly no wonder drugs. So how did they stay well? Perhaps their survival depended on Mother Nature, as expressed in Her herbs and plants, fruits, roots, and barks. Today, those very medications and miracle drugs you take are simply derivatives of the same herbs, barks, and roots that Mother Nature still provides in abundance. The herbs and their uses that I'm about to share with you can be studied more fully in two excellent books: *Philosophy of Divine Nutrition*, by Rev. Donald Thomas, and *Back to Eden*, by Jethro Kloss. The following herbs and fruits are healthy, nontoxic, and surprisingly, are often found on your kitchen shelf—however, when introducing a new herbal remedy into your diet it is always wise to consult an experienced nutritionist or herbalist.

Natural Foods

NUMBER 1 PERSON

For those born on the 1st, 10th, 19th, or 28th, the following herbs and fruits are good: bay leaves, oranges, lemons, apples, figs, raisins, grapefruit, barley, borage, ginger, chamomile, nutmeg, spinach, cloves, and honey. Avoid oily, fatty foods whenever possible.

NUMBER 2 PERSON

If you were born on the 2nd, 11th, 20th, or 29th, the following foods are for you: lettuce, plenty of fresh water, melons of all kinds, cucumbers, cabbage, asparagus, prunes, okra, carrots, apples, turnips, kale, lemons, cauliflower, strawberries, linseed, endive. Avoid hot, spicy foods in your diet.

NUMBER 3 PERSON

Born on the 3rd, 12th, 21st, or 30th, include some of following in your diet: borage, cherries, parsnips, grapes, sage, parsley, peaches, celery, beets, nutmeg, comfrey, saffron, olives, rhubarb, almonds, mint, hazelnuts, and wheat products of all kind. Avoid overstrained nerves and overwork.

NUMBER 4 PERSON

Born on the 4th, 13th, 22nd, or 31st, the following are for you: Solomon's seal, coconut, wintergreen, pilewort, romaine, lima beans, bananas, okra, lentils, marigold, spinach, and medlars. Your state of mind is your best medicine. You tend to be receptive to cures administered through the use of electrical treatments, hypnosis, and mental suggestion. Avoid highly seasoned foods.

NUMBER 5 PERSON

If you were born on the 5th, 14th, or 23rd, include the following for a natural balance: carrots, nuts of all kinds, parsnips, cloves, mace, hops, ginseng, peas, parsley, oats in all forms, thyme, caraway seeds, apricots, hyssop, string beans, rye products in all forms, cherries, buckwheat, and cranberries. Rest and relaxation is your best medicine. Get plenty of sleep.

NUMBER 6 PERSON

Those born on the 6th, 15th, or 24th, should include the following in their diet: beans of all kinds, rose leaves, pears, apricots, almonds, cherries, dates, raspberries, melons, radishes, brussels sprouts, squash, walnuts, vervain, and limes. Avoid rich, fattening foods.

NUMBER 7 PERSON

Born on the 7th, 16th, or 25th, you should include: plenty of fresh water, fruit juices of all kinds, cabbage, lettuce, cucumbers, celery, chicory, hops, sorrel, endive, oats, honey, prunes, pineapples, dates, onions, watercress, and linseed. Avoid repressed emotions and moods.

NUMBER 8 PERSON

If you were born on the 8th, 17th, or 26th, select the following for your diet: spinach, angelica, wild carrots, celery, marshmallow, Solomon's seal, turnips, savory, figs, blessed (holy) thistle, psyllium seeds, dates, and ragwort. Try to have one meatless meal per week. Avoid feelings of intense loneliness.

NUMBER 9 PERSON

Born on the 9th, 18th, or 27th, take the following: garlic, peppers, onions, radishes, tomatoes, nettle juice, hops, rhubarb, leeks, danewort, apricots, apples, eggplant, mustard greens, mustard, and relish. Avoid rich food and watch alcohol consumption.

Health: The
Rosicrucian Way

In the chapter on "Health and Illnesses" you discovered the correlation between your date of birth number and the illnesses commonly associated with it. Let me introduce you to another health barometer—one that is not new at all, but very old. According to the ancient Rosicrucian Order, from birthday to birthday one's health can undergo dramatic changes. However, the Rosicrucians believed that as long as we were in harmony with ourselves, nature, and our universe, the end result would be a longer, healthier, and happier way of life. What more can one ask for?

This mystic order observed that in every 52-day period, from birthday to birthday, a change of some sort occurs. Have you ever wondered, when faced with a health crisis, whether it would be best to go ahead with that operation? What about starting that new diet or exercise program? All this and more has been carefully considered.

From birthday to birthday, there are seven periods of 52 days each. To keep track of your seven 52-day periods, start with your birth day. This is considered day 1. Now, count forward another 51 days on your calendar. This completes period number 1. Next, count forward another 51 days from where you last stopped. This is period number 2. Continue this method until you come

back around to your next birthday, for a total of seven
periods. If you want to read more about how these
cycles affect the health and mind, I recommend *Self-
Mastery and Fate with the Cycles of Life*, by Dr. H.
Spencer Lewis. The following is an outline of the seven
periods and how your health is likely to be affected in
each of them.

A 52-Day Cycle and Your Health

PERIOD 1 (52 Days)

• Your vitality is generally at its best. Health that's
  below normal quickly returns.
• Good period to plan an operation.
• An especially good period for deep breathing, walking,
  and other outdoor activities.
• Avoid straining the eyes.

PERIOD 2 (52 Days)

• Tendency toward rapid changes in the health.
• Problems develop with the stomach, bowels, blood-
  stream, nerves, aches, and pains.
• Keep a cheerful and contented attitude of mind.

PERIOD 3 (52 Days)

• Period of accidents and sudden operations.
• Injury through fires, sharp instruments, falls, and sudden blows.
• Watch your blood pressure; avoid strain and overwork.

PERIOD 4 (52 Days)

• Time of restlessness, uneasiness, and stress on the
  nervous system.
• Avoid excessive reading, planning or overworking the
  mind.
• Rest and sleep is needed more during this period than
  at any other time.

PERIOD 5 (52 Days)

- Tendency to overindulge in things of the flesh.
- Good period for recovery from fevers, chronic conditions, or other afflictions.
- Stay alert, since mental suggestions from others, as well as your surroundings, affect the mind during this time.

PERIOD 6 (52 Days)

- Skin, throat, the reproductive system, and kidneys may be affected.
- Avoid mental strain, overwork, or too much pleasure of a physical nature.
- Drink plenty of fresh water and take part in lots of outdoor activities.

PERIOD 7 (52 DAYS)

- Physical and mental vitality is generally at its lowest.
- Not a good time for taking medicine or having an operation.
- Try to avoid lingering colds or flare-ups of chronic conditions.

VI.

The Subject of Money

Numerology and Money

Money is defined as "a medium of exchange for goods and services." It takes on different meanings for different people. To some, money may mean security and happiness. To others, it could mean pleasure or a means to an end. Then there's the other side of money—how to attract it. Ever heard someone ask, "Why is so and so making plenty of money and I'm not?" Or, "If I was born on the same day as a famous personality, why aren't I rich?"

Although your birth number and Zodiac sign play a part, your place of birth, education, parental upbringing, and a host of other factors must also be taken into consideration. I, too, have wondered why a person born the same month and day as someone rich and successful will have no money at all. In the world of Numerology there are other considerations aside from your month, day, and year of birth. For example, is your name in harmony with your date of birth? Is it in harmony with your destiny number, your pinnacle period, or your personal year?

Your name is just as important as your date of birth; from a numerical viewpoint, it has a lot to do with success or failure. Since a name may go through a variety of changes, your birth date is the constant indicator, much like a needle on a compass pointing north. This is why each case has to be examined individually. Even if we had the same birth date, chances are, you and I will never suffer from the same diseases, nor marry at the same time, nor reach peaks of success at the same time, so differences in the capacity to attract money become very understandable.

Your Chances for Attracting Money

NUMBER 1 MONEY PERSON

If you were born on the 1st, 10th, 19th, or 28th of the month, you may regard money as a means to an end, or as a way to further your name, reputation, or position in life. Your best way of making money is by entering into fields and occupations that are new, different, and original. As your birth number suggests authority over others, so you have the potential of making money by striking out on your own, by going into business for yourself. It's important to be self-motivating—depend primarily on YOU. Develop an attitude of success; have a clear conscience about making money—and plenty of it. Establish good credit; borrow only through established institutions. April and August, followed by February are the months your business or partnerships are likely to prosper. Double-check cosigning notes or making loans to those born in January, May and October.

Millionaire 1 Personalities:

Richard Pryor	December 1, 1940
Dolly Parton	January 19, 1946
Yves St. Laurent	August 1, 1936
Rod Stewart	January 10, 1945
Lee Marvin	February 19, 1924
William Paley	September 28, 1901
David Susskind	December 19, 1920
Jacqueline Kennedy Onassis	July 28, 1929
Smokey Robinson	February 19, 1940

NUMBER 2 MONEY PERSON

If your birth day is the 2nd, 11th, 20th, or 29th of the month, you may be shy about making money, especially on your own. One of the best ways for you to make money is by accumulating it slowly over the years. For you, money isn't often made over night. And it comes from occupations and careers having to do with the public in some way. Pooling your talents, skills, and resources with people who share your monetary goals will accelerate your financial gains. Teaming up to help others will pay off later in financial dividends. Shopping for bargains adds more coins to your money mountain. Your best business or financial partners are those born in the months of May, July, October, and sometimes January. Be careful of loaning money to or asking for money from those born in April, November, and January.

Millionaire 2 Personalities:

TV personality Oprah Winfrey	January 29, 1954
Burt Reynolds	February 11, 1946
Michael Jackson	August 29, 1958
George Burns	January 20, 1896
Jerome Robbins	October 11, 1918
Bob Hope	May 29, 1903
Gloria Vanderbilt and Sidney Poitier	both born on February 20, 1924
Burt Lancaster	November 2, 1913
Salvador Dali	May 11, 1904
Aristotle Onassis	January 20, 1906

NUMBER 3 MONEY PERSON

Born on the 3rd, 12th, 21st, or 30th of the month, you may be the type that lives for the moment. This can result in a drain on your savings and other resources. Your best way of building your financial future is by having a success-oriented attitude. The bigger you think, the bigger you'll win. The word "fail" is not in your vocabulary —an attitude that gets you off to a good start. Equating money with status and position is an equally strong motivating factor. Building a good line of credit and paying your bills promptly add to your advantage. Matters concerning money can be expected around March, May, October, and December. Financial stress may come through those born in February, June, August, and September.

Millionaire 3 Personalities:

Bill Cosby	July 12, 1937
Jack Nicklaus	January 21, 1940
Dick Clark	November 30, 1929
Eddie Murphy	April 3, 1961
Wayne Newton	April 3, 1941
Placido Domingo	January 21, 1941
Kenny Rogers	August 21, 1938
Joan Rivers	October 12, 1935
Frank Sinatra	December 12, 1915
Paul Anka	July 30, 1941
Larry Hagman	September 21, 1931

NUMBER 4 MONEY PERSON

If your date of birth is on the 4th, 13th, 22nd, or 31st of the month, you're are a 4 person. You have the potential of making money through odd or unusual methods. Money may also come to you in extremes—you may have lots of it at one time, and almost none at another. You may be generally indifferent to money but have a way of stretching it once you've got it. Keeping good financial records, budgeting, and living within your means increases your nest egg. Shop for bargains. Take advantage of discounts and rebates and you're sure to get ahead. Business and money matters generally occur during months of February, June, and August. Financial stress tends to develop with those born in the months of January, May, and October

Millionaire 4 Personalities:

Stevie Wonder	May 13, 1950
Neil Simon	July 4, 1927
Walter Cronkite	November 4, 1916
Harrison Ford	July 13, 1942

Oscar de la Renta	July 22, 1932
Phil Collins	January 31, 1951
William Shatner	March 22, 1931
Clint Eastwood	May 31, 1930
Dan Rather	October 31, 1931
L. Ron Hubbard	March 13, 1911
Joseph Papp	June 22, 1921
Henry Ford II	September 4, 1917

NUMBER 5 MONEY PERSON

A birth date on the 5th, 14th, or 23rd, suggests that living for the moment affects your pocketbook. You don't have the best reputation for saving. You may feel drawn to make your money by taking chances, risks, and gambles. Make better use of your time and you'll do better financially. Having more than one iron in the fire will pay off later on. Since 5 is a media number, use radio, television, newspapers, and the like to promote your talents. If you remember to pay yourself first before paying others, you'll find your personal account growing rapidly. Success with money generally comes in February, May, June, September, and October. The reverse is the case for January, March, and December, as well as with those born in these months.

Millionaire 5 Personalities

Johnny Carson	October 23, 1935
George Lucas	May 14, 1944
Julio Iglesias	September 23, 1944
Ralph Lauren	October 14, 1939
Michael Caine	March 14, 1933
Raymond A. Kroc	October 5, 1902
Bruce Springsteen	September 23, 1949
Prince Charles of England	November 14, 1948
Diane Keaton	January 5, 1946
Otto Preminger	December 5, 1906
Vincent Sardi	July 23, 1915

NUMBER 6 MONEY PERSON

In my research notes on multimillionaires, your birth dates on the 6th, 15th, or 24th head the list. One of the swiftest ways to start accumulating money is by assuming full responsibility for your actions, deeds, victories, and defeats. Another financial building trait you have is your sense of value. When it comes to business, you're a natural. And you know a bargain when you see one. Since your birth number is associated with teamwork, you'd do well by letting others in on the action. You have magnetic qualities that naturally draw the help and assistance you need. However, thoughts of failure or worrying about what others may think of you can block your financial riches if you're not mindful. Deal with money matters during March, May, July, October, and December. Those who were born in the months of February, April, and August may alter your financial destiny.

Millionaire 6 Personalities:

Sylvestor Stallone	July 6, 1946
Ivan Boesky	March 6, 1939
Lucille Ball	August 6, 1910
Howard Hughes	December 24, 1905
J. Paul Getty	December 15, 1892
Alfred Bloomingdale	April 15, 1916
Merv Griffin	July 6, 1925
Bjorn Borg	June 6, 1956
Shirley MacLaine	April 24, 1934

NUMBER 7 MONEY PERSON

If your date of birth is the 7th, 16th, or 25th of the month, you're a 7 money person. In your case, money is usually accumulated by slow and intuitive means. A deep understanding of your money motives seems to steer you more clearly and directly toward your monetary goals. In my survey of over a hundred multimillionaires, it came as no surprise that those born under the birth number 7 ranked in last place. After all, 7 is spiritual in nature, not material. Creative visualization is one of your success formulas for financial attraction. See the material things you want out of life in your mind's eye. You don't do well chasing after dollars. Rather, make use of the knowledge and skills you've acquired over the years. Others pay handsomely for important information. Since this is an information and technological age, your expertise may prove to be a blessing. Do business with those born in March, May, July, and August. Persons born in January, April, and November could prove a financial disaster.

Millionaire 7 Personalities:

Kareem Abdul-Jabbar	April 16, 1947
Liberace	May 16, 1919
Sean Connery	August 25, 1930
David Frost	April 7, 1939
Elton John	March 25, 1947
George Harrison	February 25, 1943
Francis Ford Coppola	April 7, 1939
Leonard Bernstein	August 25, 1918
Conrad Hilton	December 25, 1887
Jerry Lewis	March 16, 1926

NUMBER 8 MONEY PERSON

Those born on the 8th, 17th, or 26th of the month acquire money and financial success through hard work and determination. Strangely enough, although the 8 represents money, power, and authority, your birth number ranks in seventh place among the multimillionaires. Start your own business if you can. Think big, think success, and you're likely to do very well. Think small and just the reverse happens. Make no bones about making money. Your birth number has dominion over material and tangible things. Don't take No for an answer, take responsibility for your gains and losses, and you will move faster toward financial independence. You would do well to wear the best of clothes on the job or when taking interviews. It seems to help in attracting money. Financially, you do well during the months of January, May, and October. Use caution with those born in February, June, August, and September.

Millionaire 8 Personalities:

Nelson Rockefeller	July 8, 1908
Mick Jagger	July 26, 1943
Diana Ross	March 26, 1944
Paul Newman	January 26, 1925
Sugar Ray Leonard	May 17, 1956
Jackie Gleason	February 26, 1916
Robert De Niro	August 17, 1943
Lauren Hutton	November 11, 1943
Muhammad Ali	January 17, 1942
Jack Lemmon	February 8, 1925
Aldo Gucci	May 26, 1909

NUMBER 9 MONEY PERSON

If you were born on the 9th, 18th, or 27th of the month, you have an excellent chance of making money. In fact, your birth number ranked three on the list of multimillionaires. Your energetic capacity, mental attitude, and strong desire to control your destiny help attract the money you need. Being unconcerned about what others think or say, in addition to your natural driving force, are qualities that quickly take you to the top. Establishing an excellent line of credit and diversifying your nest egg gives you a giant leap forward toward monetary growth and financial independence. In business, you tend to do well during April, August, November, and December. Be wary of those born in May, July, and October.

Millionaire 9 Personalities:

Yoko Ono	February 18, 1933
Reggie Jackson	May 18, 1946
Cary Grant	January 18, 1904
Steven Spielberg	December 18, 1947
Richard Nixon	January 9, 1913
Martina Navratilova	October 18, 1956
Elizabeth Taylor	February 27, 1932
Hugh Hefner	April 9, 1926
Billy Joel	May 9, 1949
Paul McCartney	June 18, 1942

How to Use Your Lucky Numbers

Without exception almost everyone wants to know their lucky or important number and how to use it to their advantage. Some want to use their lucky number for making important dates and decisions or for taking interviews. Others will want to know their lucky number for entertainment purposes, for speculation, marriage, first dates, or for success in their plans.

The first thing you need to know is what is your lucky number? The second, is how to increase the power of your lucky number once you've found it. Your lucky or important number is determined from your date of birth —it's just that simple. Thousands of years of observations by those interested in Numerology have proven that the date you were born is the luckiest and most important number for you. For example, take someone born August 14th (1+4=5), 5 is that person's lucky number. For a person born December 7th, 7 would be the lucky number.

So, now that you've found your lucky number, how do you increase its power? First, you must begin to concentrate on it. Begin to look forward to the day your lucky number appears in the month. If your lucky number is 5, any date of the month adding up to the number 5, such as the 5th, 14th (1+4=5) and 23rd (2+3=5), offers you the best chance for success. The person with 3 as a lucky number would best use the 3rd, 12th ($1+2=3$), 21st ($2+1=3$), and 30th ($3+0=3$) of the month to speculate, make decisions, take tests, have interviews, etc.

This rule applies to all numbers with the exception of 4 and 8. Because of the peculiar, sudden, and sometimes turbulent qualities of the numbers 4 and 8, their power should NOT BE INCREASED. An alternate number should be used instead. Persons born under the numbers 4 and 8 encounter difficulty and misfortune more often than any others. Therefore, the 4 person should choose the number 1 as their lucky or important number, and act on dates adding up to the 1st, 10th ($1+0=1$), 19th ($1+9=10/1$), and 28th ($2+8=10/1$) of the month. The 8 person should choose the number 3 and use dates adding up to the 3rd, 12th ($1+2=3$), 21st ($2+1=3$), and 30th ($3+0=3$), for important plans, speculations, and actions.

When you begin using the rule of determining your lucky and important number, and then increasing its power, you'll begin to notice a marked improvement in your personal and business affairs. The changes will not be immediate or overnight, but should be noticeable in the short space of about 3 months. It depends on how much you concentrate on increasing the power of your lucky number.

Analysis of a Lottery

Does your state have a lottery system? Lotteries have experienced phenomenal growth throughout the entire United States and other parts of the world. In North America the biggest lottery to date took place in New York on August 21, 1985. The amount of the lottery was over 41 million dollars. Before this multimillion-dollar biggie, the record jackpot was in Chicago on the 3rd of September 1984. If you'll notice, both of these humongous lotteries took place on a number 3 date. Interestingly enough, the single winner of the New York lottery was born on the 21st—$2 + 1 = 3$.

In the case of the August 21st drawing, the first number to be drawn was 30—$3 + 0 = 3$. It took 3 days to determine the winners—and there were 3. Strangely, one of the 3 winning tickets was held by a group of 21 factory workers from Mt. Vrnon, NY. They called themselves the "lucky 21"—$2 + 1 = 3$. According to press reports, they formed their pool around 3 o'clock on the afternoon of the drawing. Celso Carcete, the factory worker who picked the lucky numbers, happens to have 12 letters in his name—$2 + 1 = 3$.

I was personally contacted by New York lottery winner, Gwendolyn Lynch, and she added further insight into this amazing pattern of 3. When she won, she shared with two others (making a total of 3), a 3.9 million dollar prize—$3 + 9 = 12; 1 + 2 = 3$.

What does all this mean? Can it be said that the number 3 seems to be lucky in some way when it comes to winning big-ticket lotteries. Not necessarily—but it does suggests strong possibilities.

Looking at these lottery winners from the angle of Astrology, we find other insights. For instance, it was found that the majority of lottery winners, at least in New York, were born under the Earth signs of Taurus, Virgo, and Capricorn—with Taurus leading. This confirmed the earlier research I did on multimillionaires. Those with a birth number of 6 (a multiple of 3), which rules the signs of Taurus and Libra respectively, led the list when it came to making the most money in this country. Those with birth numbers adding up to 3 (sound familiar?) followed second.

In the final analysis, can a lottery be won using a Numerology system? Judging from the numerous lottery publications on the market today, one gets the impression that there must be some system. But is it a definite one? The New York Lottery's own research showed that most of the winners never had a system, but chose their numbers randomly or in an association with some personal event, etc.

To my knowledge, no numerologist has ever won these lotteries. This is not to say you can't win using a system. Many have tried, and perhaps even succeeded to a degree. I have theories of my own based upon my limited research in this area, but they haven't proved consistent. Remember, a lottery is a game of chance, with the odds heavily favoring the house. If you're a lottery player, your best bet is to stay within your budget and to know when to stop.

Using Your Birth Date to Win at Lotto

Although there are numerous newsstand guides and tip sheets, in my long experience of reading people, I've found the best guide to winning at lotto and other games of chance comes from your birth date, coupled with the best times to use this informtion. Over the years, many people have informed me that their lucky numbers came up shortly after our consultation. I'd like to share with you the lucky numbers, days, and months associated with your birth day, so if you're a lotto player, this section should boost the odds of your winning.

But do me a favor first. Before looking up your birth day information, think back to the times you've won anything, no matter how big or small, and ask yourself the following questions: What day(s) did you win? What month(s) did the win(s) occur? Was there a number or series of numbers associated with the win(s), such as the date or address number? Now, look up your birth day to determine your lucky numbers, days, and months. This chart also applies to family members and friends. Suppose one night you dream about Uncle Joey. Find Uncle Joey's birth day and select his numbers in addition to your own. Good Luck!

[A note about the chart: When you find your month and date of birth, your lucky numbers will appear in ORDER OF IMPORTANCE, as will the days. Your months are *UNDERSCORED* in order of importance.]

JANUARY

Date	Lucky Numbers	Days	Months
1ST	1–4–8	SUN–SAT	JAN–APR–AUG
2ND	2–7–8	MON–SAT	JAN–MAY–JULY–OCT
3RD	3–6–8	THU–FRI–SAT	JAN–MAR–MAY–OCT–DEC
4TH	4–1–8	SUN–SAT	JAN–FEB–AUG
5TH	5–6–8	WED–FRI–SAT	JAN–JUN–MAY–SEPT–OCT
6TH	6–3–8	FRI–THU–SAT	JAN–MAR–MAY–OCT–DEC
7TH	7–2–8	MON–SAT	JAN–MAR–MAY–JULY–OCT
8TH	8–3–6	SAT–THU–FRI	JAN–MAR–MAY–OCT–DEC
9TH	9–6–8	TUE–FRI–SAT	JAN–APR–MAY–OCT–NOV
10TH	1–4–8	SUN–SAT	JAN–APR–AUG
11TH	2–7–8–11	MON–SAT	JAN–MAY–JULY–OCT
12TH	3–6–8	THU-FRI-SAT	JAN–MAR–MAY–OCT–DEC
13TH	4–1–8	SUN–SAT	JAN–FEB–AUG

Date	Lucky Numbers	Days	Months
14TH	5–6–8	WED–FRI–SAT	JAN–MAY–JUN–SEP–OCT
15TH	6–3–8	FRI–THU–SAT	JAN–MAR–MAY–OCT–DEC
16TH	7–2–8	MON–SAT	JAN–MAY–JULY–OCT
17TH	8–6–3	SAT–FRI–THU	JAN–MAR–MAY–OCT
18TH	9–6–8	TUE–FRI–SAT	JAN–APR–MAY–OCT–NOV
19TH	1–4–8	SUN–SAT	JAN–APR–AUG
20TH	2–7–8	MON–SAT	JAN–MAY–JULY–OCT
21ST	3–4–1	THU–SUN	FEB–MAR–AUG–DEC
22ND	4–1–5–22	SUN–WED	FEB–JUN–AUG–SEP
23RD	5–4–1	WED–SUN	FEB–JUN–AUG–SEP
24TH	6–2–7	FRI–MON	MAR–MAY–JULY–OCT
25TH	7–2–4	MON–SUN	FEB–JUN–JULY–AUG
26TH	8–4–1	SAT–SUN	JAN–FEB–JULY–AUG
27TH	9–4–1	TUE–SUN	FEB–APR–AUG–NOV
28TH	1–4–9	SUN–TUE	FEB–APR–AUG–NOV
29TH	2–7–4–11	MON–SUN	FEB–JUN–JULY–AUG
30TH	3–4–1	THU–SUN	FEB–MAR–AUG–DEC
31ST	4–1–5	SUN–WED	FEB–JUN–AUG–SEP

FEBRUARY

Date	Lucky Numbers	Days	Months
1ST	1–4–9	SUN–TUE	FEB–APR–JUN–AUG
2ND	2–7–4–1	MON–SUN	FEB–JUN–JULY–AUG
3RD	3–4–1	THU–SUN	FEB–MAR–AUG–DEC
4TH	4–1–5	SUN–WED	FEB–JUN–AUG–SEP
5TH	5–4—1	WED–SUN	FEB–JUN–AUG–SEP
6TH	6–2–7	FRI–MON	MAY–JULY–OCT
7TH	7–2–4	MON–SUN	FEB–JUN–JULY–AUG
8TH	8–4–1	SAT–SUN	JAN–FEB–JULY–AUG
9TH	9–4–1	TUE–SUN	FEB–APR–AUG–NOV
10TH	1–4–9	SUN–TUE	FEB–APR–JUN–AUG
11TH	2–7–4–1–11	MON–SUN	FEB–JUN–JULY–AUG
12TH	3–4–1	THU–SUN	FEB–MAR–AUG–DEC
13TH	4–1–5	SUN–WED	FEB–JUN–AUG–SEP
14TH	5–4–1	WED–SUN	FEB–JUN–AUG–SEP
15TH	6–2–7	FRI–MON	MAY–JULY–OCT
16TH	7–2–4	MON–SUN	FEB–JUN–JULY–AUG
17TH	8–4–1	SAT–SUN	JAN–FEB–JULY–AUG
18TH	9–4–1	TUE–SUN	FEB–APR–AUG–NOV
19TH	1–4–9	SUN–TUE	FEB–APR–JUN–AUG
20TH	2–7–3	MON–THU	MAR–MAY–JULY–OCT–DEC
21ST	3–6–9	THU–FRI–TUE	MAR–APR–MAY–OCT–NOV–DEC

Date	Lucky Numbers	Days	Months
22ND	4–1–3–22	SUN–THU	FEB–MAR–AUG–DEC
23RD	5–6–3	WED–FRI–THU	MAR–MAY–JUN–SEP–OCT–DEC
24TH	6–3–9	FRI–THU–TUE	MAR–APR–MAY–OCT–NOV–DEC
25TH	7–2–3	MON–THU	MAR–MAY–JULY–OCT–DEC
26TH	8–3–6	SAT–THU–FRI	JAN–MAR–MAY–OCT–DEC
27TH	9–3–6	TUE–THU–FRI	MAR–APR—MAY–OCT–NOV–DEC
28TH	1–4–3	SUN–THU	FEB–MAR–APR–AUG–DEC
29TH	2–7–3–11	MON–THU	MAR–MAY–JULY–OCT–DEC

MARCH

Date	Lucky Numbers	Days	Months
1ST	1–4–3	SUN–THU	FEB–MAR–APR–AUG–DEC
2ND	2–7–3	MON–THU	MAR–MAY–JULY–OCT–DEC
3RD	3–6–9	THU–FRI–TUE	MAR–APR–MAY–OCT–NOV–DEC
4TH	4–1–3	SUN–THU	FEB–MAR–AUG–DEC
5TH	5–6–3	WED–FRI–THU	MAR–MAY–JUN–SEP–OCT–DEC
6TH	6–3–9	FRI–THU–TUE	MAR–APR–MAY–OCT–NOV–DEC
7TH	7–2–3	MON–THU	MAR–MAY–JULY–OCT–DEC
8TH	8–3–6	SAT–THU–FRI	JAN–MAR–MAY–OCT–DEC
9TH	9–3–6	TUE–THU–FRI	MAR–APR–MAY–OCT–NOV–DEC
10TH	1–4–3	SUN–THU	FEB–MAR–APR–AUG–DEC
11TH	2–7–3–11	MON–THU	MAR–MAY–JULY–OCT–DEC
12TH	3–6–9	THU–FRI–TUE	MAR–APR–MAY–OCT–NOV–DEC
13TH	4–1–3	SUN—THU	FEB–MAR–AUG–DEC
14TH	5–6–3	WED–FRI–THU	MAR–MAY–JUN–SEP–OCT–DEC

Date	Lucky Numbers	Days	Months
15TH	6–3–9	FRI–THU–TUE	MAR–APR–MAY–OCT–NOV–DEC
16TH	7–2–3	MON–THU	MAR–MAY–JULY–OCT–DEC
17TH	8–3–6	SAT–THU–FRI	JAN–MAR–MAY–OCT–DEC
18TH	9–3–6	TUE–THU–FRI	MAR–APR–MAY–OCT–NOV–DEC
19TH	1–4–3	SUN–THU	FEB–MAR–APR–AUG–DEC
20TH	2–7–3	MON–THU	MAR–MAY–JULY–OCT–DEC
21ST	3–6–9	THU–FRI–TUE	MAR–APR–MAY–OCT–NOV– DEC
22ND	4–1–9–22	SUN–TUE	FEB–APR–AUG–NOV
23RD	5–9–6	WED–TUE–FRI	APR–MAY–JUN–SEP–OCT–NOV
24TH	6–9–3	FRI–TUE–THU	MAR–APR–MAY–OCT–NOV–DEC
25TH	7–2–6	MON–FRI	MAR–MAY–JULY–OCT
26TH	8–9–6	SAT–TUE–FRI	JAN–APR–MAY–OCT–NOV
27TH	9–3–6	TUE–THU–FRI	MAR–APR–MAY–OCT–NOV–DEC
28TH	1–4–9	SUN–TUE	FEB–APR–AUG–NOV
29TH	2–7–6–11	MON–FRI	MAR–MAY–JULY–OCT
30TH	3–9–6	THU–TUE–FRI	MAR–APR–MAY–OCT–NOV–DEC
31ST	4–1–9	SUN–TUE	FEB–APR–AUG–NOV

APRIL

Date	Lucky Numbers	Days	Months
1ST	1–4–9	SUN–TUE	FEB–APR–AUG–NOV
2ND	2–7–6	MON–FRI	MAR–MAY–JULY–OCT
3RD	3–9–6	THU–TUE–FRI	MAR–APR–MAY–OCT–NOV–DEC
4TH	4–1–9	SUN–TUE	FEB–APR–AUG–NOV
5TH	5–9–6	WED–TUE–FRI	APR–MAY–JUNE–SEP–OCT– NOV
6TH	6–9–3	FRI–TUE–THU	MAR–APR–MAY–OCT–NOV– DEC
7TH	7–2–6	MON–FRI	MAR–MAY–JULY–OCT
8TH	8–9–6	SAT–TUE–FRI	JAN–APR–MAY–OCT–NOV
9TH	9–3–6	TUE–THU–FRI	MAR–APR–MAY–OCT–NOV–DEC

Date	Lucky Numbers	Days	Months
10TH	1–4–9	SUN–TUE	FEB–APR–AUG–NOV
11TH	2–7–6–11	MON–FRI	MAR–MAY–JULY–OCT
12TH	3–9–6	THU–TUE–FRI	MAR–APR–MAY–OCT–NOV–DEC
13TH	4–1–9	SUN–TUE	FEB–APR–AUG–NOV
14TH	5–9–6	WED–TUE–FRI	APR–MAY–JUN–SEP–OCT–NOV
15TH	6–9–3	FRI–TUE–THU	MAR–APR–MAY–OCT–NOV–DEC
16TH	7–2–6	MON–FRI	MAR–MAY–JULY–OCT
17TH	8–9–6	SAT–TUE–FRI	JAN–APR–MAY–OCT–NOV
18TH	9–3–6	TUE–THU–FRI	MAR–APR–MAY–OCT–NOV–DEC
19TH	1–4–9	SUN–TUE	FEB–APR–AUG–NOV
20TH	2–7–6	MON–FRI	MAR–MAY–JULY–OCT
21ST	3–9–6	THU–TUE–FRI	MAR–APR–MAY–OCT–NOV– DEC
22ND	4–1–9–22	SUN–TUE	FEB–APR–AUG–NOV
23RD	5–6–9	WED–FRI–TUE	APR–MAY–JUN–SEP–OCT– NOV
24TH	6–3–9	FRI–THU–TUE	MAR–APR–MAY–OCT–NOV– DEC
25TH	7–2–6	MON–FRI	MAR–MAY–JULY–OCT
26TH	8–6–3	SAT–FRI–THU	JAN–MAR–MAY–OCT–DEC
27TH	9–6–3	TUE–FRI–THU	MAR–APR–MAY–OCT–NOV–DEC
28TH	1–4–2	SUN–MON	APR–MAY–JULY–AUG
29TH	2–7–6–11	MON–FRI	MAR–MAY–JULY–OCT
30TH	3–6–9	THU–FRI–TUE	MAR–APR–MAY–OCT–NOV–DEC

MAY

Date	Lucky Numbers	Days	Months
1ST	1–4–2	SUN–MON	FEB–APR–JULY–AUG
2ND	2–7–6	MON–FRI	MAR–MAY–JULY–OCT
3RD	3–6–9	THU–FRI–TUE	MAR–APR–MAY–OCT–NOV– DEC
4TH	4–1–2	SUN–MON	FEB–JUN–JULY–AUG
5TH	5–6–9	WED–FRI–TUE	APR–MAY–JUN–SEP–OCT–NOV
6TH	6–3–9	FRI–THU–TUE	MAR–APR–MAY–OCT–NOV–DEC

Date	Lucky Numbers	Days	Months
7TH	7–2–6	MON–FRI	MAR–MAY–JULY–OCT
8TH	8–6–3	SAT–FRI–THU	JAN–MAR–MAY–OCT–DEC
9TH	9–6–3	TUE–FRI–THU	MAR–APR–MAY–OCT–NOV– DEC
10TH	1–4–2	SUN–MON	FEB–APR–JULY–AUG
11TH	2–7–6–11	MON–FRI	MAR–MAY–JULY–OCT
12TH	3–6–9	THU–FRI–TUE	MAR–APR–MAY–OCT–NOV– DEC
13TH	4–1–2	SUN–MON	FEB–JUN–JULY–AUG
14TH	5–6–9	WED–FRI–TUE	APR–MAY–JUN–SEP–OCT–NOV
15TH	6–3–9	FRI–THU–TUE	MAR–APR–MAY–OCT–NOV–DEC
16TH	7–2–6	MON–FRI	MAR–MAY–JULY–OCT
17TH	8–6–3	SAT–FRI–THU	JAN–MAR–MAY–OCT–DEC
18TH	9–6–3	TUE–FRI–THU	MAR–APR–MAY–OCT–NOV–DEC
19TH	1–4–2	SUN–MON	FEB–APR–JULY–AUG
20TH	2–7–6	MON–FRI	MAR–MAY–JULY–OCT
21ST	3–6–5	THU–FRI–WED	MAR–MAY–JUN–SEP–OCT–DEC
22ND	4–1—5–22	SUN–WED	FEB–JUN–AUG–SEP
23RD	5–6–9	WED–FRI–TUE	APR–MAY–JUN–SEP–OCT
24TH	6–5–9	FRI–WED–TUE	APR–MAY–JUN–SEP–OCT
25TH	7–2–5	MON–WED	FEB–JUN–JULY–SEP
26TH	8–5–6	SAT–WED–FRI	JAN–MAY–JUN–SEP–OCT
27TH	9–5–6	TUE–WED–FRI	APR–MAY–JUN–SEP–OCT– NOV
28TH	1–4–5	SUN–WED	FEB–APR–JUN–APR–SEP
29TH	2–7–5–11	MON–WED	MAY–JUN–JULY–SEP–OCT
30TH	3–5–6	THU–FRI–WED	MAR–MAY–JUN–SEP–OCT–DEC
31ST	4–1–5	SUN–WED	FEB–JUN—AUG–SEP

JUNE

Date	Lucky Numbers	Days	Months
1ST	1–4–5	SUN–WED	FEB–APR–JUN–AUG–SEP
2ND	2–7–5	MON–WED	MAY–JUN–JULY–SEP–OCT

Date	Lucky Numbers	Days	Months
3RD	3–5–6	THU–FRI–WED	MAR–MAY–JUN–SEP–OCT–DEC
4TH	4–1–5	SUN–WED	FEB–JUN–AUG–SEP
5TH	5–6–9	WED–FRI–TUE	APR–MAY–JUN–SEP–OCT–NOV
6TH	6–5–9	FRI–WED–TUE	APR–MAY–JUN–SEP–OCT–NOV
7TH	7–2–5	MON–WED	FEB–JUN–JULY–SEP
8TH	8–6–5	SAT–FRI–WED	JAN–MAY–JUN–SEP–OCT
9TH	9–5–6	TUE–WED–FRI	APR–MAY–JUN–SEP–OCT–NOV
10TH	1–4–5	SUN–WED	FEB–APR–JUN–AUG–SEP
11TH	2–7–5–11	MON–WED	MAY–JUN–JULY–SEP–OCT
12TH	3–6–5	THU–FRI–WED	MAY–MAY–JUN–SEP–OCT–DEC
13TH	4–1–5	SUN–WED	FEB–JUN–AUG–SEP
14TH	5–6–9	WED–FRI–TUE	APR–MAY–JUN–SEP–OCT–NOV
15TH	6–5–9	FRI–WED–TUE	APR–MAY–JUN—SEP–OCT–NOV
16TH	7–2–5	MON–WED	FEB–JUN–JULY–SEP
17TH	8–6–5	SAT–FRI–WED	JAN–MAY–JUN–SEP– OCT
18TH	9–5–6	TUE–WED–FRI	APR–MAY–JUN–SEP–OCT– NOV
19TH	1–4–5	SUN–WED	FEB–APR–JUN–AUG–SEP
20TH	2–7–5	MON–WED	MAY–JUN–JULY– SEP–OCT
21ST	3–6–5	THU–FRI–WED	MAR–MAY–JUN–SEP–OCT–DEC
22ND	4–1–2–7–22	SUN–MON	FEB–JUN–JULY–AUG
23RD	5–2–7	WED–MON	MAY–JUN–JULY–SEP–OCT
24TH	6–2–7	FRI–MON	MAR–MAY–JULY–OCT
25TH	7–2–6	MON–FRI	MAR–MAY–JULY–OCT
26TH	8–2–7	SAT–MON	JAN–MAY–JULY–OCT
27TH	9–3–6	TUE–THU–FRI	MAR–APR–MAY–OCT–NOV–DEC
28TH	1–4–2–7	SUN–MON	FEB–JULY–AUG
29TH	2–7–6–11	MON–FRI	MAR–MAY–JULY–OCT
30TH	3–2–7	THU–MON	MAR–MAY–JULY–OCT–DEC

JULY

Date	Lucky Numbers	Days	Months
1ST	1–4–2–7	SUN–MON	FEB–JULY–AUG
2ND	2–7–6	MON–FRI	MAR–MAY–JULY–OCT
3RD	3–2–7	THU–MON	MAR–MAY–JULY–OCT–DEC
4TH	4–1–2–7	SUN–MON	FEB–JUN–JULY–AUG
5TH	5–2–7	WED–MON	MAY–JUN–JULY–SEP
6TH	6–2–7	FRI–MON	MAR–MAY–JULY–OCT
7TH	7–2–6	MON–FRI	MAR–MAY–JULY–OCT
8TH	8–2–7	SAT–MON	JAN–MAY–JULY–OCT
9TH	9–3–6	TUE–THU–FRI	MAR–APR–MAY–OCT–NOV–DEC
10TH	1–4–2–7	SUN–MON	FEB–JULY–AUG
11TH	2–7–6–11	MON–FRI	MAR–MAY–JULY–OCT
12TH	3–2–7	THU–MON	MAR–MAY–JULY–OCT–DEC
13TH	4–1–2–7	SUN–MON	FEB–JUN–JULY–AUG
14TH	5–2–7	WED–MON	MAY–JUN–JULY–SEP
15TH	6–2–7	FRI–MON	MAR–MAY–JULY–OCT
16TH	7–2–6	MON–FRI	MAR–MAY–JULY–OCT
17TH	8–2–7	SAT–MON	JAN–MAY–JULY–OCT
18TH	9–3–6	TUE–THU–FRI	MAR–APR–MAY–OCT–NOV–DEC
19TH	1–4–2–7	SUN–MON	FEB–JULY–AUG
20TH	2–7–6	MON–FRI	MAR–MAY–JULY–OCT
21ST	3–2–7	THU–MON	MAR–MAY–JULY–OCT–DEC
22ND	4–1–5–22	SUN–WED	FEB–JUN–AUG–SEP
23RD	5–1–4	WED–SUN	FEB–JUN–AUG–SEP
24TH	6–2–7	FRI–MON	MAR–MAY–JULY–OCT
25TH	7–2–1–4	MON–SUN	MAR–JULY–AUG
26TH	8–1–4	SAT–SUN	JAN–FEB–JULY–AUG
27TH	9–1–4	TUE–SUN	FEB–APR–AUG–NOV
28TH	1–4–9	SUN–TUE	FEB–APR–AUG–NOV
29TH	2–7–1–4–11	MON–SUN	FEB–JULY–AUG
30TH	3–1–4	THU–SUN	FEB–MAR–AUG–DEC
31ST	4–1–5	SUN–WED	FEB–JUN–AUG–SEP

AUGUST

Date	Lucky Numbers	Days	Months
1ST	1–4–9	SUN–TUE	FEB–APR–AUG–NOV
2ND	2–7–1–4	MON–SUN	FEB–JULY–AUG

Date	Lucky Numbers	Days	Months
3RD	3–1–4	THU–SUN	FEB–MAR–AUG–DEC
4TH	4–1–5	SUN–WED	FEB–JUN–AUG–SEP
5TH	5–1–4	WED–SUN	FEB–JUN–AUG–SEP
6TH	6–2–7	FRI–MON	MAR–MAY–JULY–OCT
7TH	7–2–1–4	MON–SUN	FEB–MAR–JULY–AUG
8TH	8–1–4	SAT–SUN	JAN–FEB–JULY–AUG
9TH	9–1–4	TUE–SUN	FEB–APR–AUG–NOV
10TH	1–4–9	SUN–TUE	FEB–APR–AUG–NOV
11TH	2–7–1–4–11	MON–SUN	FEB–JULY–AUG
12TH	3–1–4	THU–SUN	FEB–MAR–AUG–DEC
13TH	4–1–5	SUN–WED	FEB–JUN–AUG–SEP
14TH	5–1–4	WED–SUN	FEB–JUN–AUG–SEP
15TH	6–2–7	FRI–MON	MAR–MAY–JULY–OCT
16TH	7–2–1–4	MON–SUN	FEB–MAR–JULY–AUG
17TH	8–1–4	SAT–SUN	JAN–FEB–JULY–AUG
18TH	9–1–4	TUE–SUN	FEB–APR–AUG–NOV
19TH	1–4–9	SUN–TUE	FEB–APR–AUG–NOV
20TH	2–7–1–4	MON–SUN	FEB–JULY–AUG
21ST	3–1–4	THU–SUN	FEB–MAR–AUG–DEC
22ND	4–1–5–22	SUN–WED	FEB–JUN–AUG–SEP
23RD	5–6–9	WED–FRI	APR–MAY–JUN–SEP–OCT–NOV
24TH	6–5–2	FRI–WED–MON	MAY–JUN–JULY–SEP–OCT
25TH	7–2–5	MON–WED	MAY–JUN–JULY–SEP–OCT
26TH	8–6–5	SAT–FRI–WED	JAN–MAY–JUN–SEP–OCT
27TH	9–5–6	TUE–WED–FRI	APR–MAY–JUN–SEP–OCT–NOV
28TH	1–4–5	SUN–WED	APR–JUN–AUG–SEP
29TH	2–7–5–11	MON–WED	MAY–JUN–JULY–SEP–OCT
30TH	3–6–5	THU–FRI–WED	MAR–MAY–JUN–SEP–OCT–DEC
31ST	4–1–5	SUN–WED	FEB–JUN–AUG–SEP

SEPTEMBER

Date	Lucky Numbers	Days	Months
1ST	1–4–5	SUN–WED	APR–JUN–AUG–SEP
2ND	2–7–5	MON–WED	MAY–JUN–JULY–SEP
3RD	3–6–5	THU–FRI	MAR–MAY–JUN–SEP–OCT–DEC

Date	Lucky Numbers	Days	Months
4TH	4–1–5	SUN–WED	FEB–JUN–AUG–SEP
5TH	5–6–9	WED–FRI–TUE	MAY–JUN–SEPT–OCT
6TH	6–5–9	FRI–WED–TUE	MAY–JUN–SEPT–OCT
7TH	7–2–5	MON–WED	MAY–JUN–JULY–SEP–OCT
8TH	8–6–5	SAT–FRI–WED	JAN–MAY–JUN–SEP–OCT
9TH	9–5–6	TUE–WED–FRI	APR–MAY–JUN–SEP–OCT–NOV
10TH	1–4–5	SUN–WED	APR–JUN–AUG–SEP
11TH	2–7–5–11	MON–WED	MAY–JUN–JULY–SEP
12TH	3–6–5	THU–FRI	MAR–MAY–JUN–SEP–OCT–DEC
13TH	4–1–5	SUN–WED	FEB–JUN–AUG–SEP
14TH	5–6–9	WED–FRI–TUE	MAY–JUN–SEP–OCT
15TH	6–5–9	FRI–WED–TUE	MAY–JUN–SEP–OCT
16TH	7–2–5	MON–WED	MAY–JUN–JULY–SEP–OCT
17TH	8–6–5	SAT–FRI–WED	JAN–MAY–JUN–SEPT–OCT
18TH	9–5–6	TUE–WED–FRI	APR–MAY–JUN–SEP–OCT–NOV
19TH	1–4–5	SUN–WED	APR–JUN–AUG—SEP
20TH	2–7–5	MON–WED	MAY–JUN–JULY–SEP
21ST	3–6–5	THU–FRI	MAR–MAY–JUN–SEP–OCT–DEC
22ND	4–1–5–22	SUN–WED	FEB–JUN–AUG–SEP
23RD	5–6–9	WED–FRI–TUE	MAY–JUN–SEP–OCT
24TH	6–3–9	FRI–THU–TUE	MAR–APR–MAY–OCT–NOV–DEC
25TH	7–2–6	MON–FRI	MAR–MAY–JULY–OCT
26TH	8–6–3	SAT–FRI–THU	JAN–MAR–MAY–OCT–DEC
27TH	9–6–3	TUE–FRI–THU	MAR–APR–MAY–OCT–NOV–DEC
28TH	1–4–2	SUN–MON	APR–JULY–AUG
29TH	2–7–6–11	MON–FRI	MAR–MAY–JULY–OCT–DEC
30TH	3–6–9	THU–FRI–TUE	MAR–APR–MAY—OCT–NOV–DEC

OCTOBER

Date	Lucky Numbers	Days	Months
1ST	1–4–2	SUN–MON	APR–JULY–AUG
2ND	2–7–6	MON–FRI	MAR–MAY–JULY–OCT–DEC
3RD	3–6–9	THU–FRI–TUE	MAR–APR–MAY–OCT–NOV–DEC
4TH	4–1–2	SUN–MON	FEB–JUN–JULY–AUG
5TH	5–6–9	WED–FRI–TUE	MAY–JUN–SEP–OCT
6TH	6–3–9	FRI–THU–TUE	MAR–APR–MAY–OCT–NOV–DEC
7TH	7–2–6	MON–FRI	MAR–MAY–JULY–OCT
8TH	8–6–3	SAT–FRI–THU	JAN–MAR–MAY–OCT–DEC
9TH	9–6–3	TUE–FRI–THU	MAR–APR–MAY–OCT–NOV– DEC
10TH	1–4–2	SUN–MON	APR–JULY–AUG
11TH	2–7–6–11	MON–FRI	MAR–MAY–JULY–OCT–DEC
12TH	3–6–9	THU–FRI–TUE	MAR–APR–MAY–OCT–NOV–DEC
13TH	4–1–2	SUN–MON	FEB–JUN–JULY–AUG
14TH	5–6–9	WED–FRI–TUE	MAY–JUN–SEP–OCT
15TH	6–3–9	FRI–THU–TUE	MAR–APR–MAY–OCT–NOV–DEC
16TH	7–2–6	MON–FRI	MAR–MAY–JULY–OCT
17TH	8–6–3	SAT–FRI–THU	JAN–MAR–MAY–OCT–DEC
18TH	9–6–3	TUE–FRI–THU	MAR–APR–MAY–OCT–NOV–DEC
19TH	1–4–2	SUN–MON	APR–JULY–AUG
20TH	2–7–6	MON–FRI	MAR–MAY–JULY–OCT–DEC
21ST	3–6–9	THU–FRI–TUE	MAR–APR–MAY–OCT–NOV– DEC
22ND	4–1–9–22	SUN–TUE	FEB–APR–JUN–AUG–NOV
23RD	5–9–6	WED–TUE–FRI	APR–MAY–JUN–SEP–OCT– NOV
24TH	6–9–3	FRI–TUE–THU	MAR–APR–MAY–OCT–NOV– DEC
25TH	7–2–6	MON–FRI	MAR–MAY–JULY–OCT
26TH	8–9–6	SAT–TUE–FRI	JAN–APR–MAY–OCT–NOV
27TH	9–3–6	TUE–THU–FRI	MAR–APR–MAY–OCT–NOV–DEC

Date	Lucky Numbers	Days	Months
28TH	1–4–9	SUN–TUE	APR–AUG–NOV
29TH	2–7–6–11	MON–FRI	MAR–MAY–JULY–OCT–DEC
30TH	3–9–6	THU–TUE–FRI	MAR–APR–MAY–OCT–NOV–DEC
31ST	4–1–9	SUN–TUE	FEB–APR–JUN–AUG–NOV

NOVEMBER

Date	Lucky Numbers	Days	Months
1ST	1–4–9	SUN–TUE	APR–AUG–NOV
2ND	2–7–6	MON–FRI	MAR–MAY–JULY–OCT–DEC
3RD	3–9–6	THU–TUE–FRI	MAR–APR–MAY–OCT–NOV–DEC
4TH	4–1–9	SUN–TUE	FEB–APR–JUN–AUG–NOV
5TH	5–9–6	WED–TUE–FRI	APR–MAY–JUN–SEP–OCT– NOV
6TH	6–9–3	FRI–TUE–THU	MAR–APR–MAY–OCT–NOV– DEC
7TH	7–2–6	MON–FRI	MAR–MAY–JULY–OCT
8TH	8–9–6	SAT–TUE–FRI	JAN–APR–MAY–OCT–NOV
9TH	9–3–6	TUE–THU–FRI	MAR–APR–MAY–OCT–NOV–DEC
10TH	1–4–9	SUN–TUE	APR–AUG–NOV
11TH	2–7–6–11	MON–FRI	MAR–MAY–JULY–OCT–DEC
12TH	3–9–6	THU–TUE–FRI	MAR–APR–MAY–OCT–NOV– DEC
13TH	4–1–9	SUN–TUE	FEB–APR–JUN–AUG–NOV
14TH	5–9–6	WED–TUE–FRI	APR–MAY–JUN–SEP–OCT– NOV
15TH	6–9–3	FRI–TUE–THU	MAR–APR–MAY–OCT–NOV– DEC
16TH	7–2–6	MON–FRI	MAR–MAY–JULY–OCT
17TH	8–9–6	SAT–TUE–FRI	JAN–APR–MAY–OCT–NOV
18TH	9–3–6	TUE–THU–FRI	MAR–APR–MAY–OCT–NOV–DEC
19TH	1–4–9	SUN–TUE	APR–AUG–NOV
20TH	2–7–6	MON–FRI	MAR–MAY–JULY–OCT–DEC

Date	Lucky Numbers	Days	Months
21ST	3–9–6	THU–TUE–FRI	MAR–APR–MAY–OCT– NOV–DEC
22ND	4–1–3–22	SUN–THU	FEB–MAR–AUG–DEC
23RD	5–6–3	WED–FRI– THU	MAR–MAY–JUN–SEP– OCT–DEC
24TH	6–3–9	FRI–THU–TUE	MAR–APR–MAY–OCT– NOV– DEC
25TH	7–2–3	MON–THU	MAR–MAY–JULY–OCT– DEC
26TH	8–3–6	SAT–THU–FRI	JAN–MAR–MAY–OCT– DEC
27TH	9–3–6	TUE–THU–FRI	MAR–APR–MAY–OCT– NOV–DEC
28TH	1–4–3	SUN–THU	MAR–APR–AUG–DEC
29TH	2–7–3–11	MON–THU	MAR–MAY–JULY–OCT– DEC
30TH	3–6–9	THU–FRI–TUE	MAR–APR–MAY–OCT– NOV– DEC

DECEMBER

Date	Lucky Numbers	Days	Months
1ST	1–4–3	SUN–THU	MAR–APR–AUG–DEC
2ND	2–7–3	MON–THU	MAR–MAY–JULY–OCT– DEC
3RD	3–6–9	THU–FRI–TUE	MAR–APR–MAY–OCT– NOV– DEC
4TH	4–1–3	SUN–THU	FEB–MAR–AUG–DEC
5TH	5–6–3	WED–FRI– THU	MAR–MAY–JUNE–SEP– OCT– DEC
6TH	6–3–9	FRI–THU–TUE	MAR–APR–MAY–OCT– NOV– DEC
7TH	7–2–3	MON–THU	MAR–MAY–JULY–OCT– DEC
8TH	8–3–6	SAT–THU–FRI	JAN–MAR–MAY–OCT– DEC
9TH	9–3–6	TUE–THU–FRI	MAR–APR–MAY–OCT– NOV–DEC
10TH	1–4–3	SUN–THU	MAR–APR–AUG–DEC
11TH	2–7–3–11	MON–THU	MAR–MAY–JULY–OCT– DEC
12TH	3–6–9	THU–FRI–TUE	MAR–APR–MAY–OCT– NOV– DEC

Date	Lucky Numbers	Days	Months
13TH	4–1–3	SUN–THU	FEB–MAR–AUG–DEC
14TH	5–6–3	WED–FRI–THU	MAR–MAY–JUN–SEP–OCT–DEC
15TH	6–3–9	FRI–THU–TUE	MAR–APR–MAY–OCT–NOV–DEC
16TH	7–2–3	MON–THU	MAR–MAY–JULY–OCT–DEC
17TH	8–3–6	SAT–THU–FRI	JAN–MAR–MAY–OCT–DEC
18TH	9–3–6	TUE–THU–FRI	MAR–APR–MAY–OCT–NOV–DEC
19TH	1–4–3	SUN–THU	MAR–APR–AUG–DEC
20TH	2–7–3	MON–THU	MAR–MAY–JULY–OCT–DEC
21ST	3–6–9	THU–FRI–TUE	MAR–APR–MAY–OCT–NOV–DEC
22ND	4–1–8–22	SUN–SAT	JAN–FEB–JULY–AUG
23RD	5–6–8	WED–FRI–SAT	JAN–MAY–JUNE–SEP–OCT
24TH	6–8–3	FRI–SAT–THU	JAN–MAR–MAY–OCT–DEC
25TH	7–2–8	MON–SAT	JAN–MAR–MAY–JULY–OCT
26TH	8–6–3	SAT–FRI–THU	JAN—MAR–MAY–OCT–DEC
27TH	9–8–6	TUE–SAT–FRI	JAN–APR–MAY–OCT–NOV—DEC
28TH	1–4–8	SUN–SAT	JAN–APR–JULY–AUG
29TH	7–2–8–11	MON–SAT	JAN–MAY–JULY–OCT
30TH	3–8–6	THU–SAT–FRI	JAN–MAR–MAY–OCT–DEC
31ST	4–1–8	SUN–SAT	JAN–FEB–JULY–AUG

What Does It Take to Be a Winner?

Beyond analyzing the outcome of a lottery, what does it take to become a lottery winner? Is it just plain luck, or are there some numerological and astrological clues? Ken Dickkerson, an occult colleague, and I made some interesting observations. For instance, the birth number of 6 tops the list of money-makers in this country. The number 6 also rules the sign of Taurus. Ken and I found that people born under Taurus won the lottery more frequently. The other Earth signs—Virgo and Capricorn—came in second and third.

Numerologically, I noticed that those with birth dates adding up to 1 did equally well. So, if you are a Taurus and a number 1 person, your chances of winning are greatly increased. In our random survey, the biggest winner was Felipe Hassell, with $11 million. He was born May 1, 1939—a Taurus and number 1 person.

Another observation we made was that a high percentage of lottery winners won their good fortune on a date in which the Sun sign was compatible with their own. For instance, Joseph Urban, an Aquarius, won his $1.7 million in his own sign. Another winner, Andrew Tegerides, born under the Fire sign of Sagittarius, won his $5 million biggie in the Fire sign of Leo. When doing the biorhythm charts of the winners, at least two of their three cycles were above the critical line. (See "Numerology and Biorhythms" and "Biorhythms in Action" for further details.

Is There a Winning System?

Is there a sure-fire system for winning the lottery? Not a hundred percent, but there are numerous systems that attempt to narrow the odds. Gail Howard, for example, won the lottery 72 times within one year—an incredible feat when you consider the odds. The editor of *Gambling Times*, Ms. Howard developed the "Wheeling System." Making use of her Wall Street background as a stockbroker, she applied business rules to lottery and the rest is history. Her Wheeling System seems to narrow the odds considerably if played consistently.

Kenneth Dickkerson, who has also done research in this area, found that when at least two biorhythm cycles were above the critical line, a person's chances of winning were greatly increased. Ken noticed that the physical cycle, which he also calls the "money cycle," produced the best outcome. His observations have given him promising results.

Tips for Winning

- Have the right attitude, and play within your means.
- Play when you're in your best cycle:

  —Play during those parts of the year that are compatible with your Sun sign.
  —Play when your biorhythm cycles—especially the physical one—are high.
  —Try to discover a winning lottery pattern in your state. You'll be surprised at the outcome.

Gambling and Horse Racing

How many of you gamble? Perhaps all of us at some time in our lives take one gamble or another. Gambling in all forms is at an all-time high today. There's lotto, bingo, sweepstakes, contests, lotteries, and "the numbers." Now the Nevada casinos are moving east to Atlantic City.

Some people have extremely good luck gambling, others are flops. Gambling, like anything else, should be kept within reason and done with a cool head—easier said than done. Almost always, the serious or long-term gambler loses in the end because the odds will always be in favor of the house.

Since there are different types of gambling, it's understandable that one person may have good luck at horse racing, while another does better at cards, or with sports contests.

To find the type of gambling where you may have some degree of luck, turn to your date of birth. A person born on May 23rd would be ruled by the number 5 $(2+3=5)$, and would do better in one of the forms of gambling listed in the number 5 section below.

Finally, you shouldn't look on gambling as a livelihood unless you have lots of money to spend—and to LOSE.

Your Lucky Bet

NUMBER 1 PERSON

Those born on the 1st, 10th, 19th, and 28th, or in April and August, usually make good gamblers in either business, speculation, or contests. As long as 1 persons avoid carelessness in speculation, they can have good streaks of fortune. While all competitive contests give the 1 person the edge, racing contests of all kinds should be avoided. Number 1 persons usually do not like to lose.

NUMBER 2 PERSON

Those born on the 2nd, 11th, 20th or 29th, or in May and July, would do well betting on the "favorites" instead of the "outsiders." Yacht races, crossword competitions, spelling bees, and bingo games are usually the best areas for number 2 persons. They have a much better chance with all contests requiring patience, detail, and intuitive feelings to win.

NUMBER 3 PERSON

Those born on the 3rd, 12th, 21st, or 30th, or in March and December, as a rule do best gambling in all fashionable and regal contests such as horse racing, yacht racing, tennis, and golf contests. Because 3 persons take excessive pride in what they do in games of chance, they should try not to be sore losers in contests, or avoid gambling entirely.

NUMBER 4 PERSON

Those born on the 4th, 13th, 22nd, or 31st, or in February and August, aren't usually lucky with gambling in any form. If the 4 person must gamble, then "outsiders" are basically the best choice to put your money on. Mechanical games of all forms. such as one-armed bandit machines, should be the next choice. Of all the numbers, the 4 person should never depend on gambling alone.

NUMBER 5 PERSON

Those born on the 5th, 14th, or 23rd, or in June and September, usually have the best luck of any of the other numbers, especially those born on the 23rd of the month. Racing of all kinds, the roulette wheel, dice, cards, games of wit, you name it, all come under the 5 domain. The 5 person, if anything, must avoid becoming addicted to gambling, as the 5 naturally takes chances.

NUMBER 6 PERSON

Those born on the 6th, 15th, or 24th, or in May and October, do well with all Earth-related contests such as horse racing, dog racing, trotters and the like. The 6 person, like the 5, is considered lucky when it comes to gambling and games of chance. However, if your lucky streak hits a bad spell—stop right away!

NUMBER 7 PERSON

Those born on the 7th, 16th, or 25th, or in March and July should take the intuitive approach if they must gamble. Choose "favorites," as opposed to "outsiders." The nature the 7 is not really to speculate, but to seek inner truth and wisdom. Contests of an analytical nature, like crosswords, math or science contests and the like, will bring greater fortune to the 7 person.

NUMBER 8 PERSON

Those born on the 8th, 17th, or 26th, or in January and October, as a rule should not gamble at all! Hard work, struggle, and effort is usually the game of life for the 8 person. If you must gamble choose contests where the odds are not too high. Choose Earth-related sports such as football, horse racing, or boxing. Your best gamble, however, is to save all the money you can.

NUMBER 9 PERSON

Those born on the 9th, 18th, or 27th, or those born in April and November, do well in all competitive contests such as wrestling, football, cock fights, bull fights, cards, roulette, and field sports. Even when 9 persons hit a run of bad luck, they usually make up for it with forceful successes.

Numerology and Horse Racing

How do you handicap horse races? Do you play by hunch, or do you work from a racing form using past performance as a guide? Whatever your method, Numerologists have come up with various formulas for determining possible winners. An Indian Numerologist from the East, for instance, feels that the Moon, along with other key planets and their movements in the heavens, greatly determines the winning outcome. Another Numerologist uses a system that combines the number of a horse's name with other factors to find winners. Finally, there is a system that uses one's own date of birth as a factor to make an easy determination of possible winners.

The system of using the date of birth is the simplest of all the other techniques in Numerology and horse racing. Other systems require more study, skill, and astrological knowledge before you can put them into practice. However, by using your birth date number, and following a few basic rules, the chances of decreasing the odds against you are maximized, which increases your chances for a possible win. This system is credited mainly to the late Cheiro, the master occultist, and it basically goes like this:

- Select a day to go to the races that's in accord with your own birth number.

- If you can, find out if there's a jockey whose date of birth matches your own and the number of the day.
- See if the jockey's birth number matches the racing numbers of any of the horses that jockey will be riding.

Let's look at a complete example. Say you were born on the 15th of the month $(1+5=6)$. Choose Friday for a day at the track since it rules the number 6, especially if the 6th, 15th, or 24th should fall on a Friday. Next, go to the races in person—this is a must in the Cheiro system. Now, if you can, find out the birth number of any jockey's that matches your own (in this case, any birth number adding up to 6). Finally, see if that particular jockey will ride horses during the day's races running under that number. Winning bets on first, second, or third places will likely be the outcome before the day is out. If you try this system, write and let us know your results.

Best Days to Play the Horses

NUMBER 1 PERSON

Those born on the 1st, 10th, 19th, and 28th, or in April and August, should choose Sunday or Tuesday for a day at the races, especially on dates adding up to the number 1.

NUMBER 2 PERSON

Those born on the 2nd, 11th, 20th, or 29th, or in May and July, should choose Monday or Friday to try their luck at handicapping, especially on dates adding up to the number 2.

NUMBER 3 PERSON

Those born on the 3rd, 12th, 21st, or 30th of the month, or in March and December, choose Thursday or Friday for handicapping especially on dates adding up to the number 3.

NUMBER 4 PERSON

Those born on the 4th, 13th, 22nd, or 31st, or in February, June, or August, should select Sunday or Wednesday for horse racing, especially on dates adding up to the number 4.

NUMBER 5 PERSON

Those born on the 5th, 14th, or 23rd, or in June or September, pick Wednesday or Friday for handicapping, especially on dates adding up to the number 5.

NUMBER 6 PERSON

Those born on the 6th, 15th, or 24th, or in May or October, should try Friday or Thursday as their day at the races, especially on dates adding up to the number 6.

NUMBER 7 PERSON

Those born on the 7th, 16th, or 25th, or in March or July, choose Monday or Sunday for horse racing, especially on dates adding up to the number 7.

NUMBER 8 PERSON

Those born on the 8th, 17th, or 26th, or in January or October, look to Saturday or Thursday for horse racing, especially on dates adding up to the number 8.

NUMBER 9 PERSON

Those born on the 9th, 18th, or 27th, or in April or November, try your luck at the races on Tuesday or Thursday, especially on dates adding up to the number 9.

Remember, no method is really foolproof, given the laws of chance. Therefore, don't look at this as a system for making a quick buck, but rather for fun and entertainment.

VII.

Numerology in History and Events

In the Beginning . . .

During my years of study in Numerology, I've received many calls and letters concerning the ethics of this occult subject. In some instances, I've been informed by certain students of religion that Numerology is "the Devil's work." Or that it's "leading people away from God." I find this rather ironic, for on the one hand, we understand the rhythm and reasons for planting, harvesting, and taking our produce to market. The Farmer's Almanac will advise you of the best times to plant certain crops, raise certain livestock, and a host of other things. If man is made in God's image, and we're the highest form of life in the animal kingdom, it's no mystery that we too must have our seasons.

I've found that, no matter what your religious belief, Numerology does not interfere. Whether your religious text is the Bible, the Koran, the Talmud, or other religious teachings, these holy works all speak in number symbology. The Bible, the world's best-selling book, is literally and symbolically filled with numbers all through its ancient and prophetic scriptures.

There are numerous examples, but I'll discuss just a few. One of the most profound uses of numbers in the Bible begins in the Old Testament, in the Fourth Book of Moses, entitled NUMBERS. In chapter 1, verses 1 and 2, God commanded Moses:

On the first [1] day of the second month [2], in the second [2] year after they were come out of the land of Egypt, saying, Take ye the sum of all the congregation of the children of Israel, after their families, by the house of their fathers, with the number of their names, every male by their polls.

The first two verses alone showed the importance and timing God placed in numbers. Moses was then further instructed by God in the same chapter, verse 3:

From twenty years [20] old and upward, all that are able to go forth to war in Israel: thou and Aaron shall number them by their armies [referring to the twelve tribes].

Finally, verses 18 and 19, chapter 1:

and they assembled all the congregation together on the first [1] day of the second [2] month, and they declared their pedigrees ... according to the number of the names, from twenty [20] years old and upward, by their polls.
As the LORD commanded Moses, so he numbered them in the wilderness of Sinai.

The balance of the verses in Chapter 1 of Numbers, as well as other chapters and verses, go into other number instructions, including naming the twelve tribes of Israel and the numbers assigned to them.
An often misunderstood numerical symbology comes from the New Testament. In Revelation, chapter 13, verse 18:

Here is wisdom. Let him that hath understanding count the number of the beast: for it is the number of a man, and his number is six hundred threescore and six [666].

For centuries, this 666 reference to the beast was a mystery to the masses. When adding 6+6+6 you get 18;

$1+8=9$; and 9 is the highest level one can attain. It represents completion, culmination, fulfillment of dreams, also the 9 planets in our solar system, the 9 months from conception to birth, and a 360 degree circle $(3+6=9)$. The 9 also represents all of humankind—the Universal Man. The 9 is assigned to the planet Mars, and denotes force, combat aggressiveness, and energy. It is strongly associated with guns, knives, explosions, warlike activity, military dominion, and fire. Would this explain humanity's warlike destructiveness, where life becomes incredibly cheap and worthless? Humans have a long history of war (mostly waged in the name of religion) and destruction, as seen in today's Middle East crisis and elsewhere.

Students of the Bible and the occult know that Jesus Christ symbolically carried the fateful numbers of 888. These 8s added together equal 24; $2+4=6$. The number 6 is ruled by Venus, the planet of Love. Was love not Christ's mission? There are other examples too numerous to name. Investigate them for yourself, and be open-minded about what you discover.

Friday the 13th

Do you have "triskaidekaphobia"— fear of the number 13? Even though we're at the door of the 21st century, the number 13, especially Friday the 13th, still tops the list of superstitions. It's been estimated that, in this country alone, this phobia costs U.S. business a little over $700 million dollars a year in absenteeism. Believe it or not, there are even those who take off work on the 13th day of the month.

If you've had a fear of the number 13, you're not alone. President Franklin D. Roosevelt feared the number 13. According to his secretary, Grace Tully, in her book *F.D.R., My Boss*, President Roosevelt would have her seated at the dinner table at the last minute if there were 13 present. In fact, it was under his administration that the official presidential swearing-in ceremony was changed from March 4th (13; $1+3=4$) to January 20th.

Then there was the case of the Apollo 13. This Apollo moon mission was launched on the 13th minute of the 13th hour, from launch pad 39 (3 divided into 39 is 13), and on the 13th of April (the 4th month: $1+3=4$). An explosion on board forced the Apollo mission and her crew to limp back to Earth, barely making the return trip. When Britain's Princess Margaret was born on August 21, 1930, the royal family waited to officially regis-

ter her birth for days after the event—after another baby
was given the birth registry number 13. But if you look at
1930, the year of Princess Margaret's birth, it still adds
up to 13. In fact the shortest rule by a British monarch
lasted only 13 days, when Lady Jane Gray was ousted by
Mary Tudor. The year in which this occurred was 1553,
which also adds up to 13). At Geneva's International
Airport, the 24-hour clock is missing the number
13—12A is in its place instead.

Then there's the case of Proctor & Gamble and the
number 13. This major corporation has the symbol of a
quarter moon and 13 stars on all of its consumer products. Each year this company receives thousands of calls
accusing them of Devil worship or Satanic influences. It
recently got so bad that an executive officer of the corporation appeared on prime time TV news to inform the
public that this was not true. There are other examples,
but ironically, every person I've met who was born on
13th of any month, has felt lucky, not unlucky.

Of all the 13 superstitions, Friday the 13th sticks out
the most. Perhaps the logic of Numerology, with the help
of Astrology, can shed some light on the subject. Each
individual number has a nature and character all its own.
Some numbers will harmonize when they come together,
and others won't. For example, the nature of the 4, when
in the presence of a number 6, is not considered harmonious. Long ago, numbers were assigned to each day of
the week. The 6 has universally been assigned to Friday,
the 4 to Sunday. If you add up 13, you get the single digit
of 4 $(1+3=4)$. Therefore, you have the combination of
the 4 and 6 coming together, in this case on Friday the
13th.

Whenever the 4 or any of its series, such as the 13th,
22nd, or 31st of the month, falls on a Friday, strange and
tragic events can and usually do occur. Consider the following examples.

- President Abraham Lincoln was assassinated on a Friday in the 4th month, April in 1865.

- President Kennedy was assassinated on Friday, November 22nd, (2 + 2 = 4) 1963. Ironically, the fearful word "assassination" has 13 letters.

- In Chicago, on Friday, February 4th, 1977 (1 + 9 + 7 + 7 = 24; 2 + 4 = 6), an elevated train hit another, knocking two cars to the street, killing 11 people and injuring nearly 200.

- Remember the ill-fated airlift of Vietnamese children in 1975? It crashed after takeoff on Friday, April 4th, killing 172 persons, mostly children. If you examine the month, date, and year of this tragic event, they're all 4s (4/4/1975 = 22; 2 + 2 = 4).

You can see from the above examples that when the 4 and 6 come together, tragedy may result. However it's important to understand that this is not always the rule.

Although the number 13 is given the connotation of being unlucky, it's really not. Perhaps the reason for this belief has to do with ancient symbology. Long ago, when people used picture symbols, the 13 was thought to represent death. They knew it as a picture on the Tarot Card labeled "Death," showing a skeleton with a scythe in his hands, cutting off human heads. In the late Middle Ages, people interpreted this to mean physical death, not realizing that, symbolically, it meant death to an old way of life and way of thinking—a change for the better.

The ancients described 13 as a "symbol of power, which if wrongly used, wreaks destruction upon itself." It was said that, "He who understands the number 13 will be given power and dominion." Numerically and astrologically, this makes sense. The 13 is composed of the numbers 1 and 3. The 1 represents the Sun, the giver of (life, light) and energy. The 3 represents Jupiter, the expansive, good luck planet. Both the 1 and 3 are naturally dominant and powerful, so it's easy to understand the "power and dominion" aspect.

However, when you add the 1 and 3, the sum is 4, which is ruled by Uranus, the planet of surprises and the unusual. Number 4 people are known to rebel against rules and regulations. Unconventional opinions, new schools of thought, and social questions of all kinds are governed by the 4. The United States of America seems to have understood the 13 very well—as you will see in the next chapter.

Numerology and the United States

The United States of America, born July 4, 1776, is an infant nation in terms of universal time and world history. Even so, this country has certainly attained "power and dominion," compared with most of the world, through its use of 13. One of the most important numbers to the United States is 4, derived from its day of birth. The number 4 has played a large role in this country's history and currency (see chapter on "Numerology and the Dollar Bill").

The number 13 adds up to 4 $(1+3=4)$, the root number of the U.S. Let's take a numerical look at the United States, and its use of 13, as well as 4.

The 13

- The United States began with 13 colonies.
- Its first flag has 13 stars and stripes.
- Its first Navy had 13 ships.
- The Declaration of Independence was signed at 1300 Locust Street in Philadelphia.
- Thomas Jefferson, the major architect of this historic document, was born on the 13th of April (4th month).
- There were 13 signers of the Declaration.
- The cornerstone of the first White House was laid on the 13th of October.

- The United States' Sun sign is 13 degrees Cancer.
- Its rising sign is 13 degrees Scorpio.
- The motto, "Don't Tread On Me," has 13 letters.
- "The White House" has 13 letters.
- "The Spirit of '76" has 13 letters.
- Neil Armstrong, the first man to land on the moon, has 13 letters in his name.
- The biggest tax cut to date was signed on the 13th of August by President Reagan.

The 4

- George Washington, the first U.S. President, was born on the 22nd of the month $(2+2=4)$.
- U.S. Presidents are elected every 4 years.
- The original swearing-in date of U.S. Presidents was the 4th of March.
- The present swearing-in date is January 20th (a period ruled by the 4).
- Only one President (F.D.R.) served 4 terms.
- F.D.R. was the first President to speak on TV at the 1939 World's Fair—1939 adds up to 22; $2+2=4$.
- Congress elects its members every 4 years.
- First Moon rock sample sent back to the U.S. was tagged number 10003, which adds up to 4.
- The deadline for tax returns is the 4th month of April.

There's more, but it's obvious the 13, and its root number 4, have had a major role in the development and laws of the United States.

Numerology and the Dollar Bill

In the last chapter, we saw examples of how the numbers 13 and 4 are interwoven into the fabric of United States history. The same is true for U.S. currency, for like the nation itself, the dollar has long held a position of dominance and influence all over the world.

Since the number 13 promises "power and dominion" for those who understand its esoteric meaning, it seems only logical that the United States would apply the same mystic understanding to the design and power of its currency.

Before you read any further, take out a $1.00 bill and look at the back. Let's start by looking at the eagle on the Great Seal:

- The Eagle holds 13 arrows in one claw.
- The Eagle holds an olive branch of 13 leaves and berries in the other claw.
- The shield in front of the Eagle has 13 stripes.
- There is a cluster of 13 stars above the Eagle's head.
- The motto, *"E Pluribus Unum,"* on the banner in the Eagle's mouth has 13 letters.
- Each of the Eagle's wings has 13 feathers.

Now, let's look at the pyramid on the other side of the Great Seal:

- The pyramid has 13 steps from the base to the top.
- The base angles of the pyramid measure 67 degrees ($6 + 7 = 13$).
- The motto, *"Annuit Coeptis,"* above the pyramid has 13 letters.
- President Washington, whose picture is on the front of the dollar bill, was born on the 22nd of February ($2 + 2 = 4$).
- The letters in Washington's last name add up to 40 ($4 + 0 = 4$).

Perhaps there's more if we dig deeper, but it's obvious that the numbers 4 and 13 have woven "power and dominion" into the history of the United States of America.

Lincoln–Kennedy: A Common Thread?

It's often been said that to get a glimpse of the future, we must study the past. There is a period or lapse of time between the past and future generally referred to as cycles. These cycles affect every living system, be it animal, human, or a nation. If one would take the time to look at the history of the 100-year cycle between the presidencies of Abraham Lincoln and John F. Kennedy, one would be amazed at the seemingly "coincidental" events that took place in their lives.

Since 1840, every President of the United States who was elected in a year ending in 0 has died in office. This 0 cycle has had a menacing effect on our history every twenty years. It was Numerologist, Irving Joshua Bush, better known as The Incredible Dr. Matrix, who brought this strange coincidence between the two Presidents to public attention. In December of 1963, he sent a letter to Martin Gardner, then a contributing columnist to *The Scientific American*, giving his findings. Below are the 16 salient points covered in Bush's letter, along with other remarkable incidents that later came to light from other sources:

- Lincoln was elected president in 1860; Kennedy in 1960 [M].*

*[M] = Matrix; [A] = Author's; [OS] = Other sources.

- Lincoln was 52 $(5+2=7)$ when elected. Kennedy was 43 $(4+3=7)$ [A].
- Lincoln served in the House of Representatives in 1847, Kennedy in 1947 [OS: *National Enquirer*].
- Lincoln was defeated for the vice-presidential nomination in 1856, Kennedy in 1956 [OS: *National Enquirer*].
- Lincoln was born in 1809 $(1+8+0+9=18; 1+8=9)$; Kennedy was born in 1917; $(1+9+1+7=18; 1+8=9)$; [A].
- The name of Lincoln, under the Chaldean system, adds up to 27 $(2+7=9)$; the name of Kennedy, under the Chaldean system, adds up to 27 $(2+7=9)$ [A].
- Both Lincoln and Kennedy had seven letters in their last name [M].
- Both presidents were born under Air signs (Lincoln was an Aquarius; Kennedy a Gemini [A].
- Both were deeply involved in civil rights issues [M].
- Both were assassinated on a Friday, in the presence of their wives [M].
- Both were shot and killed by a bullet that entered the skull from behind [M].
- Lincoln was killed in Ford's Theatre; Kennedy was killed in a car manufactured by Ford [M].
- Lincoln died at age 56; Kennedy died at age 46 [A].
- Both Lincoln and Kennedy were shot and killed in the "period of the 9," April and November respectively [A].
- Lincoln was shot April 14th $(4+1+4=9)$; Kennedy was shot November 22nd $(1+1+2+2=6$, the 9 upside down) [A].
- Both men were succeeded by their Vice-presidents, whose last names were Johnson. Both were southern Democrats and former Senators [M].
- Andrew Johnson was born in 1808; Lyndon Johnson was born in 1908. [MA], [A], or [OS].
- Both vice-presidents were born under Earth signs (Andrew was a Capricorn; Lyndon a Virgo) [A].
- Both Andrew Johnson and Lyndon Johnson had thirteen letters in their names [M].
- Andrew Johnson died on the 31st of the month $(3+1=4)$; Lyndon Johnson died on the 22nd of the month $(2+2=4)$ [A].

- Lincoln's assassin, John Wilkes Booth, was born in 1839; Kennedy's assassin, Lee Harvey Oswald, was born in 1939 [M].
- Both Booth and Oswald were ruled by a common planet, Venus (Booth was a Taurus; Oswald a Libra) [A].
- Both John Wilkes Booth and Lee Harvey Oswald had fifteen letters in their names [M].
- Booth shot Lincoln in a theater; Oswald was arrested in a theater [OS: *National Enquirer*].
- Both assassins were themselves shot and killed before their trials [M].
- Both Mary Lincoln and Jacqueline Kennedy could speak French [OS: *Cycles: The Mysterious Forces That Trigger Events*].
- Both women married their husbands at age 24 [A].
- Both lost a son while in the White House [M]; and both sons died of respiratory conditions [OS: *National Enquirer*].
- Robert, Lincoln's surviving son, moved to 3104 N Street in Georgetown [OS: *Cycles: The Mysterious Forces That Trigger Events*].
- John, Kennedy's surviving son, also lived at 3104 N Street in Georgetown [OS: *Cycles: The Mysterious Forces That Trigger Events*].
- Both widows politely declined all further invitations to the White House [OS: *Cycles: The Mysterious Forces That Trigger Events*].

Do you still feel these events were merely coincidences between two outstanding presidents in U.S. history?

A Presidential Chart: Ronald Reagan

In my weekly "Numbers and You" column in December of 1980, I wrote a two-part article on new President-Elect, Ronald Reagan. My interest was piqued because he, like myself, is an Aquarian. But more importantly, he had just become the fifth Aquarian President in U.S. history.

Aquarius, ruled by Uranus, has always been associated with the unique, the unusual. For example, the President to serve the shortest term in office was an Aquarian (William Henry Harrison, March 4–April 4, 1841). The President to serve the longest was an Aquarian (Roosevelt). The first President to be assassinated while in office was an Aquarian (Lincoln). And the oldest President ever elected to office? You guessed it, an Aquarian (Reagan). Another point, all the Aquarian Presidents have died in office—except Reagan.

In my 1980 column, I explained that since Ronald Wilson Reagan was born on February 6, 1911, the number 6 would be considered important in his life in some special way. Using the Chaldean system of numbers, I gave examples of the startling repetition of the number 6 in his life and career.

When he took office, there were references made to the Bible—chapter 13, verse 18, of the Book of Revelation—alluding to President Reagan as "the beast (666)".

Perhaps the reason for this was that a few years before the election, several popular movies—*The Exorcist*, *The Omen* (a trilogy), and *The Heretic*—were released. These movies concerned the Devil's being reborn in human form and his eventual rise and take-over of the White House. *The Omen* suggested the mark of 666, found at the base of his skull, would confirm his arrival. When it was noted that Ronald Wilson Reagan had 6 letters in his first, middle, and last name, there were those who really got carried away.

However, the biblical reference to 666 is to the universal man. Adding up the three 6's you get 18; $1+8=9$ —the universal number of 9. The 9 is ruled by the planet Mars and is warlike in nature. Haven't humans been warlike with one another—killing and maiming in the name of God, religion, and politics? Man himself is "the beast." When people rob and hurt each other they are beastlike. Perhaps this is why the biblical number given to Christ was 888. Adding the three 8s together, they total 24; $2+4=6$, the number of love. Was it not the purpose of Christ to teach love to us all?

Nonetheless, President Reagan, numerically speaking, is a true example of the 6. Take the following:

- He was born on the 6th of February.
- There are 6 letters in his first, middle, and last name.
- The name, President Reagan, has 15 letters—$1+5=6$.
- He was president of the Screen Actors Guild 6 times.
- He attended Eureka College, which has 6 letters in its name.
- His college football jersey was 33; $3+3=6$.
- His first child, Maureen Reagan, was born in 1941, which adds up to 15; $1+5=6$.
- The First Lady, Nancy Reagan, was born on the 6th of July.
- They married on March 4, 1952 ($3+4+1+9+5+2=24$; $2+4=6$).
- The name, Nancy, adds up to 15 under the Chaldean system ($1+5=6$).
- He was elected the 33rd ($3+3=6$) Governor of California.

- He won that election on November 6, 1966.
- His first try for the office of President was in 1968 (adds up to 24; 2 + 4 = 6).
- His second attempt in 1980 was successful, making him the oldest President ever elected to office, at age 69 (6 + 9 = 15; 1 + 5 = 6).
- He won by a landslide election on November 4, 1980 (1 + 1 + 4 + 1 + 9 + 8 + 0 = 24; 2 + 4 = 6).
- His inauguration suit cost $1500, which adds up to 6.
- One of his first presidential pledges was to upgrade the Navy to a fleet of 600 ships.
- Just 69 days (6 + 9 = 15; 1 + 5 = 6) after being sworn in as President, there was an attempted assassination on his life.
- President Reagan, on that fateful day, March 30, 1981, was going through a 6 personal day.
- The bullet wound left a 6-inch scar.
- "Rawhide" is his Secret Service code name. "Rawhide" adds up to 24 under the Chaldean system (2 + 4 = 6).
- His first trip as President outside the country was to Canada, which is a number 6 nation under the Chaldean system.
- Canada's Prime Minister at that time was Pierre Trudeau, a Libra, ruled by the number 6.
- President Reagan left for his first official vacation on the 6th of August.
- During his 6th year in office, his administration was rocked by the Irangate scandal. His 6th year in office was 1986 (adds up to 24; 2 + 4 = 6).

There are more examples of the 6 in President Reagan's life. There are also instances of the influence of the number 4, which rules his Zodiac sign of Aquarius. For instance, his first wife, Jane Wyman, was born on the 4th of January. He married his second wife, Nancy, on the 4th of March. He became the 40th President of the United States. His landslide election to the Presidency took place on the 4th of November. The lowest point in his Presidency and popularity in the nation took place in his 76th year (7 + 6 = 13; 1 + 3 = 4).

There's another point of interest about this particular

President. Starting in 1840, and every 20 years thereafter until now, Presidents elected in a year ending in 0 have died in office. Only seven Presidents to date have died in office. Incredibly, four out of the seven were Aquarians. Remember, there have only been four until President Reagan became the fifth Aquarian. What about President Reagan? Will he live out his term, thereby breaking the "Tecumseh Curse" (Tecumseh was the Native American who had a curse put on W. H. Harrison and the United States) that has been haunting this nation since 1840?

Strangely enough, of the four Aquarian Presidents to die in office, three of them died in the month of April. President Reagan nearly lost his life to an assassin's bullet just two days shy of April, if you'll remember. Of the three previous Aquarian Presidents, all won re-election, as did President Reagan (re-elected in 1984). All three died within one year after their re-election to the office.

President Reagan thus far has broken that rule. However, the pressing issue of a possible presidential scandal, coupled with age and personal health problems leading to several operations, certainly suggests that he should use the greatest of care in completing his Administration. This will make him the first Aquarian President of the United States ever to do so.

Failure of a Shuttle Mission

On Tuesday, January 28, 1986, the world was shocked and saddened by the unexpected explosion of the space shuttle *Challenger*, with her crew of seven astronauts. After the numbing effect wore off, we began to realize the magnitude of the nation's loss. Questions began to be asked about why it had happened? What went wrong? Could it have been avoided? At times, individuals, projects, even nations are given signs of warning in advance. The fact that the shuttle mission was delayed seven times, even up to the very morning of that fateful lift-off, may have been such a sign. Naturally, with hindsight, many answers are possible. However, given the laws of cycles and numbers, could further clues be possible with Numerology?

Progressed Chart of the United States

In Mundane Astrology and Numerology the events of nations and communities are the focus of attention rather than individuals. We did a progressed chart for the United States, born on July 4, 1776, known in Numerology as the personal year. We simply took the birth month and date of the nation, July 4, and added these numbers to the year we wanted information about. In this case it was 1986. When these three were added together, it gave us an 8 personal year for the United States ($7+4+1+9+8+6=35$; $3+5=8$).

Before going any further, let me lay the numerical foundation. Each of us has both positive and negative numbers that are important in some way. For example, the United States' key numbers are the $4=1$; $2=7$. This was determined from the birth number and Zodiac sign. However, it is even more important to know what the opposition numbers are in order to minimize their effects. The opposition numbers for the United States are 6, 8, and 9.

These key numbers or opposition numbers may not seem significant until you lay out the events related to them:

United States: Key Numbers and Opposition Numbers

Best Days: Sunday and Monday.

Best Dates: 1st, 2nd, 4th, 7th, 10th, 11th, 13th, 16th, 19th, 20th, 22nd, 25th, 28th, and 31st of the month.

Best Months: late January through February; late May through June; late June into July and August.

Caution Days: Friday, Saturday, Tuesday.

Caution Dates: 6th, 8th, 9th, 15th, 17th, 18th, 24th, 26th, 27th.

Caution Months: Late December through January; late March through April and May; late September through October and November.

The purpose of laying out the basic chart in this way is to discover a pattern that could be useful or preventive in nature. If the past can be used as a guidepost to the future, perhaps it would be wise to study the laws of nature, numbers, and the universe a little closer. If you look at the stress side of the United States through historical events, the pattern becomes clear.

United States: Stress Months

JANUARY

This is a stress month for the United States. Remember the plane that crashed and fell into the Potomac River just after takeoff at a Washington, D.C., airport, causing much loss of life? That happened in January. Remember the three astronauts, who were killed in a practice run on the launch pad? That occurred on Friday, January 27, 1967. Notice how the opposition day, date, and month came together? This most recent tragedy of losing seven astronauts, along with a billion dollars in equipment, took place on Tuesday, January 28, 1986. Again, an opposition day, month, and year (1986 adds up to 24; $2+4=6$) came together.

APRIL

The first President of the United States to be assassinated—Abraham Lincoln—died in this month. Two other Presidents died in this month as well—Roosevelt and Harrison. It was also in April that the ill-fated attempt to rescue the Iranian hostages met with tragic and embarrassing political results. And if you remember, after less than two months in office, President Reagan had an attempt made on his life just a day or two shy of April 1980. Dr. Martin Luther King, Jr., was also assassinated in this month. All of these events changed the course of history.

MAY

Only one United States President was born in May—Harry S Truman. It was under the Truman administration that the decision was made to drop the Atom Bomb on Japan. The actual event took place on the 6th of August, 1945. That month, day, and year add up to a 6 universal day.

OCTOBER

The stock market crash of 1929 took place in this month. In fact, it also occurred on a Tuesday—an opposition day and month coming together. President McKinley was shot in late September. Lee Harvey Oswald, the alleged assassin of President John F. Kennedy, was born on the 18th of this month—an opposition month and day.

NOVEMBER

President Kennedy was assassinated in this month, on a Friday, in Dallas—an instance of an opposition month, day, and place coming together. The Ayatollah Khomeini's factions took over the U.S. embassy in Iran in the month of November 1979.

There are many other examples. When I analyzed the seven *Challenger* astronauts' birthdays and names, almost all of them were numerically in opposition on that fateful day.

Hopefully, one day, the science of Numerology and other occult studies will be given the serious attention they deserve. It could make all the difference in the world.

Dr. Martin Luther King, Jr.: A Numerical Biography

Not long ago, the United States enacted a law establishing its tenth official holiday, this one honoring Dr. Martin Luther King, Jr., who was born on January 15, 1929. His key numbers are 6, 8, and 3, determined from the Chaldean method of Numerology. Of the three numbers, 6 is his most important. This was determined from his date of birth on the 15th of the month (1+5=6). Are these numbers really significant in his life? You be the judge:

- His first name was changed from Michael to Martin at age 6 [6].
- The name Martin has 6 letters [6].
- He enrolled in Morehouse College at the young age of 15 (1+5=6) [6].
- He completed his doctorate at age 24 (2+4=6) [6].
- He married Coretta Scott also at age 24 (2+4=6) [6].
- When he was jailed during the Montgomery Boycott, his prison number was 7089 (7+0+8+9=24; 2+4=6) [6].
- His final book, *The Trumpet of Conscience* was published in 1968 (1+9+6+8=24; 2+4=6) [6].
- 1968 was also the year of his assassination, which adds up to 6 [6].
- Reversing '68, 1986 was the year Dr. King's birthday became a national holiday.

The numbers 8 and 3 were also important in the life of Dr. Martin Luther King, Jr.

- Dr. King's original name was Michael Luther King, which contained 17 letters $(1+7=8)$ [8].
- His new first name, Martin, totals 17 $(1+7=8)$ [8].
- The sum of his entire name, Martin Luther King, adds up to the single digit of 8 [8].
- Dr. King was graduated from Morehouse College in an 8 personal year [8].
- His famous March on Washington also took place in an 8 personal year [8].
- Dr. King won the Nobel Peace Prize at age 35 $(3+5=8)$ [8].
- He was named "Man of the Year" by *Time Magazine* in an 8 personal year [8].
- He became the prime mover of the Montgomery Boycott in 1956 $(1+9+5+6=21; 2+1=3)$ [3].
- He authored his first book, *Stride Toward Freedom*, in a 3 personal year [3].
- He authored his next to last book in a 3 personal year [3].
- He was only 39 when he was killed by an assassin's bullet $(3+9=12; 1+2=3)$ [3].
- His name and deeds were recognized by a national holiday on what would have been his 57th birthday $(5+7=12; 1+2=3)$ [3].

Numbers in Human Achievements

In my newspaper columns I've often made reference to numbers and events concerning individuals and nations. But numbers in human achievements tell another story. The publishers of the *Guinness Book of Records* understand this very well. From cover to cover, each page documents outstanding achievements in various fields, and without exception, these achievements are expressed in the form of numbers.

Take the case of human achiever, Dr. Donald Thomas. Since 1978 he's been listed as a rare breed, the person who has spoken the longest time in recorded history. There have only been 8 others, plus Dr. Thomas, who have spoken longer than any other human being on this Earth.

It is my great pleasure that I happen to know Dr. Thomas personally. He used my system of numbers to break not only the record for one of the longest sermon but just recently used numbers again to break another Guinness record. This time it was for the longest after-dinner speech; it lasted 19 hours and 20 minutes.

Dr. Thomas and I have known each other since the Tree of Life days. Before his first attempt, we discussed his lucky numbers. Born on September 21, 1953, we concluded his key numbers were 3, 6, and 9. These numbers are in direct harmony with one another. What made it all the more fortunate in his case was that his name contained 12 letters; under the Chaldean system, this added up to the single digit of 3 $(1+2=3)$. Based upon this information, Dr. Thomas made his decision and the rest is history. The following is a numerical outline of Dr. Donald Thomas' two Guinness records:

FIRST GUINESS RECORD—WORLD'S LONGEST SERMON

- Dr. Thomas was born on the 21st $(2+1=3)$.
- He began his sermon on September 18th $(1+8=9)$.
- He started at 12 noon $(1+2=3)$.
- He ended his sermon 3 days later, on his birthday, September 21st $(2+1=3)$ at 9 A.M. [9].
- He was 24 years old at the time $(2+4=6)$.
- The old record was 72 hours $(7+2=9)$.
- Dr. Thomas beat the record by 21 hours $(2+1=3)$.
- He spoke for 93 hours without a stop, and only 6 people in recorded history had ever done so [3 and 6].
- His 93-hour sermon was taken from his book, *Philosophy of Divine Nutrition*, published in 1977 (adds up to 24; $2+4=6$).

SECOND GUINNESS RECORD—LONGEST AFTER-DINNER SPEECH

- Dr. Thomas began his speech on June 21st (a 6 month; $2+1=3$ day).
- The cost of the dinner was $15 $(1+5=6)$.
- The cost of the lecture was $3 (3).
- He began his speech at 6:30 that evening in the Grand Ballroom at the City College of New York $(6+3+0=9)$.
- He ended his after-dinner speech 19 hours and 20 minutes later, to become the record holder $(1+9+2+0=12; 1+2=3)$.
- As of 1986, the *Guinness Book of Records* (the year adds up to 24; $2+4=6$) lists Dr. Thomas under two categories.

Numerology and Plane Crashes

Do you fly often? Are you afraid of flying? I for one don't like to fly often, and when I do I'm always concerned about takeoffs and landings. Recently I discovered that takeoffs and landings are the most critical phases of the flights we take. After weeks of numerical research on this subject, I came up with some interesting facts. The year 1984 saw the lowest death toll in the history of aviation. Only 224 persons died in commercial air flights worldwide. Ironically, 1985 was just the reverse. In that year, aviation accidents accounted for more loss of life globally—close to 2,000 persons—than in any previous year.

Most experts in the aviation field feel that wind sheers and mechanical and/or operational errors are some of the major causes of these accidents—but is there more to it than that? Is there perhaps an occult pattern to all of this? Going back to the beginning of passenger aviation, I analyzed over 70 commercial air crashes. The results of my research—presented below as questions and answers—is not intended to discourage flying in any way, but when your life is on the line, it pays to check everything.

Question: Under what signs, months, and days do most airplane crashes occur?

Answer: The month of August, or the sign of Leo, heads the list of air crashes. In fact, the month of August recorded the highest air casualties in history.

The months of June and December, representing the signs of Gemini and Sagittarius respectively, follow close behind. Why accidents occur in these months in particular hasn't yet been determined—at least not by me—but they do represent the elements of Fire and Air.

When I focused my attention on the particular days of the week that air crashes occurred, Sunday by far led the list with fifteen. A close second was Tuesday, with fourteen. Coming neck and neck for third place were Monday and Friday with thirteen each. These four days alone accounted for over 50 percent of the accidents. It's interesting to note that Sunday and Tuesday are Fire days, just as August and December are Fire months.

Question: Which months and days account for the least number of air crashes?

Answer: Going back over the last sixty-four years in aviation, only three air crashes occurred in the month of October. And in two of the incidences, the casualties were low. Right behind October was the month of May, with only four air crashes over the sixty-four-year period. As for the safest day, the day with the lowest number of air casualties, was Thursday with only four. And what makes it more interesting is that not one of these occurred in the United States, which makes Thursday the safest day to fly in this country.

Question: Under which number or days of the month did most of the air crashes occur?

Answer: The numbers 4 and 6 tied for first place with twelve accidents each. As for the 4 series, the 4th of the month led the list, whereas only one crash took place on the 13th $(1+3=4)$. Looking at the 6 series, the 15th $(1+5=6)$ headed this fatal date list, whereas only one accident took place on the 6th of the month. The numbers 1 and 3 tied for second place. The 1st of the month led. In the 3 series, the 3rd of the month led. In fact, these four digits (4, 6, 1 and 3) accounted for over 50 percent of the accident dates.

Question: Under which numerical digit did the least number of air crashes occur?

Answer: The 8 had the lowest amount of fatal air crashes. This makes it perhaps the safest date series to take an air journey. In fact, the last number 8 date on which a fatal air occurrence took place was back in November 26th ($2+6=8$) in the year 1979 (a year that adds up to 26; $2+6=8$).

More has been observed from this research, but what all this ultimately means has yet to be determined and validated.

Numerology and Fires

F ire is perhaps the most destructive element in nature. Fires and earthquakes take turns for first place as the leading cause of heavy death tolls. Fires and explosions alone have wiped out entire communities. This was the case in Minnesota on September 1, 1984, when a forest fire burned 480 square miles, destroying a total of six towns. Most people remember the infamous Chicago Fire that occurred on Saturday, October 8, 1871. But did you know that on the very same day in another part of the country the town of Peshtigo, Wisconsin, lost 1,152 of its citizens by fire—five times as many people as were killed in Chicago Fire? In addition, over 2 billion trees were destroyed—the Chicago Fire destroyed over seventeen thousand buildings. And we all know about the recent loss of homes and natural resources by fire in California. Naturally, there are fires or explosions every day, but when they take a heavy toll on life and property, it calls for a closer investigation.

Question: In what months did most major fires and explosions occur? On what days did most of them take place?

Answer: The month of December led the list, with the month of May coming in second. Running neck and neck for third place were the months of October and No-

vember. These four months alone accounted for nearly
50 percent or more of the these occurrences. For instance, in December 1980, there was the Stouffer Inn fire
in Upstate New York that killed the key executives of a
computer company, which later folded as a result. Many
of these major disasters took place on a Saturday, closely
followed by Thursday, Wednesday, and Sunday.

Question: During which months and days did the least
number of fires and explosions occur?

Answer: January, May, and March, in that order,
headed the safer list, accounting for only seven major
fires and explosions. As to safe days, while Monday
came out on top, the days were spread pretty much
evenly across the board.

Question: What numerical influence accounted for
most fires and explosions?

Answer: Dates adding up to 1, 4, and 7 headed this
tragic list. Focusing a little closer, we saw that for dates
under the 1 series, the 1st of the month accounted for 50
percent of such accidents, whereas the 19th of the month
produced the least. In the 4 series, the 13th of the month
$(1+3=4)$ headed this list, although the 4th of the month
ranked lowest. In the 7 series, the 7th of the month accounted for over 50 percent of all fires.

Question: Under which numerical influence did the
least number of fires occur?

Answer: Dates in the 5 and 9 series produced the least
amount of tragedies by fire and explosion. In both cases,
they occurred under different dates.

Fire is certainly nothing to play with.

Numerology Tidbits from Real Life

In the preceding sections of this book, we have gone into the various forms of Numerology as it affects the individual and events. I would now like to introduce you to a new phase of the mystic art—Mundane Numerology. Mundane Numerology deals with actual events and happenings as they affect the world, nations, communities, and individuals—whether for good or bad.

One such example of Mundane Numerology involves the numbers 4 and 8. These two numbers, when strongly associated with each other in people's lives, usually warn of circumstances and events that are seemingly out of their control. Oftentimes, sudden, strange, and unexpected misfortunes come into their lives.

Son of Sam

One recent example of this plaything of fate—the relation between the 4 and 8—can be seen in the "Son of Sam" murder case. Son of Sam, better known as the "44 Caliber Killer" (whose real name was David Berkowitz), caused the biggest manhunt to date in New York City. Psychologists, psychiatrists, and, yes, even Numerologists and biorhythm experts were called into the case to determine Son of Sam's pattern of murder and mayhem, and when and where his next attack was likely to occur.

I came to the following conclusions before the actual capture of Son of Sam, as documented in my booklet, "Numerology and Its Application to Events." From the dates and events, as well as the places where the attacks occurred, I determined that the 44 Caliber Killer was probably ruled by the key numbers 4 and 8. Let's look at some instances:

- "44 Caliber Killer" (4+4=8) [8].
- The first attack was on July 29, 1976, which is ruled by the House of the 1=4 [1=4].
- The killer made 8 known attacks [8].
- Of the 8 attacks, he killed or wounded 13 people (1+3=4) [8=4].
- 4 of the 8 attacks were on days adding up to the number 4 and 8 [4=8].
- Most of the victims were attacked at places or addresses adding up to the numbes 4 and 8 [4=8].
- The last attack was on July 31 (3+1=4) [4].
- The name of his last victim, killed on July 31, adds up to the number 8 [8].
- The name, "Son of Sam," contains 8 letters [8].
- The hotline number for leads to the Son of Sam case began with the numbers 844 [8=4]).

I presented this information to my Numerology class in the summer of 1977, before the actual capture of Son of Sam that August. The following information, which continues this amazing 4=8 pattern, was documented from major New York newspapers. These clues were used to track down and arrest the killer. You be the judge of the importance of the numbers 4 and 8 in this instance:

- A $35 parking ticket (3+5=8) helped trace the killer [8].
- It was issued for parking on Bay 17 (1+7=8) Street, on the morning of July 31 (3+1=4) [8=4].
- Near fire hydrant #40 (4+0=4) [4].

- The ticket was written from the 62nd Precinct (6 + 2 = 8) [8].
- Son of Sam was captured in August (8th month) [8].
- August rules the House of the 1 = 4 [4 = 1].
- Son of Sam was arrested in front of his home at 35 (3 + 5 = 8) Pine Street (the number of the building has since been changed) [8].
- Rent on his studio apartment at 35 Pine Street was $265 a month (2 + 6 + 5 = 13; 1 + 3 = 4) [4].
- When arrested, he had $4 in his possession [4].
- Son of Sam was then taken to the 84th Precinct in Brooklyn [8 & 4].
- He was interrogated on the 13th floor of that Precinct [4].
- Son of Sam was adopted at 17 (1 + 7 = 8) months of age [8].
- He entered the Army 4 days after his 18th birthday [4].
- He became a specialist 4th Class in the Army [4].
- He previously lived with his father at 107 Loop Drive, in the Bronx, on the 17th floor [8].
- He worked at a Bronx Post Office, on the 4 p.m. to midnight shift [4].
- His salary at the Post Office was $13,000 a year [4].
- A biorhythm chart pattern on Son of Sam by a Long Island company indicated that his next likely attack, just before his capture, would have been August 13th (8th month, 4 day) [8 & 4].

And, yes, there's still more. But I think you'll get the point from the above list. This is a perfect example of how the key numbers 4 and 8 can be interwoven into the destiny of an individual to produce sudden, strange, and unexpected misfortunes.

Now, I'd like to present two more real-life examples centering around the number 4, which is also a Uranus number. It is said that the number 4, like its ruling planet, runs a fine line between genius and insanity. The 4 rules things that are of a sudden, unexpected, and mysterious nature. Moods of despondency and depression, mental disorders, and sudden and unexplainable types of illnesses and accidents, as well as suicides, are governed by this number. As a result, the mental outlook of persons influenced by the number 4 is most important.

Freddie Prinze

Let's take the case of the late comic genius, Freddie Prinze. The number 4 had its influence throughout the major events of his life and career. Unfortunately, this brilliant young man ended his life as a result of pressure and despondency. The following was documented from newspapers on the weekend of his tragic and premature death on January 28, 1977:

- Freddie Prinze was born on June 22, 1954 (2+2=4), which made him a number 4 person [4].
- There are 13 letters in the name Freddie Prinze (1+3=4) [4].
- He grew up in New York on 157th Street (1+5+7=13; 1+3=4) [4].
- He married Kathy Cochrane, whose name has 13 letters [4].
- His wife's first name, Kathy, adds up to 13 in the Chaldean system [4].
- His marriage took place in 1975 (1+9+7+5=22; 2+2=4) [4].
- He married on the 13th of September [4].
- It was his 1st marriage, and her 3rd (1+3=4) [4].
- Kathy was born on January 28th—the month of January is ruled by the number 4 [4].
- His wife filed for divorce on the 13th of December [4].
- Because of depression, and perhaps marital problems, Freddie Prinze shot himself on the morning of January 28th, around 4 a.m. [4].
- Prinze was rushed to UCLA Medical Center. The letters U C L A add up to 13 in the Chaldean system [4].
- 4 members of the family were present at the hospital [4].
- Freddie Prinze was buried on January 31st (3+1=4) [4].

- Prinze was 22 years old at the time of his death (2+2=4) [4].
- Freddie Prinze's popular TV show, "Chico and the Man," appeared on Channel 4 in New York City.

Stevie Wonder

Our next example is the musical genius, Stevie Wonder. Stevie was born on May 13 (1+3=4), 1950. His important number is calculated from his date of birth, which is the 13th. Therefore, Stevie is a number 4 person. The number 4 represents the Sun and the planet Uranus, and the Zodiac signs of Aquarius and Leo. The 4 also has the number 1 as its interchangeable number, which is always been expressed 4–1 when associated with a person's life. Here are a few examples of the number 4 in the life of Stevie Wonder:

- Stevie was born on May 13th (1+3=4), 1950 [4].
- His first successful single record was "Fingertips," which adds up to 40 [4].
- Stevie's first wife, Syreeta, was born on August 13th [4].
- Stevie was involved in a car accident that nearly took his life in August 1973. August is governed by the number 4 [4].
- The accident took place in Durham, NC. Durham adds up to 4 [4].
- Stevie has a $13 million contract with Motown [4].
- Advance sales on his album, "Songs in the Key of Life," was 1.3 million orders [4].
- In 1975 (1+9+7+5=22; 2+2=4), Stevie won 5 Grammy Awards [4].
- Also in 1975, Stevie's first child was born in April, the 4th month [4].
- Stevie's second child was born in April 1977, again the 4th month [4].
- Stevie's second wife, the mother of Aisha and Kita, is named Yolanda, which adds up to 4 [4].

Tony

The last example comes from my personal files, and it deals with the number 8. For the sake of privacy, we'll just call this 8 person "Tony." Tony is what I consider a classic example of an 8. The 8 has always played an important part in his personal and business affairs, as you'll see in a moment. Like the 4, when the number 8 is dominant in a person's life, it can carry with it sudden, strange, and unexpected misfortunes.

However, this is not always the case with an 8, I'm glad to say. This 8 person has so far proved to be an exception to the rule. I'll divide his case into two parts —personal and business.

On the personal side:

- Tony was born on July 26th $(2+6=8)$ [8].
- He married in 1970 $(1+9+7+0=17; 1+7=8)$ [8].
- The marriage took place in the month of August, the 8th calendar month; and the original wedding day was set for the 8th [8].
- He was age 26 at the time of the marriage $(2+6=8)$ [8].
- His first apartment was on a street adding up to 8 [8].
- He was involved in an auto accident that totaled his car, hospitalized his wife, yet left him without a scratch on December 7, 1978 (12/7/78 = $1+2+7+1+9+7+8=35; 3+5=8)$ [8].
- He now resides at Bert Court in Long Island, which adds up to the number 8 in Chaldean Numerology [8].

On the business side:

- His first job was at 26 Court Street $(2+6=8)$ [8].
- His present job started in January, a month that is governed by the number 8 [8].
- His company has 8 letters in its name [8].
- The real name "Tony" is known by has 8 letters [8].
- His office was located at a building numbered 880 [8].
- His first executive-level promotion came on June 22, 1978 (6/22/1978 = $6+2+2+1+9+7+8=35; 3+5=8)$ [8].

- He supervised an 8-man staff [8].
- His staff later grew to 17 (1 + 7 = 8) [8].
- At the same time he had responsibilities covering 26 states (2 + 6 = 8) [8].
- He relocated to new headquarters in a building numbered 575 (5 + 7 + 5 = 17; 1 + 7 = 8) [8].
- He received his second executive-level promotion in January, a month that is governed by the number 8, in 1979 (1 + 9 + 7 + 9 = 26; 2 + 6 = 8) [8].
- His staff grew to 35 persons (3 + 5 = 8) [8].
- His third executive-level promotion came at age 35 (3 + 5 = 8) [8].
- He turned 35 in the year 1979 (1 + 9 + 7 + 9 = 26; 2 + 6 = 8) [8].
- His new office is in room 1808 (1 + 8 + 0 + 8 = 17; 1 + 7 = 8) [8].
- His immediate vice-president has 8 letters in his last name [8].

Of course there's more, but the point of all these examples are that numbers, regardless of your station in life, have a profound influence on you. As you can see from the above examples, the key numbers of most individuals, determined from their date of birth, follow them throughout their career and lifetime.

What is your date of birth number? Has it been dominant in your life? If so, I hope it has been a good experience. It's also important to remember that whatever fate your key number might destined you for can be reprogrammed by your positive actions—if you apply the knowledge and wisdom of the wonderful science of Numerology.

Trends and Predictions

One day in the offices of the publisher, my editor, Cheryl Woodruff, suggested I do a chapter on predictions. To be honest, this is an area I try to stay out of. Yes, as a numerologist, I've made successful predictions of a Super Bowl game, three major fights, world events, even two Guinness World records (see chapter on "Numbers in Human Achievements") in which I had a part. While there have been a number of outstanding men and women since the dawn of civilization who have had the "gift" to see into the future, they're still very rare birds.

Take Nostradamus, born in the early 1500s, his predictions are still being fulfilled after hundreds of years. Then there's Cheiro, a master occultist in his own day, his skills were sought the world over by those in high places. *Cheiro's World Predictions*, written in the early 1930s, are, like Nostradamus' still coming to pass.

Another such remarkable person was Edgar Cayce, who seemed to be an average man. But upon entering deep trance, he was able not only to diagnose someone accurately by phone or letter, he could tell them what to use as a remedy. The Mayo brothers, the surgeons who founded the Mayo Clinic, also had gifts along these lines.

After long and careful thought, I would like to share with you a number of "trends" Numerically affecting us now and into the future. While the word "predictions" conjures up a feeling of looking into the future and telling in detail what's about to happen, "trends" implies a probable outcome based upon past experience. It also allows for "misses," without ignoring the overall significant message or outcome.

As we discussed in the chapter on "Numerology and the United States," the 6 is one of the opposition numbers to the nation, along with 8 and 9. Note the following examples of trends just with the number 6:

- Civil War: 1860 (= 15; 1 + 5 = 6).
- World War I: 1914 (= 15; 1 + 5 = 6).
- World War II: 1941 (notice the reversal of the last two numbers; the year adds up to 6).
- Korean War: 1950 (= 15; 1 + 5 = 6).
- The Vietnam War and the Civil Rights Movement took heavy toll on the Nation during the decade of the 1960s.

Trends for 1987

This is the year of the 7. The general trend will favor those under the sign of Cancer, Pisces, or anyone born on the 7th, 16th, but especially the 25th of the month. Since 7 is a Water element, industries related to liquids and water in some way should prosper. With Fire in opposition to a Water year, industries such as steel, automobiles, and construction are likely to be at an all-time low, especially from mid August into September. Cities and countries such as Annapolis, Brazil, Istanbul, Hollywood, Mexico, Santiago, Senegal, and Tallahassee are the ones likely to make noticeable headlines.

The year will be an opposition one for the United States. Since endings and completion lie ahead in the 9 year, this suggests that things are coming to a head. The months of February, and especially April (between the 8th through the 14th, and the 22nd through the 30th), as well as June, August, September, and November are indicated as stressful.

Trends for 1988

This is the year of the 8—the year that Nostradamus predicted a severe earthquake like no other. His poetic messages suggest that the month of May would be the time. Numerically I could agree with this, as 1988 adds up to 26; $2 + 6 = 8$, an Earth number. The month of May rules the Earth period of Taurus. Another note to add to this is that from my own personal research, almost without exception, any time a major earthquake occurred in this month, it was either on the 4th, 13th, 22nd, or 31st —every single date adding up to 4. So, if Nostradamus is right again (and let's hope he misses this time—he rarely does) and THE earthquake occurs in May, these 4 dates may offer a warning clue.

This year of the 8 will favor Capricorn, and in a minor way Libra, as well as those born on the 8th, 17th, but especially the 26th of the month. The mood of the world will be a conservative, take-no-chances attitude. Since 8 is an Earth element, industries dealing with products of the Earth (trees, minerals, mining, oil, excavations) will be more in demand. With 8 ruling real estate, we're likely to see prices for property, as well as rents and mortgages, going sky high. Places like Buffalo, Cleveland, Cuba, Gambia, Guyana, Sacramento, and Tulsa should be more in the news during '88.

The United States will be in an election year. Interestingly enough, there have only been five Presidents with a one-syllable last name (Polk, Grant, Hayes, Taft, and Ford). There has only been one Gemini President (Kennedy). Based on this alone, chances are slim that Vice-President Bush (one-syllable name and a Gemini) will be elected President of the United States, unless President Reagan were unable to serve the rest of his term.

The 8 cycle of the nation suggests that new names and faces not previously known to the general public will run for the office. The nation as whole will take bold, innovative steps, but financial debts and policies could be seriously questioned in March, April, July, and December. May suggests a concern for the health of someone high up in the Capital. August could see some explosive issues for the country if events aren't brought under control.

Trends for 1989

This is the year of the 9—a year favorable to Aries and Scorpio, or anyone born on the 9th, 18th, but especially the 27th of the month. The 9 represents the element of Fire; it is a volatile, explosive number. Therefore, outbreaks of fires are likely to dominate the news, especially during February and November. The construction, auto, and steel industries should be on the upswing again. Denver, Detroit, Philadelphia, Phoenix, Savannah, Silver Springs, and Tampa are a few of the cities likely to dominate the news in a positive way.

The United States will be passing through a period of transition between its neighbors and allies. Mass movements will flourish across the country, but they will be movements more of anger than peace. April will be especially stressful to the nation as a whole, nearly leading to a possible undeclared war. The third week of that month should be the make-or-break point for the country. Women will insist on being heard, not only in the home but in the nation as well.

Trends for 1990

This is the year of the 1, a year that may prove favorable in some way for Leo and Aries, and anyone born on the 1st, 10th, especially the 19th, and 28th of the month. The nation, and the world as a whole, will take a more assertive stand about getting things done. Politically oppressed countries will gain their independence, as well as set the tone and tenor of their new direction. Like 1989, 1 is a Fire number, bringing increasing benefits to all industries dealing with this element. Atlanta, Boston, Houston, Knoxville, and New York are just a few of the cities that should do well this year.

Numerically, the United States will be passing through the Jupiter cycle, or the number 3. As a result, the nation will find consumer spending up (especially in February and November) particularly in the area of big-ticket items. The nation should move ahead with a positive, upbeat approach to resolve whatever needs to be done. March, May, and December will challenge the country this year.

Trends for 1991

A 2 year, favoring those born under Cancer and Taurus, and those born on the 2nd, 7th, 11th, 16th, especially the 20th, the 25th, or 29th of the month. Mass movements on a global scale will be formed against our blowing ourselves out of existence. As 2 is ruled by the Water element, we may see an increase in floods, tidal waves, and heavy rains. Look for women to take the lead on the national and international stage. In this year, peace-keeping efforts will either be made or broken, especially during the months of March, July, and December. Places likely to be in the news more this year are Austin, Baltimore, Barcelona, Brooklyn, Charleston, Cincinnati, Harlem, Leningrad, Los Angeles, and Miami.

The United States will be passing through a Uranian cycle, which matches the birth number of the nation itself. This cycle also denotes the odd and unusual, the sudden and unexpected. The nation will take austere measures concerning its economy during the months of February and November. The nation will almost be forced to take a "waste not, want not" attitude. Inventions and innovative techniques should come to the fore as well. April and May will test the nation concerning possible breakups with some of her key friends and allies.

Trends for 1992

This is the year of the 3, another year of the Jupiter cycle. It will favor Pisces and Sagittarius, or anyone born on the 3rd, 12th, especially the 21st, and the 30th of the month. A 3 cycle year usually suggests generosity and expansion. As a result, consumer spending around the world should increase. Since 3 is a Fire number, expect related industries to move ahead of the rest.

Energy will be spent to recapture our lost youth, with emphasis on losses through drugs, improper education, and lack of parental guidance. The entertainment industry, governments, and religious orders should make a strong showing this year. Places here and around the world likely to dominate the headlines will be Andover, Cuba, Grenada, Haiti, Kingston, Manhattan, Memphis, Moscow, San Antonio, and Toledo, to name a few.

The United States will also be passing through a 5 personal year, or Mercury cycle. Since this region of the world is ruled by Gemini, or Mercury, the nation as a whole will be working on making changes for the better. This, being another election year for the nation, a somewhat youthful President—in age or attitude—will take the helm of the U.S. government. As 5 is an Air number, expect the aerospace, airline, and travel-related industries to be a dominant force in the economy. January, March, especially April, October, and December are the months likely to be stressful as a whole.

Trends for 1993

This is the year of the master number 22 (or 4). It favors Aquarius and Gemini, and those born on the 4th, 13th, especially the 22nd, and 31st of the month. This universal year should give the world collectively an opportunity to act as "master builders" for the betterment of all its citizens. The underdog nations, as well as the poor and "have nots" of society, will refuse to be ignored. Winners will become losers and losers will become winners. Places that are likely to capture the attention of the world in the news this year are Albany, Atlantic City, Barbados, Buenos Aires, Dayton, Jackson, London, Richmond, Salt Lake City, and Washington, D.C.

The United States may find this year a blessing as well as a curse. On the one hand, the year 1993 matches the birth number of the country, but on the other hand, the nation's personal year cycle is opposing it. There's likely to be a large amount of civil unrest throughout the country, serious threats of war, or getting indirectly involved in one. Social institutions will be challenging the policies of the states as well as the nation as a whole. February, March, September, November, and December are the months that will pull at the fabric of this nation and its citizens.

Trends for 1994

This is the year of the 5. It will favor Gemini, Virgo, and Aquarius, or anyone born on the 5th, 14th, and especially the 23rd of the month. Travel, space exploration, as well as the business and scientific community should see a favorable upturn in activities. The communications industry will assume an even bigger role in the nation, and in what they project around the world. The places capturing most of the headlines will be Acapulco, Athens, Cairo, Caracas, Chicago, Nashville, Nicaragua, Oakland, Palm Beach, Rio de Janeiro, Santa Cruz, and Trenton.

This year the nation will adopt a rather reflective and discriminating posture toward its citizens as well as its friends and allies. Secret deals of far-reaching consequences later on are likely to be made during this cycle year. In this cycle the nation may also find skeletons coming out of its closet that may shock even the most patriotic citizens. On the other hand, scientific advances and research should make some astounding discoveries related to physics and nature. Care for the nation has to be exercised during the months of January, February, August, October, and November.

VIII.

Things of Interest

Music, Music, Music

Music is the universal art of emotional expression through the voice, instruments, or other means. Music is universally beloved by young and old, rich and poor. Through Numerology a great deal can be determined about the type of music a person is likely to enjoy. For instance, one person may like rich and forceful music, another may prefer music that is sweet and romantic. Others will be drawn to spiritual or religious music, while still others may be into up-tempo disco sounds.

Numerology even goes as far as helping you select the musical instruments that are in accord or harmony with you. Look to your date of birth for the answer. A person born on the 2nd of December has the number 2 as his important number. Then check below to find the type of music and musical instruments best suited to you.

Choosing Your Music

NUMBER 1 PERSON

Those born on the 1st, 10th, 19th, or 29th, or in February, April, and August, will basically prefer original, forceful, and energetic music. Music for the 1 person is clean, fresh, creative, and straight to the point without the frills. Dynamic, brassy music with full rich tones attracts the 1 person. Musical instruments that vibrate under the number 1 are: drums, conga, saxophone, xylophone, bugle, piano, bassoon, gourd, cowbell, and tambourine.

NUMBER 2 PERSON

If you were born on the 2nd, 11th, 20th or 29th, or in May and July, you'll basically enjoy soft, gentle, sweet and romantic type of music. The 2's choice of music is usually centered around the themes of love, peace, and understanding. For example, that singer of love songs, Barry White, carries this number in his name and in his music. Musical instruments that vibrate under the number 2 are: the voice, harp, harmonica, banjo, trombone, french horn, steel pan, drums, lyre, piano, and castanets.

NUMBER 3 PERSON

Those born on the 3rd, 12th, 21st, or 30th, or born in March and December, like the 1 person, enjoy full, rich, and energetic music. Disco music with its strong social appeal and bright lights attracts the 3 very much. The 3 person usually likes music that is youthful and in today's popular style. Musical instruments that vibrate under the number 3 are: horns, oboe, mandolin, cello, saxophone, trumpet, violin, zither, chimes, and ukulele.

NUMBER 4 PERSON

Those born on the 4th, 13th, 22nd, or 31st, or in February, June, and August, basically enjoy odd and unusual types of music. Today's electronic music has a strong attraction to the number 4 nature. Music with rhythms of surprise and suddenness hold the 4's attention, yet at the same time music of a traditional nature fascinates and soothes the nerves. Musical instruments that vibrate under the number 4 are: electronic instruments of all kinds, bagpipes, saxophone, the voice, gourd, rattles, cow bells, xylophone, piano, zanza, drums, tuba, and fife.

NUMBER 5 PERSON

If you were born on the 5th, 14th, or 23rd, or in June and September, you enjoy music that is lively, active, up-tempo, and free in its expression. On the one hand, 5s like music that gives freedom of movement and expression, such as the disco music now on the scene. On the other hand, their listening taste is very broad—they like all types of music, from reggae to opera. Musical instruments that vibrate under the number 5 are: kalimba, conch, timbales, violin, piccolo, marimba, trumpet, zither, harpsichord, and piano.

NUMBER 6 PERSON

Those born on the 6th, 15th, or 24th, or in May and October, are basically attracted to all beautiful, sweet, and romantic music—especially when it's for the voice. Because love and romance is important to the 6, music must also have this in feeling and emotion. Therefore, soft and harmonious music stays at the top of the 6 list. Musical instruments that vibrate under the number 6 are: the voice, oboe, marimbas, clarinet, trumpet, timpani, cello, zither, shekere, mandolin, and chimes.

NUMBER 7 PERSON

If you were born on the 7th, 16th, or 25th, or in February, July, and August, you basically enjoy spiritual, mystical, and inspirational music—it's about truth, wisdom, and knowledge as expressed in the musical universe. Generally the 7 person prefers soft, quiet, and peaceful music rather than the loud, bright sounds of disco. Musical instruments that vibrate under the number 7 are: harp, harmonica, banjo, lyre, french horn, steel pan, piano, trombone, and drums.

NUMBER 8 PERSON

Those born on the 8th, 17th, or 26th, or in January and October, are basically drawn to philosophical and religious music. Blues, which expresses moods of depression, despondency, and a deep nature has a strong appeal to the 8. Church music—religious music of any kind—will receive respect from an 8. The musical instruments that vibrate under the number 8 are: guitar, flute, cymbals, cornet, bells, trumpet, clarinet, zither, and chimes.

NUMBER 9 PERSON

Those born on the 9th, 18th, or 27th, or in April and November, will like music that has force, richness, and energy in its elements. Music of an impulsive, bold, and brassy nature will be in the 9's record collection. Feelings of strength and determination will be important musical themes for the 9. Musical instruments that vibrate under the number 9 are: organ, bass, lute, viola, sax, bongos, shekere, conga, cello, drums, horns, and gongs.

Numerology and Hobbies

With today's shorter work week, there is more hobby, leisure, and recreational time than ever before. The dictionary defines hobbies as anything that gives pleasure and creates stimulus and interest in something other than a nine-to-five job. Many times hobbies grow into a profession or occupation, as in this writers' case.

Hobbies often relieve tension and boredom, produce relaxation, enjoyment, creativity, and an inner feeling of self-satisfaction and self-worth. Hobbies are as diverse as people, and those best suited to your enjoyment can be determined from your birth date. A person born November 14 ($1 + 4 = 5$) would choose the number 5 section below for hobbies and interests related to the nature and disposition of his or her ruling key number. Find your single birth date number and look below.

Choosing Hobbies

NUMBER 1 PERSON

Born on the 1st, 10th, 19th, or 28th of the month, or in April and August, you'll find pleasure in such hobbies as: acting, community work, engraving, games of all kind, horseback riding, history, inventing, martial arts, outdoor sports, photography, skiing, traveling.

NUMBER 2 PERSON

Those born on the 2nd, 11th, 20th, or 29th of the month, or in May and July, will find pleasure in: acting, akido, all types of collecting, babysitting, cooking, crocheting, dancing, designing, drawing, fishing, modeling, novelties, painting, poetry, sailing, swimming.

NUMBER 3 PERSON

If you were born on the 3rd, 12th, 21st, or 30th of the month, or in March and December, you'll find pleasure in such hobbies as: autograph collecting, boxing, decorating, gambling, horseback riding, hunting, jewelry making, magic, music, painting, photography, social clubs, public speaking, storytelling, traveling, and writing.

NUMBER 4 PERSON

Those born on the 4th, 13th, 22nd, or 31st of the month, or in February and August, will find pleasure in: Astrology, collecting odds and ends, electronics (TV and radio), flying, inventing, martial arts, mechanics, music, novelty items, Numerology, sculpture, and travel.

NUMBER 5 PERSON

Born on the 5th, 14th, or 23rd of the month, or in June and September, you'll find pleasure in such hobbies as: all forms of communications, calligraphy, crossword puzzles, being a disc jockey, flying, gambling, graphology, jogging, martial arts, modeling, music, racing, swimming, traveling, and writing.

NUMBER 6 PERSON

Those born on the 6th, 15th, or 24th of the month, or in May and October, will find pleasure in: ceramics, cooking, crocheting, dancing, designing, being a disc jockey, doll collecting, jogging, knitting, landscape gardening, modeling, music, sewing, singing, social clubs, sports in general, and weaving.

NUMBER 7 PERSON

If you were born on the 7th, 16th, or 25th of the month, or in March and July, you'll find pleasure in such hobbies as: Astrology, book collecting, fishing, magic, music, nature studies, Numerology, painting, photography, poetry, puzzles of all kind, reading, Scrabble, skiing, and writing.

NUMBER 8 PERSON

Those born on the 8th, 17th, or 26th of the month, or in January and October, will find pleasure as a government volunteer, or in antique collecting, boxing, bricklaying, coin collecting, excavating, folklore, geology, magic, nature studies, occult or religious studies, philosophy, pottery, taxidermy, rock collecting, and skiing.

NUMBER 9 PERSON

If you were born on the 9th, 18th, or 27th of the month, or in April and November, you'll find pleasure in such hobbies as: all outdoor sports, acrobatics, carpentry, etching, gun collecting, horseback riding, hunting, jogging, magic, mechanics, repairing, tool collecting, train collecting, traveling, and wood carving.

Numerology and Sports

Sports and recreational activities are not only more fun today, they've grown into a multibillion dollar industry. Sports and recreation offer a wonderful outlet for the mind and body at all ages. Sports such as basketball and football have grown so sophisticated that one must be mentally sound as well as be physically fit and alert to play.

The diversity of sports and recreation today encourages family participation on all levels, while at the same time, allowing for individual sportsmanship. Sports have grown in popularity so much that they dominate most of Saturday's and Sunday's TV viewing.

To find the sports and recreational interests most compatible with you, look to your date of birth number for the answer. For instance, a person born July 26th $(2+6=8)$ would look in the 8 section.

As you will see below, there are several sports activities that overlap one another. For example, although jogging is primarily under the rulership of the numbers 4 and 5, jogging is so popular today that all ages and classes of people born under other numbers also find pleasure in this sport.

Since some sports and recreational activities might cause physical stress, it would be wise to follow a few basic rules:

- See your doctor for a physical checkup.
- Start Slow! Build up your strength.
- Use common sense about what you can endure, to avoid mental and physical harm to yourself.

Choosing Your Sports

NUMBER 1 PERSON

Those born on the 1st, 10th, 19th and 28th of the month, or in April and August, can be bold and aggressive in acrobatics, athletics of all kind, amusements of all kind, archery, bowling, camping, checkers, chess, fencing, hockey, karate, racing, soccer, track and field, and weight lifting.

NUMBER 2 PERSON

If you were born on the 2nd, 11th, 20th, or 29th of the month, or in May and July, you should look into akido, badminton, billiards, canoeing, diving, fishing, ice skating, martial arts, table tennis, tennis, t'ai chi ch'uan, sailing, softball, swimming, volleyball, and water skiing.

NUMBER 3 PERSON

Born on the 3rd, 12th, 21st, or 30th of the month, or in March and December, you'll find much amusement with archery, basketball, bowling, exploring, fencing, fishing, handball, horseracing, hunting, karate, kung fu, ping pong, volleyball, weight lifting, and wrestling.

NUMBER 4 PERSON

Those born on the 4th, 13th, 22nd, and 31st of the month, or in February and August, will find odd and surprising pleasures in amusements of all kinds. Try bicycling, electronic sports games, checkers, chess, exploring, frisbee, high jump, jogging, martial arts, polo, racing, roller skating, sky diving, tennis, track and field, and jogging.

NUMBER 5 PERSON

Those born on the 5th, 14th, and 23rd, or in June and September, will find movement, change, and variety in auto racing, bicycling, checkers, chess, frisbee, handball, high jump, jogging, judo, roller skating, running, skate boarding, sky diving, sprinting, swimming, tennis, and track and field.

NUMBER 6 PERSON

If you were born on the 6th, 15th, and 24th of the month, or in May and October, you'll find fun and pleasure in amusements of all kinds, but especially with ball games. Try basketball, bowling, football, golf, handball, horse racing, table tennis, polo, softball, stickball, stoopball, tennis, table pool, and volleyball.

NUMBER 7 PERSON

Born on the 7th, 16th, and 25th of the month, or in March and July, you should have fun investigating acrobatics, akido, badminton, billiards, bowling, canoeing, chess, deep-sea diving, fishing, ice skating, jogging, sailing, skating, swimming, and tennis.

NUMBER 8 PERSON

Those born on the 8th, 17th, and 26th of the month, or in October and January, should seriously consider archery, ball games of all kinds, boxing, chess, golf, horse racing, ice hockey, karate, long-distance running, mountain climbing, polo, weight lifting, wrestling, and jogging.

NUMBER 9 PERSON

If you were born on the 9th, 18th, or 27th of the month, or in April and November, you'll enjoy competitive sports of all kinds, such as acrobatics, auto racing, baseball, boxing, bullfights, fencing, football, golf, hunting, karate, motorcycling, soccer, target or skeet shooting, tennis, and weight lifting.

Numerology and Cars

Why did you choose your present car? Was it because of its size, price, color, or performance? Or was it something else? Whatever your reason, it's always best to select an automobile in harmony and agreement with your date of birth. Let's say, for example, that you were born on the 14th of the month. Your best choice of a car would be one that added up to the number 5. In my research, I was amazed at how many people owned cars either matching their birth number or their Zodiac sign. Because there are so many makes and models of cars, only the more popularly known ones are listed below.

Choosing Your Car

NUMBER 1 PERSON

Born on the 1st, 10th, 19th, or 28th, of if you're a Leo or Aries, your best selection would be: Ambassador, AMX, Bobcat, Cadillac, Caravan, Catalina, Chevette, Excalibur, Galaxie, Gran Fury, Gran Torino, Hornet, Laguna, Lancer, Mustang II, Newport, Nova, Pacer, Rambler, Tempo, Toronado, Town Car, Zephyr.

NUMBER 2 PERSON

Born on the 2nd, 11th, 20th or 29th, or under Cancer, make your choice: Accord, Alfa Romeo, Apollo, Blazer, Camry, Centurion, Coupe De Ville, Cutlass Supreme, Daimler, Dart, Dasher, Fuego, Fury III, Granville, LTD, Omega, Peugeot, Plymouth, Pontiac, Sirocco, Sentra, Skyhawk, Skylark, Subaru, Supra, Trans Am, Ventura, Versailles, Volvo.

NUMBER 3 PERSON

Those born on the 3rd, 12th, 21st, or 30th, or under the sign of Pisces or Sagittarius, will find an attraction to the: Aries, Audi, BMW, Brava, Brougham, Calais, Charger, Ciera, Ford, Karmann Ghia, LeMans, LeSabre, Mark III, Maserati, Oldsmobile, Rabbit, Reliant, Road Runner, Stanza, Super Beetle, Triumph, Valiant.

NUMBER 4 PERSON

Born on the 4th, 13th, 22nd, or 31st, or if you're an Aquarius, you should find an unusual attraction to the: Alliance, American Motors, Aspen, Barracuda, Cavalier, Chevrolet, Concord, Cougar, Cressida, Daytona, Fiesta, Fleetwood, Grand Prix, Honda, Javelin, Mark IV, Polara, Scooter, Starlet, Tercel, Phaeton, Thunderbird, Toyota Celica.

NUMBER 5 PERSON

Born on the 5th, 14th, or 23rd, or if you're a Gemini or Virgo, you'd do well selecting the following: Aries K, Audi Coupe, Audi Fox, Bavaria, Buick, Caprice, Civic, Comet, Convert, Cutlass, Datsun, Diplomat, Dodge, Electra, Electra 225, Fairmount, Fiat, Gremlin, GTO, Hyundai, Isuzu, Jaguar, Laser, Laguna, Lotus, Lynx, Mark V, Matador, Mercedes, Monte Carlo, Park Avenue, Pulsar, Regal, Sunbird, Volkswagen.

NUMBER 6 PERSON

If you were born on the 6th, 15th, or 24th, or you happen to be a Taurus or Libra, choose: Astre, Bonneville, Capri, Chrysler, Cobra, Coronet, Delta 88, Duster, Eldorado, Escort, Gran Marquis, Jetta, Maverick, Monza, Porsche, Prelude, Regency, Skylark, Somerset, Town Coupe, Toyota, Vega, Corvette, Volare.

NUMBER 7 PERSON

Born on the 7th, 14th, or 25th, or if you're a Pisces or Cancer, you'll find a magnetic attraction to the: Arrow GT, Austin Marina, Celica, Cimarron, Continental, Corona, Firebird, Horizon, Imperial, LeBaron, Maxima, MG, Mirage, Pinto, Saab, Swinger, Trans Am, Volvo.

NUMBER 8 PERSON

Born on the 8th, 17th, or 26th, or under the sign of Capricorn, you'd do best with the: AMC, Audi 5000, Austin Healy, Celebrity, Century, Challenger, Citation, Colt, Cordoba, Corolla, Eagle, Fury, Gran Sport, Granada, Malibu, Mazda, Montego, Mustang, New Yorker, Omni, Rebel, Renault, Seville, Sirocco, Starfire, Torino.

NUMBER 9 PERSON

Born on the 9th, 18th, or 27th, or if your sign is Aries or Scorpio, you'd do well getting the following: Avenger, Camaro, Citroën, Cordia, Concord, Corvette, Cougar XR7, Dart Swinger, Delta Royale, Elite, Encore, Fifth Avenue, Futura, Impala, Lincoln, Marquis, MGB, Monaco, Monarch, Nissan, Phoenix, Riviera, Rolls Royce, Sedan De Ville, Suburban, Turismo.

Numerology and Gift Giving

A gift is anything that is given, such as a present or donation. Gift giving takes place all year long for one reason or another, be it a birthday or anniversary. However, Christmastime seems to put more emphasis on giving gifts. Perhaps, like yours truly, you may have encountered the "decisions, decisions" syndrome. Hopefully, this chapter will narrow your guesswork by guiding you to buy those gifts associated with the birth number and Zodiac sign of the recipient.

To find the best type of gift for someone—including yourself—keep the following in mind:

- First, find the person's date of birth. For instance, someone born on the 14th of the month is a number 5 person (1 + 4 = 5).
- For a second choice in selection of gifts, find the person's Zodiac sign, which is usually different from the birth number.
- Finally, if the gift selections don't seem to match exactly what you want, look for gifts listed under your own birth number or Zodiac sign.

The following is just a representative listing of the thousands of possible gifts to be given.

Choosing the Right Gift

THE NUMBER 1 PERSON

If the person was born on the 1st, 10th, 19th, or 28th of the month, or under the Zodiac sign of Aries or Leo, they would probably like a watch, painting, tie, candlesticks, jewelry box, hat, pajamas, briefcase, towel set, humidifier, cookware, razor, space saver, slide projector, tool set, leg warmers, pillows, glassware, gloves, or skates. Or, give this person a year's subscription to *Creative Ideas*, *Golf Digest*, *Hunting*, *Money*, *Photography*, *Playboy*, *Forbes*, *Metropolitan Home*, *Newsweek*, *Business Week*, *Entrepreneur*, *Handyman*, *Cruise Travel*, *Esquire*, *Homeowner*, *Vogue*, *Income Opportunities*, *New Woman*, *Savvy*, *Video*, or *Writer's Digest*.

THE NUMBER 2 PERSON

A number 2 person born on the 2nd, 11th, 20th, or 29th, or under the sign of Cancer or Taurus, would find pleasure and surprise in the following gift items: Teapot, hobby set, pocketbook, perfume, stroller, C.B. radio, infantwear, stationery, stoneware, vest, cutting board, rockers, shaver, percolator, hot brush, piano, camera, scissors, bed sheets, calculator, slacks, or plants. If you don't have a gift in mind, you can get them a year's subscription to *Cookbook*, *Bon Appetit*, *Cooking Light*, *Crochet*, *Ebony*, *Family Computing*, *Organic Gardening*, *Good Food*, *Mother Earth News*, *Parenting*, *True Story*, *World's Greatest Love Stories*, *Contest Newsletter*, *Fly Fisherman*, *Homeowner*, *1,001 Home Ideas*, *Creative Quilting*, *Redbook*, *Refunder's Digest*, *Prevention*, or *Health*.

THE NUMBER 3 PERSON

Let's say you know someone born on the 3rd, 12th, 21st, 30th, or under the sign of Pisces or Sagittarius. It's a cinch they're likely to enjoy a handbag, gown, dishes, pants, record album, cassette player, flatware, skillet, furniture, grill, hair clipper, sleepwear, airpump, carpet sweeper, moccasins, turtleneck, or headwear. Why not give a gift subscription to *American Photographer*, *Catholic Digest*, *New Woman*, *Popular Photography*, *Country Music*, *Organic Gardening*, *Golf Digest*, *Motor Trend*, *People*, *Photographic*, *Playboy*, *Connoisseur*, *Fashion Knitting*, *Games*, *Modern Photography*, *Sheet Music*, *Soap Opera*, *Star*, *Tennis*, or *Stereo Review*.

THE NUMBER 4 PERSON

A 4 person, born on the 4th, 13th, 22nd, or 31st, or under the sign of Aquarius, would find an unusual appeal with gifts such as a fruit bowl, VCR, earrings, pipe, computer, blanket, griddle, microwave, tool set, chess set, coffee maker, ironing board, heater, wallet, watch, projector, minicam, belt, or electronic games of all kind. Perhaps you could give this person a subscription to *Architectural Digest*, *The Atlantic*, *Early American Life*, *Homeowner*, *Omni*, *Alfred Hitchcock*, *Americana*, *Analog*, *50 Plus*, *Handyman*, *Natural History*, *Popular Science*, *Flying*, *Country Journal*, *Electric Company*, *Family Computing*, *Compute*, *Ellery Queen*, *Handcrafts*, or *Psychology Today*.

THE NUMBER 5 PERSON

If you know someone born on the 5th, 14th, or 23rd, of the month, or under the sign of Gemini or Virgo, they should enjoy the following: traveling kit, calculator, pen & pencil set, pendant, VCR, vest, spice set, bath oil, can opener, slippers, curlers, shaver, oven, book, skates, skis, or luggage. If that doesn't work, try giving them a subscription to *Bicycling*, *California*, *Car & Driver*, *Esquire*, *Income Opportunities*, *Life*, *Money*, *Motor Cyclist*, *Flying*, *People*, *TV Guide*, *Drugs*, *Fortune*, *Omni*, *Rolling Stone*, *Changing Times*, *Cycle World*, *Leisure*, *Automobile*, or *Business Week*.

THE NUMBER 6 PERSON

Persons born on the 6th, 15th, or 24th, or under Taurus or Libra, would enjoy receiving gloves, perfume, sweater, slacks, painting, decorative piece, bakeware, copper, silverware, furniture, coat, handkerchief, comforter, hosiery, or cutlery. They could easily enjoy a year's subscription to *Grit*, *Ladies Home Journal*, *Harper's Bazaar*, *Needlework & Crafts*, *Prevention*, *Essence*, *Sports Illustrated*, *Sports Afield*, *Baseball Digest*, *Consumer's Digest*, *Homeowner*, *Freebies*, *Redbook*, *Refunder's Digest*, *Working Mother*, *Ebony*, *Cooking Light*, *Parents*, or *People*.

THE NUMBER 7 PERSON

Someone born on the 7th, 16th, or 25th, or under the sign of Pisces or Cancer, would probably like having a teapot, stationery, hobby set, bracelet, robe, bath towels, walkie talkie, bedspread, camera, jacket, silverware, a good book, wall décor, painting, scissors, hot brush, frypan, or reading light. On the other hand, it may not be a bad idea to give them a subscription to *Alfred Hitchcock*, *Field & Stream*, *Jet*, *Natural History*, *Popular Science*, *The Christian Science Monitor*, *Drugs*, *Omni*, *Health*, *Country Journal*, *Cruise Travel*, *Psychology Today*, *Ski*, *Stereo Review*, *Travel-Holiday*, *Vegetarian Times*, *Writer's Digest*, *Astrology*, *Bassin*, or *Compute*.

THE NUMBER 8 PERSON

If the person was born on the 8th, 17th, or 26th, or under the sign of Capricorn or Libra, take seriously the following selections: blender, gift certificate, step stool, toiletries, raincoat, bakeware, iron, scale, blouse, radio, raincoat, or flatware. Or better yet, why not a gift subscription to *Forbes*, *Early American Life*, *Fortune*, *Newsweek*, *Time*, *Americana*, *Catholic Digest*, *50 Plus*, *Income Opportunities*, *Money*, *Yankee*, *American History*, *Business Week*, *Home*, *Town & Country*, *Practical Homeowner*, *Life*.

THE NUMBER 9 PERSON

Someone born on the 9th, 18th, or 27th, or born under the sign of Aries or Scorpio, would appreciate a clock, juicer, skates, crock pot, razor, shaver, chair, computer, rocker, towel set, humidifier, heater, electronic games and gadgets. Suggested magazine subscriptions could be *American Photographer*, *New Woman*, *Sports Afield*, *Baseball Digest*, *Newsweek*, *Time*, *Outdoor Life*, *U.S. News*, *Hunting*, *Motor Cyclist*, *Playboy*, *Tours & Resorts*, *Automobile*, *Entrepreneur*, *Esquire*, *Flying*, *Good Food*, *Inside Sports*, *Military History*, or *Motor Trend*.

Happy gift giving!

Numerology and Consumer Products

Have you ever thought about consumer products and the numbers associated with them? Numbers other than price are interwoven into many of the things you buy. Is it an accident that a product will often have a number as part of its title? How about 7-Up soda as a start? What about Clorox 2 bleach?

Numbers often have a strong association with the purpose or image of the product. For example, take the breakfast cereal, Product 19. The 19 adds up to the single digit of 1 $(1+9=10; 1+0=1)$. The number 1 is associated with energy, get up and go, something new, something original. Take another example, Chanel No. 5 perfume. The number 5 is associated with sexual attraction, sex appeal, animal magnetism. What could be a better number for this product? Was it by accident or design?

One man selected a number on gut feeling and made a fortune. His name was H. J. Heinz of "Heinz 57 Varieties," known for his beans. Originally selling pickles and fresh garden vegetables, his persistence and business acumen later developed into a product line of over sixty varieties of beans, vegetables, soups, and the like. Although his variety of products went past 57, he chose to keep that number. He felt the magical last digit 7 had an "alluring significance to people of all ages." There must have been something to it, because today over 900 million cans of beans alone are sold—and that's only one of the Heinz 57 varieties.

The following is only a partial listing of common household products with numerical titles found on your grocer's shelf:

Formula 409 [cleaner]	Super 80 [disinfectant]
666 Cough Syrup	Humphrey's 11
V-8 Vegetable Juice	5-Alive Fruit Beverage
9 Lives Cat Food	Purina 100 Cat Food
Colt 45 [beer]	Old English 800 [beer]
Alberto VO 5	Hairline 25
612 Plus Repellant	707 Ant & Roach Spray
Brut 33 Deodorant	Product 19
40% Bran Flakes	Clorox 2
Bold 3 Detergent	A-1 Sauce
Heinz 57 Sauce	7-Up [soda]
Seven Seas Dressing	

Keep in mind the above is just a random sampling of grocer-related items. When it comes to other areas, the same holds true. What about that sporty Cougar XR7? What about that luxury Electra 225? The list goes on. The airline industry flies a variety of makes and models of planes ranging from the DC-10 to the 747. Then there's the drug industry with its endless list. The computer and electronics industry, among others, oftentimes have numbers in their product names. The next time you're in the kitchen or looking in your medicine cabinet, take notice. You'll be surprised.

Questions Asked of Me

In the eighteen years I've studied Numerology, I've discovered that wherever I lectured or appeared, people asked me certain basic questions about this subject. Take the following:

Question: Is there a close relationship between Numerology and Astrology?

Answer: Yes. I would go as far as saying they're first cousins. Where an Astrologer may use the language of planets and signs, a Numerologist talks of numbers and how their various aspects concern this ancient craft.

Question: Which came first, Numerology or Astrology?

Answer: My answer is, Numerology came first. I can hear you saying, "Of course you'd say that, being a Numerologist." But let me explain it another way, a common sense way. My reason for believing that numbers and Numerology had to precede Astrology is the fact that Astrologers must have certain information from you to cast a horoscope. The one thing needed is your date of birth. How do you give them your birth date? Why, in numbers of course.

Astrologers must know the exact time and location of your birth in order to determine your correct ascendant and so on. After they have this information, they must then prepare your chart to determine what degree your Sun sign is in, and what degree your rising sign and Moon are in, among a host of other numerical aspects. Is there any wonder I believe that Numerology preceded Astrology?

Question: Why are both your name and birth day analyzed in Numerology?

Answer: The reason is, Numerically, your name tells quite a lot about you as a person. It reveals your natural talents, skills, and abilities, even if you haven't had the benefit of a formal education. Your name represents what you can do naturally, without training. On the other hand, your birth day reveals the destiny or path that you're here to follow, as well as the lessons that have to be learned on God's green Earth.

Question: Is it true that Numerology is easy to learn since the numbers only go from 1 to 9—in no time you must be a pro?

Answer: I felt that way when first introduced to the science of numbers. I felt that all one had to do was to know how to count from 1 to 9—after all, I had ten fingers. Yet, after eighteen years of study on this fascinating subject, there is so much I still have to learn. In fact, really good or exceptional Numerologists usually have at least twenty-five years of experience under their belts. So it's not as simple as it appears, although the applications and techniques are remarkably easy to learn.

Question: Is there only one basic number that rules the life of a person?

Answer: Yes and no. Yes, in some cases, a number or series of numbers may be repetitive in a person's life. No, in the sense that we are composed of a mixture of numbers. For instance, while a person may have been born under the Sun sign of Aries, there's more to that individual than just the Sun sign. There's the rising sign, denoting appearance. Then there's the Moon sign, denoting individuality. So in the world of Numerology, one is often composed of a mixture of numbers. This is the reason each of us has to be analyzed in our entirety before any firm conclusions can be reached.

Question: It's been said numbers have vibrations, what does that mean?

Answer: Each of the numbers from 1 to 9 has its own individual vibration, which is simply another word for frequency or rate of motion. Case in point: Take your favorite radio or TV program. Each station has its own call numbers or channel number, based on the strength of its frequency. In reality, we can't see or touch these frequencies we're bombarded with each day, but the laws of physics prove they exist. The same holds true in the world of Numerology. Just because you can't see, taste, or touch these numbers, doesn't mean they don't exist, or that they don't affect or influence your life in some profound way.

Question: Can Numerology tell us about matters of love, romance, business, and health?

Answer: Without a doubt, the ways in which the occult world of numbers affects areas of your life would astound you. First, when it comes to choosing partners for business and romance, Numerology is one of the quickest and most accurate methods to use. Even your health is affected to a large degree by the numbers found in your name, but especially in your birth day. The original material in this book on tracing your family tree, childbirth, your personal week, etc., suggests there's a lot yet to be discovered.

Question: Do you need a degree or certain level of education to learn Numerology? What about finding a teacher?

Answer: One of the beauties of Numerology is its simplicity of application. A degree or certain level of education is not a requirement. You simply have to learn the symbols—and there are many—associated with each number. Later on, hopefully, you will learn how to synthesize and interpret these numbers from a person's name and birth date.

As for a teacher, there seems to be an emergence of occult teachers across the country. There's no doubt that you should be able to find someone in your area. You can usually find good instructors at psychic fairs, metaphysical lectures, and other related events. As a last resort, you can do as I did. Simply read as many books on the subject as you can. Then reread them again and again for further understanding, and apply what you've learned by analyzing your family, friends, and loved ones.

For you as an individual, you may find more personal enjoyment and satisfaction in Astrology than Numerology. Each of us is special. You'll ultimately find your own niche if you follow your inner guide. Whichever area of the occult you decide to study, be patient, allow yourself time to learn and master the fundamentals. You'll be rewarded in the end.

IX.

Numerology
and Beyond

The Sacred Number 7

Of all the numbers from one to nine, the number 7 is universally considered the spiritual, mystical, occult, and lucky number. Among all the great religions there is no disagreement that the number 7 is the number of God and all things mystic. It has long been associated with priests, monks, seers, mystics, researchers, technicians, artists, and musicians. Even in games of chance, the lucky 7–11 wins out, especially in craps and at the roulette wheel.

The 7 is found in all forms expressed in nature and in human life. The number 7 represents the search for truth, wisdom, understanding, and perfection; after all, God "blessed the seventh day" (Genesis 2:3).

In Nature, the 7 is found in the:

- 7 days of the week.
- 52 (5 + 2 = 7) weeks in the year.
- 7 major planets (Saturn, Jupiter, Mars, Venus, Mercury, the Moon, and the Sun).
- 7 colors in a rainbow.
- 7 notes in a musical scale.
- 7 major metals (lead, tin, iron, quicksilver, gold, copper, silver).
- 7 Wonders of the World.
- Complete luna (Moon) cycle, which averages 28 days (4 x 7).
- 7 phases of the Moon.

In humans, the 7 represents the:

- 7 natural divisions of the brain.
- 7 functions of the nervous system.
- 7 compartments of the heart.
- 7 major organs (heart, brain, liver, kidneys, lungs, gall bladder, reproductive system).
- 7 holes in the body (nostrils (2), ears (2), mouth, rectum, penis/vagina).
- 7 psychic centers (chakras) in the body.
- Menstrual cycle of women averages 28 days (4 x 7).
- A minor wound heals in about 7 days.
- Depending on the size and extent of a wound, it will heal in days adding to the multiple of 7 (7, 14, 21 days, etc.).
- The mind and body undergo basic physiological changes every 7 years:

  —Age 7: age of reason.
  —Age 14: age of puberty.
  —Age 21: age of physical maturity.
  —Age 28: age of mental maturity (1st complete Moon cycle in humans, astrologically).
  —Age 49: or 7 x 7; a critical or climacteric period in human life.

In general, the 7 denotes:

- "7-year itch."
- "7th inning stretch."
- "7th heaven."
- 7 Archangels.
- 7 deadly sins (pride, avarice, lust, wrath, idleness, gluttony, envy).
- 7 virtues (faith, hope, charity, justice, prudence, temperance, strength).
- 52 (5 + 2 = 7) cards make a deck.
- In the Bible, Joshua's forces marched 7 times around the walls of Jericho, the trumpets were sounded 7 times, and the walls came tumbling down.
- In Mecca, the holy city of Islam, a Muslim's pilgrimage is completed by going around the sacred Kabba stone 7 times.

And the list goes on. In the examples above, one can see the tremendous yet subtle influence of the 7.

One must not feel that the other numbers do not have important roles to play in the universal scheme of things —they do. However, out of all nine numbers, the 7 was blessed with a special role and purpose.

The Secrets of Thought Reading

How many times have you regretted not acting on your first impressions or hunches? Your first impressions of numbers that come into the mind are also important. It has long been understood by those involved in occult or mystical studies that there is a certain cosmic process that takes place in the conscious and subconscious mind. This process is based on the fact that if the mind is concerned with a particular matter, any number or set of numbers automatically coming into the mind bear a direct relationship to the nature of the thought.

This is because numbers are symbols. Each number from 1 to 9 has, since ancient times, symbolically possessed a certain nature and character. On a conscious level, we're not usually aware of how number symbols relate to our thoughts. Curiously, however, the subconscious mind clearly seems to understand the meaning of the number symbols.

Our thoughts exist basically on two levels. One side is known as the conscious mind. The other, more hidden side, is the subconscious mind. It is the subconscious mind that is the memory bank of the brain. Like the elephant, it never forgets. This is why hypnotists and others who deal with reaching the subconscious mind can get an individual to recall many facts, events, and experiences that have been long forgotten by the conscious mind. In

Numerology the same result can be achieved by reaching into the subconscious and arriving at an answer simply by selecting a number or a series of numbers.

For instance, the number 6 may come into someone's mind. The average person may be unaware of the qualities and nature of the 6, or any other number, and may not give it a second thought. But to an Astrologer, Numerologist, mystic, seer, Rosicrucian, or others, this number can open up a world of symbols and information when properly understood. The Astrologer may interpret the 6 as belonging to the planet Venus, which governs the signs of Taurus and Libra, and as a result, the concern may be about an individual born under these influences. A Numerologist may interpret the 6 as having to do with the home, family, or loved ones.

What I'm about to share with you is a method of reaching the subconscious mind by the thought selection of numbers. This is nothing new and was demonstrated with much success to the master Astrologer Sepharial (1864–1929) by a swami from the East. Later, Astrologer Sydney Omarr carried this further in his "thought dial" concept.

Both Sepharial and Omarr agree that the following steps are necessary to get the right results. First, relax. Then, allow the question to form clearly in your mind, being as specific as possible. Now, Sepharial suggests that you write down the first nine numbers that come into your mind. To these nine numbers, add the number 3. Add up the ten figures to get your answer. Omarr's method is even simpler. He suggests that you simply write down the first three numbers that come to mind, then add up the three numbers to get a single digit.

Let's try it. I ask myself, "What am I thinking of?" Then I take the first three numbers that come to mind—2, 1, and 7 = 10; 1+0=1. The number 1 and its symbols will be the clue in this particular case. Now, take your thoughts and questions, relax and concentrate. Choose the first three numbers that come to mind, add them up, and check for meanings below.

Thought Reading Answers

If the total adds up to the single number of 1:

- Yes is definitely the answer to the question.
- The person in question was born under the signs of Leo or Aquarius, or on dates adding to the single number of 1 or 4.
- Consciously, the subject's question may concern new projects, activities, friends, and circumstances. All indications are that the subject should start going his or her own way, rather than following others at this time. Move ahead and take charge. Subconsciously, there's an inner desire to be free and independent; make a change and begin things anew.

If the total adds up to 2:

- No is definitely the answer to the question.
- The person in question was born under the sign of Cancer or on dates adding to the single number of 2, 6, or 7.
- On the conscious level, the subject's question relates to the opposite sex and concerns related to change. Partnerships of some kind appear to be important. Patience and tact are the best approach to your question. Subconsciously, there's an inner desire for peace and harmony; security is also important. Wait—things will develop slowly.

If the total adds up to 3:

- Yes is the answer to the question, but not as definitely as with the 1.
- The person in question was born under the signs of Pisces or Sagittarius, or on dates adding up to 3 or 6.
- Consciously, the question relates to the subject's pride and ambition. The subject has a need to be independent and expressive in some way. On the subconscious plane, there's an inner desire to rise above others, to make a name for oneself. Confusion may be the underlying concern.

If the total adds up to 4:

- No is the answer to the question, but not as definitely as 2.
- The person in question was born under the sign of Aquarius or Leo, or on dates adding up to 1 or 4.
- At the conscious level, the subject's question relates to hard work, routines or details. You need to structure and organize yourself as much as possible. Do not rush—take your time. Subconsciously, there's an inner concern relating to health or material restrictions.

If the total adds up to 5:

- Yes is definitely the answer to the question.
- The person in question may have been born under the signs of Gemini or Virgo, or on dates adding up to 5 or 6.
- Consciously, the subject's question is of a sexual nature or relates to the opposite sex. The subject's concern is to make changes, to move about with more freedom and less restrictions. On the subconscious plane, there's a deep inner need to communicate with others as well as to experience greater variety.

If the total adds up to 6:

- No is definitely the answer to the question.
- The person in question may have been born under the signs of Taurus or Libra, or on dates adding up to 6 or 3.
- The subject's question on the conscious level relates to home, or to his or her domestic or love life in some way. The concern also relates to duty or responsibility of some kind for someone. Inwardly, the subconscious mind is making a strong appeal to be loved, recognized, or appreciated.

If the total adds up to 7:

- Yes is the answer to the question, but with some delay.
- The person in question was born under the sign of Cancer or Pisces, or on dates adding up to 7 or 2.

- The subject's question on the conscious level relates to his or her deep inner feelings. Also indicated are questions that may relate to the deception of the self and others in some way, even repression of the emotions. Subconsciously, there's an inner desire to be left alone and to get away from it all. However, there's also an inward desire to seek wisdom, knowledge, and inner truth about a particular matter.

If the total adds up to 8:

- No is the answer to the question, but may be a Yes later on.
- The person in question was born under the sign of Capricorn or on dates adding up to 8 or 4.
- On the material or conscious level, the subject's question relates to money, finances, business, marriage, or some other personal achievement or recognition. The question relates to hard work and effort, backed by strong concentration of purpose. Subconsciously, there's an inner concern for things religious and philosophical.

If the total adds up to 9:

- Yes is the answer to the question.
- The person in question was born under the signs of Aries or Scorpio, or on dates adding up to 9 or 3.
- Consciously, the subject's question relates to bringing matters to a close with someone or something. The question further suggests nothing new should be started now, no matter how sweet the offer. Deep down, subconsciously, situations and circumstances are about to come to an end—generally for the better.

Finding Lost Objects

Have you ever lost anything such as your wallet, money, or keys? Have you ever misplaced something around your home or office and were at your wit's end trying to find it? Losing things is not a new problem. The ancients of long ago, through their constant study of the occult sciences, were able to determine where to look for missing objects and things.

The ability to find lost things was another ability demonstrated to the late master Astrologer, Sepharial, by his swami-teacher from the Orient. The swami asked Sepharial to take an object not known to him, to concentrate on that object, then give him the first number that came to mind. From the number that Sepharial gave, the swami was able to describe the object in detail (a postage stamp), and even give its value. Sydney Omarr, today's famed Astrologer, also adapted this technique in his "thought dial" concept, better known as TD.

How does this correlation between a number and a lost object work? The principal of locating lost objects through numbers starts in the subconscious mind. Here's how it works. First, both Sepharial and Sydney Omarr say that you should be as relaxed as possible. Once the subject relaxes, have him or her concentrate on the missing object or thing to be located. Next, have them write down the first set of numbers that come to mind.

Sepharial suggests you write down the first 9 numbers that come into your mind. To these 9 numbers, add the number 3, which makes for a total of ten figures. Add all ten numbers together and read the interpretation given for the final number.

Sydney Omarr's method is even simpler. Omarr suggests that you write only 3 numbers and add them up until you arrive at one single digit.

Let's take an example using Omarr's method: Our object is a missing wallet. First, relax. Next concentrate on the missing object. Finally, write down the first three numbers that come to mind. In this example, the numbers I selected were 4, 1, and 8 = 13 (1+3=4). We then read the interpretation given below for the final number of 4. There appears to be much validity to the method.

Finding Lost objects

If your total adds up to the single number of 1, it suggests:

- The object is likely to be found in a southerly direction, particularly in the main part of the house, such as the living room or bedroom.
- The object is likely to be found near white linen or cloth in the main part of the house.
- If you're still having difficulty locating the object, a young child should be questioned.

If the total adds up to 2, it suggests:

- The object is likely to be found in a southerly direction, particularly near a sink, basin, or bowl.
- The object is likely to be found with someone's assistance, particularly from a female.
- The object may be near a tank, pool, stretch of water, or near fine linen.

If the total adds up to 3, it suggests:

- The object is likely to be found in a northerly direction, in between papers, books, or documents, or in a passage.
- The object may have been mislaid near your work or office, or near books or papers, but it is safe.
- Look in a box or case that folds in two; or question a young child.

If the total adds up to 4, it suggests:

- The object is in your possession but has been forgotten.
- The object may be found in a northeasterly direction, perhaps on a shelf. It should be quickly recovered.
- Look in a closet where the coats are kept, or near neckwear.

If the total adds up to 5, it suggests:

- The object is likely to be found in a westerly direction with little or no effort. Particularly look near or under headgear, such as a hat, fez, or turban.
- Try another part of the house where clothes are kept.
- The object may be on a ledge, or on something oblong. Next, look where the wife's or husband's shoes are kept.

If the total adds up to 6, it suggests:

- Although the odds of finding the object are not great, look either in the extreme east or west, wherever shoes, sandals, or boots are kept.
- The object is likely to be in or around a rack, a stand, or a shelf.
- The wife or husband is likely to have an answer. Lastly, look through your personal effects.

If the total adds up to 7, it suggests:

- Chances are the object may not be found. However, search for it in the east. Next, find something white and round—it may be there.

- There may be deception or withholding of information in connection with the missing object.

If the total adds up to 8, it suggests:

- The object is likely to be found in a northerly direction, particularly a shelf or horizontal ledge. Next, try a cabinet.
- The object may be found where valuables or money are kept.
- Begin at your feet when you start looking—you'll soon have the object in view.

If the total adds up to 9, it suggests:

- The object may be found in an easterly direction, particularly among the childrens' clothing.
- The object is as good as found—put your hand on a shelf or search among clothing.
- The missing object is in the family circle—try the childrens' room. Next, try looking among old effects or in a dark place or corner.

Those wishing more details on the subject of numbers and lost objects should read: *The Kabala of Numbers* by Sepharial, and *Thought Dial* by Sydney Omarr. In the meantime—happy hunting!

Your Passions and Weaknesses

What are your passions, innermost wants, drives, and desires? Do you know in what areas of life your weaknesses and Karmic challenges lie? Thanks to Numerology, these questions can be answered through your name numbers. The method of arriving at these answers can be found by using the "Table of Traits," or the "Magic Box."

Each of us have certain inner needs, wants and desires as well as flaws and weaknesses which require further development. But in what areas of life, and in what way?

The purpose of the Table of Traits, or Magic Box, is to determine how many times a particular number or numbers are repeated in your name. The more a particular number is repeated, the more intense is that desire or passion in the area the numbers represent. And the reverse is also true—when a number or numbers are missing in your name, they point to weaknesses or challenges. They indicate your Karma and areas that must be overcome and developed in order to make you a well-rounded person.

The Table of Traits, or Magic Box, looks like this:

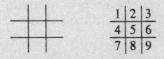

1	2	3
4	5	6
7	8	9

On the left is the Magic Box without the numbers filled in. As you can see, it is constructed like the tic-tac-toe box you played with as a youngster. Each box represents certain abilities and characteristics that will be explained. The box on the right is the how the Magic Box looks when the numbers are filled in, showing where each number from 1 to 9 should be placed. Now, let's fill in the Magic Box.

```
K A T H R Y N     A N I C E      H I L L
2 1 2 8 9 7 5     1 5 9 3 5      8 9 3 3
```

2	2	3
	3	
1	2	3

If you look carefully at the name above—Kathryn Anice Hill—you'll see that the number 1 is repeated twice in the name, and the total number of 1s (in this case two) is placed in the first box, at the top left. The number 2 is also repeated twice. The total number of 2s is placed in the middle box at the top. The number 3 is repeated three times. The total number of 3s is placed in the top right box. Continue with the rest of the numbers in this manner until each box is filled in or left blank. In the above analysis, Kathryn's passion or most repeated numbers, are the 3, 5, and 9 (repeated three times each). Kathryn's Karma and areas of weakness are the numbers 4 and 6, which are missing in her name).

Now take your name, putting each number under the letters of your name (see chart on page 16), and construct your Magic Box to determine what numbers are repeated most and what numbers are missing. Ideally, each square should be filled in, but often this is not the case. Below is a brief meaning of what each square represents, and a discussion of the presence or absence of the numbers found in them.

Magic Box Numbers

BOX #1:

Represents your ability to rely upon yourself and your own resources. Your ability to stand alone, make decisions, and be independent of others. Denotes your will, pride, and ego. Three 1s are average.

Many 1s: Strong desire to dominate, be in control, or take the lead. Very aggressive, forceful, original, determined, and demanding of others and self.

Few/No 1s: Lacks self-confidence; others tend to dominate the will. Indecisive, unable to decide or stick to decisions, lacks sunny disposition.

BOX #2:

Represents your ability to work in harmony and cooperation with others. Also denotes your ability to be patient, to attend to details, to be considerate and understanding of others, especially in domestic or romantic matters. One 2 is average.

Many 2s: Usually oversensitive and emotional. May be too dependent on others; a natural collector of things; has power of persuasion, very psychic and observant; love of details and concepts.

Few/No 2s: Impatient with self and others, moody, impressionable, weak, shy. Lacks ability to cooperate with others, lacks consideration and understanding.

BOX #3:

Represents your ability to be creative and self-expressive, especially in artistic ways. Also represents ones ability to be positive, optimistic and socially outgoing. Also denotes your ambition and desire to get ahead. One 3 is average.

Many 3s: Very ambitious, very positive, artistic, and expressive. Confident, strong need to be popular, a social animal, talkative, dictatorial.

Few/No 3s: Inferiority complex, inarticulate, superficial, boastful, socially shy, lacks ambition or drive, leans toward overindulgence.

BOX #4:

Represents your ability to endure, work, and attend to details. This box or area of life denotes the ability to establish order and systems, routines and methods, to organize and structure things. One 4 is average.

Many 4s: Strong desire to work and deal with life in practical ways; and an equally strong desire to be different from others. Such a person is very methodical, mechanically and mathematically inclined, and able to reform and reverse the rules of things.

Few/No 4s: Unable or slow to accept change; rigid or narrow in outlook; is moody and critical, especially of self; lacks concentration and organization.

BOX #5:

This area of life represents the ability to handle the right use of freedom; the ability to deal with change and the unexpected. Also denotes one's ability to deal with life experiences. Three 5s are average.

Many 5s: Strong desire to be free and independent, and to deal with the public in some way. This person is very changeable and curious, has literary talents; may overindulge in matters of sex, drink, or drugs.

Few/No 5s: Inability or lack of desire to accept change or to deal with people. Has difficulty adjusting to life experiences. May need to learn the hard way; can misuse freedom and change.

BOX #6:

This is the area of life that deals with home, family, loved ones, and other domestic matters. Represents an ability to handle duty and responsibility. Also denotes an ability to make adjustments when needed, to create harmony, and to accept things the way they really are. One 6 is average.

Many 6s: Strong concerns about family ties and relationships. A need to take on responsibilities or counsel others in some way. Desire to comfort. Can become a domestic tyrant.

Few/No 6s: Inability to deal with commitments or to make adjustments. Slow to make decisions; poor judgment of people and situations; there will be challenges in the home or love life.

Box #7:

This box shows an ability to analyze and take things apart; to look beneath the surface of things; the ability to handle theories and fundamentals of a technical nature; to comprehend the unseen. One 7 is average, but is often missing in a name.

Many 7s: Very analytical and technical turn of mind; a strong desire to gather knowledge, to be independent, to understand the unseen. There is an equally strong need for privacy and peace and quiet. Many 7s are rare.

Few/No 7s: Suggests a need to look deeper into matters when approached; a need to develop a more analytical mind; little concern for religion and the unseen; superstitious and pessimistic.

Box #8:

This area of your life denotes material and financial matters. It represents the world of judgment, concentration of purpose, and the ability to handle power, authority, and achievement. Three 8's are average.

Many 8s: Strong desire for money, important positions, and material achievements. Such a person is philosophical and serious-minded, with a desire to organize; can be a religious zealot.

Few/No 8s: Lack of judgment, especially in the material and financial world. Can be despondent, even morbid, if not positive. Unable to concentrate on purposes, especially those of a long-term nature.

BOX #9:

Shows the ability to get along with your fellows and to have a broad outlook; the ability to sacrifice for the good of all. The ability to determine one's destiny. Three 9's are average.

Many 9s: Strong desire to be one's own master and control one's destiny; great concern with the problems and events of the world. This person has much courage, energy, and leadership and organizational ability.

Few/No 9s: Lack of compassion; lack of direction and inspiration; impulsive and quick tempered; has a narrow outlook and little concern for anyone else.

Failure and Success

Failure means an inability to succeed at, to accomplish, or even attempt a certain task. Failure is a frustrating experience, but lessons can be learned from the experience however. If nothing else, you learn not to repeat them, for if you continue to make the same mistakes, life becomes one failure after another—and how sad.

But why do we fail? It's been found that your attitude plays an important role. If you think you can do something—you will. If you think you can't—guess what? Numerology can give additional insight into why we fail. This is determined from the negative side of your birth number. Understanding your negative potential is just as important as knowing your positive traits.

Negative Personal Number Traits

THE 1 PERSON

Born on the 1st, 10th, 19th, or 28th of the month, you usually fail for two major reasons. First, you may be overly weak and dependent on others. Secondly, your ego may get in the way of common sense and sound advice. Bragging, boasting, and dominating a conversation can turn others away. Impatience, pushiness, and arrogance don't help either.

THE 2 PERSON

Those born on the 2nd, 11th, 20th, or 29th, fail due to shyness and lack of self-confidence. You may not be as forceful as you should. This could lead to additional setbacks. Pettiness, narrowness of mind, and a deceptive approach with others could bring on further problems. Moodiness has to be kept under control.

THE 3 PERSON

If you were born on the 3rd, 12th, 21st, or 30th of the month, you tend to fail either because of excessive ambition, or no ambition at all. At the extreme of the ambitious end, you may brag a lot, show off in front of others, or do anything to get attention. Having a dictatorial attitude in your dealings will rub people the wrong way. On the other hand, having no ambition at all could lead to excessive whining and overindulgence.

THE 4 PERSON

A person born on the 4th, 13th, 22nd, or 31st of the month generally fails because of antisocial behavior and misunderstandings. Watch how your mood swings affect yourself and others. Maintain an upbeat attitude to avoid conflict. An inability to express your feelings and emotions could lead to needless frustration. Try to avoid acting strangely, or being rude or cold with others—it won't help.

THE 5 PERSON

If you were born on the 5th, 14th, or 23rd of the month, perhaps more than any other number, you tend to fail because a goal, purpose, objective, or direction wasn't established early in life. Not sticking with anyone or anything very long could be part of the problem. Overindulgence in drugs, sex, or alcohol is also high on your list of problems. Gambling your money away only compounds the problem. Carelessness, vulgarity, and procrastination also add fuel to your failures.

THE 6 PERSON

People born on the 6th, 15th, or 24th of the month generally encounter failure because of stubbornness. Selfishness, jealousy, and worrying about your creature comforts also slow your progress. Being a domestic tyrant, gossiping, and interfering in the affairs of others are the best ways to rush head-on into failure.

THE 7 PERSON

Born on the 7th, 16th, or 25th of the month, you tend to fail because of needless worry, negative thought patterns, and a lack of faith more than anything else. Using cunning ways, deceit, and falsehood take you even further away from success. Using drugs, or cheating, satiric and sarcastic tactics slide you deeper into the bowels of failure.

THE 8 PERSON

If you were born on the 8th, 17th, or 26th of the month, you stray from success because of severe misunderstandings and melancholy feelings. Greed and avarice on your part could also be a factor. Hoarding material possessions, intense scheming, and outright bullying is guaranteed to nail your coffin.

THE 9 PERSON

People born on the 9th, 18th, or 27th of the month generally fail because of an inability to control impulsiveness, a quick temper, or excessive alcohol consumption. You have to avoid being led by others, especially through the use of flattery. Having a combative attitude, bad habits, and aimless daydreaming is like handing yourself failure on a tarnished platter.

Numerology and Success

"It is so easy to be successful, if one can only get the right inspiration."

—Cheiro, Master Occultist

According to the dictionary, "success" means the achievement of something desired, planned, or attempted—it also means any outcome or result, no matter how big or small. Researchers have found that out of every 100 persons, only 20 will be successful. The other 80 will lead average lives or be failures.

Ironically, succeeding is much easier than failing. You have the ability to succeed, to make the most of your talents, skills, and abilities. The problem is that, while some of us take advantage of what we have, most of us don't.

How does one become successful? What are the main ingredients that go into success? How can Numerology be used to insure successs? Those involved in the field of positive thinking have found that our personal outlook on life and ourselves has a lot to do with it.

Case in point: Do you see half a glass of water as half full or half empty? What's your basic attitude toward life? Going back to the dictionary, "attitude" is defined as a state of mind or feeling toward a particular person, place, or thing. Let's say you have a job or assignment you don't like. Chances are, your attitude—the way you feel—will be negative. As a result, you don't put your best into it.

This principal of attitude comes into play in our judgments of others, even of ourselves. Those who are successful in life tend to have a good attitude or feeling about themselves. They know who they are, what they're about, and what they wish to do or be. Ask any successful person and you'll see what I mean.

Enthusiasm is another key element for success. Enthusiasm is contagious. It rubs off easily on others. People tend to bubble over with you when your enthusiasm is strong and sincere. Use plenty of it if you want to get ahead.

How does Numerology tie in with success? How does it apply? As with anything, you must first have the proper mental attitude. If your attitude about the subject of Numerology is full of misconceptions, superstition, or disbelief, I doubt seriously if it will be of help. Your basic attitude has already decided—one way or the other. This is true for anything in life. On the other hand, if you feel positive about Numerology, the speed of your success can be accelerated by following a few simple rules.

First, determine your birth number from the day of the month you were born. If you were born on the 25th of the month your number is 7 $(2+5=7)$. Once your birth number is found, begin to look forward to all the dates in the month that match your own birth number. They should be important in some way. In our example, the 7 birth number person should look forward to the 7th, 16th, and 25th of the month.

Save your best plans, projects, or major moves for dates that match your birth number. You'll become more successful. On these dates take control. Sit in the driver's seat and steer your plans in the direction you wish to go. You'll find less resistance, less waste of time and precious energy. Just try it for yourself.

Numerology and Meditation

Meditation is a healing force for the mind, body, and spirit and meditating with numbers is a wonderful tool for both inner and outer transformation. There are as many ways to meditate as there are spiritual schools of thought. Whichever method, school, or technique you choose, the essence is to be at peace with yourself and the world. However, there is a common approach among the different schools, and it's this:

- Find a quiet place for at least five minutes.
- Take several deep breaths.
- Relax as much as possible.

Because the nature of the mind is to wander, due to the ever alert five senses, it's best to visualize, rather than to try keeping the mind still. In the case of Numerology, it's best to focus on the particular number you have in mind.

In a Numerology meditation you have a choice of two techniques. First, you can focus on your date of birth. For instance, if you were born on the 31st of the month, you would be a number 4 person $(3 + 1 = 4)$. Since this is your key number, focus on it first. The second approach trusts the subconscious mind to come up with answers. First, think about the concern or person you have in mind. Next, select any three numbers that come to mind. Then add the numbers to arrive at one single digit. As a helpful hint, visualize the number, then try as best you can to associate any relationship to it. Let's say you chose the number 7. See the 7 in your "mind's eye" and try to associate any symbol, relationship, or experience you may have had with the number 7 in the past or present.

Meditations on the Numbers

MEDITATION FOR THE NUMBER 1

Visualize a oneness of purpose. Realize the oneness of God is part of the divine scheme of things. See yourself setting goals, being in control, making decisions, taking charge of your life. Visualize the new things that you wish to do. See yourself in action, whatever or wherever that may be. Set no limitations in your mind, for you are the pioneer. With mental vision and a positive approach to life, you're sure to reach your goals.

MEDITATION FOR THE NUMBER 2

Think of yourself in partnership with the universal mind and spirit. See yourself as a light reflection for others to see their way by in the dark passages of life. Giving and sharing warms the coldest hearts among those coming into your influence. You want to establish harmony, beauty, and above all love. Exercising patience generally proves to be a blessing. Be open and receptive to what is being offered. Be sympathetic to those in need, or who do not know the way.

MEDICATION FOR THE NUMBER 3

Visualize the best part of yourself—the part of you that lies hidden and really needs to be expressed. Visualize youth and vitality all around you. Recall those wonderful experiences of your youth, that time in your life filled with carefree moments. Think positive, think big, and get big results. Visualize growth, good fortune and fun as part of this numerical influence. See yourself coming alive.

MEDITATION FOR THE NUMBER 4

Meditate upon the divine order of the universe and your divine role in the scheme of things. "As above, so below," is an ancient spiritual maxim. See yourself establishing order on a smaller scale—in your personal life and the environment around you. There are no walls or boundaries that are not there to offer a lesson—to demonstrate that even in the most confusing of situations or circumstances, there is order. Visualize in your mind the type of world you want in the future for yourself and others. The future as well as the past holds the key to what keeps one's present house in order.

MEDITATION FOR THE NUMBER 5

Visualize yourself as the wind. You know no limits, no bounds. You have no ties. Visualize yourself changing, breaking away from your old way of doing things. Like the 5 senses, be open to the opportunities around you, and to communications of all kind. Visualize your mind as fertile as the banks of the Nile—soaking up knowledge, learning, teaching, and helping others to aspire to a higher order in the total scheme of things.

MEDITATION FOR THE NUMBER 6

You are the cosmic Mother or Father setting the example for others. Visualize yourself as the hub of the wheel around which everything revolves, offering help, assistance, and human comfort wherever you can. See the beauty, dignity, and grace in yourself and others that lies beneath the surface. Now is the time to act as a role model, demonstrating the goodness in all of us, pointing the way to a better way of life.

MEDITATION FOR THE NUMBER 7

This is the natural home of meditation, visualization and all things mystical. See yourself under divine protection from On High. Recognize the wonderment of God's wisdom in the nature of things. See yourself as a magnet, attracting others you meet along the way to a deeper, more cosmic understanding of the causes and effects that rule human life, nature, and the universe. Find peace within yourself. Walk with confidence, knowing you are divinely protected wherever you go.

MEDITATION FOR THE NUMBER 8

Visualize the power in you—the power to make a change for the better. Imagine yourself a philosopher, sharing the wisdom of your past and present experiences with others. Create the feeling and conviction that your deep inner strength will see you through, no matter what happens, no matter how great the stress, or how hard the struggle. Know that it is only a test of a higher order, challenging you to find your way on life's stage, to play the ultimate role you must serve.

MEDITATION FOR THE NUMBER 9

See yourself as one with the cosmos, in complete harmony with universal time and space. Visualize yourself as all encompassing, knowing that you too are part of the universal mind that is filled with endless knowledge waiting to serve you. Rise above all limitations, knowing that we are all simply a universal reflection of God. Visualize yourself as an influence for good for those who come into your sphere. Set the example by spiritual actions and deeds.

A Closing Word

Seven years after the publication of the original version of NUMBERS AND YOU, the tremendous stress and pressures of everyday life haven't changed—if anything daily living has become even more complex. And just as before, many of you readers are still looking for intelligent answers and practical solutions to everyday problems through the science of Numerology.

By using this book as a reference guide to help yourself and others, hopefully your life from this day forth will be a better one. Examine the information presented here, experiment with the universal principles...then *you* make the final judgement. Although I've had many letters over the years confirming the validity of what you have read remember you are always the final judge.

Numerology in and of itself is not a cure. However, over the tens of thousands of years, this occult science has proven to be astonishingly accurate. In essence, your personal numbers are simply "indicators" of what you have been, what you are right now...what you're likely to be—if you chose to explore the cosmic relationship between Numbers and You.

PERPETUAL CALENDAR

DIRECTIONS: The number given with each year in the key above is number of calendar to use for that year.

3

JANUARY	FEBRUARY	MARCH	APRIL
MAY	JUNE	JULY	AUGUST
SEPTEMBER	OCTOBER	NOVEMBER	DECEMBER

4

JANUARY	FEBRUARY	MARCH	APRIL
MAY	JUNE	JULY	AUGUST
SEPTEMBER	OCTOBER	NOVEMBER	DECEMBER

5

JANUARY	FEBRUARY	MARCH	APRIL
MAY	JUNE	JULY	AUGUST
SEPTEMBER	OCTOBER	NOVEMBER	DECEMBER

6

JANUARY	FEBRUARY	MARCH	APRIL
MAY	JUNE	JULY	AUGUST
SEPTEMBER	OCTOBER	NOVEMBER	DECEMBER

7

JANUARY	FEBRUARY	MARCH	APRIL
MAY	JUNE	JULY	AUGUST
SEPTEMBER	OCTOBER	NOVEMBER	DECEMBER

8

JANUARY	FEBRUARY	MARCH	APRIL
MAY	JUNE	JULY	AUGUST
SEPTEMBER	OCTOBER	NOVEMBER	DECEMBER

These are perpetual-calendar reference grids numbered **9** through **14**, each containing twelve monthly calendars. Day-of-week columns are headed **S M T W T F S**.

9

JANUARY	FEBRUARY	MARCH	APRIL
MAY	JUNE	JULY	AUGUST
SEPTEMBER	OCTOBER	NOVEMBER	DECEMBER

10

JANUARY	FEBRUARY	MARCH	APRIL
MAY	JUNE	JULY	AUGUST
SEPTEMBER	OCTOBER	NOVEMBER	DECEMBER

11

JANUARY	FEBRUARY	MARCH	APRIL
MAY	JUNE	JULY	AUGUST
SEPTEMBER	OCTOBER	NOVEMBER	DECEMBER

12

JANUARY	FEBRUARY	MARCH	APRIL
MAY	JUNE	JULY	AUGUST
SEPTEMBER	OCTOBER	NOVEMBER	DECEMBER

13

JANUARY	FEBRUARY	MARCH	APRIL
MAY	JUNE	JULY	AUGUST
SEPTEMBER	OCTOBER	NOVEMBER	DECEMBER

14

JANUARY	FEBRUARY	MARCH	APRIL
MAY	JUNE	JULY	AUGUST
SEPTEMBER	OCTOBER	NOVEMBER	DECEMBER

About the Author

Lloyd Strayhorn was first introduced to Numerology in 1969, following a deep interest in Astrology. The next seven years were devoted to study and research on the theory, meaning, nature, and practical applications of Numerology. In 1976, he began teaching Numerology in the classroom as well as privately. In 1978, he began writing his first column, and since 1979 his weekly syndicated column has been carried in over 120 newspapers across the country.

Mr. Strayhorn has made numerous radio and TV appearances on such shows as: "Tony Brown's Journal," "The Oprah Winfrey Show," "The Morning Show," hosted by Regis Philbin, and "The Joe Franklin Show." Since 1981, he has hosted his own daily radio talk show, "Numbers and You," on WLIB-AM (1190) in New York City, as well as his very popular "Cosmic Forecast" that airs twice daily on WBLS-FM (107.5), also in New York. In 1984, Mr. Strayhorn began publishing his bimonthly newsletter, NUMBERS AND YOU.

All readers interested in sharing the experiences or in receiving information about NUMBERS AND YOU workshops are invited to write to the author in care of his publisher, Ballantine Books, 201 East 50th Street, New York, NY 10022.